Lights in the Distance

Also by Daniel Trilling

Bloody Nasty People:
The Rise of Britain's Far Right

DANIEL TRILLING

Lights in the Distance

Exile and Refuge at the Borders of Europe

PICADOR

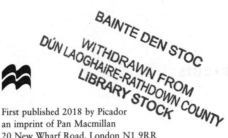

First published 2018 by Picador
an imprint of Pan Macmillan
20 New Wharf Road, London N1 9RR
Associated companies throughout the world
www.panmacmillan.com

ISBN 978-1-5098-1561-6

9 8 7 6 5 4 3 2 1

A CIP catalogue record for this book is available from the British Library.

Map artwork by ML Design
Typeset in 11.5/15 pt Sabon LT Std by Jouve (UK), Milton Keynes
Printed and bound by CPI Group (UK) Ltd, Croydon, CR0 4YY

Contents

Introduction

The history of migration is a history of controls on the movement of all but a wealthy elite. In the past, states sought to restrict the movement of their own populations, through slavery or serfdom, or poor laws and vagrancy acts; today the right to move freely within one's own territory is enshrined in the 1948 Universal Declaration of Human Rights. Instead, the movement of people across international borders is tightly controlled and regulated. As a proportion of the world population, the number of international migrants has stayed relatively steady: roughly 3 per cent since 1960, according to the sociologist Hein de Haas.

This might seem surprising in an age where goods, communication and certain kinds of people can move with greater ease than ever before, but globalization is a highly unequal process. Although the proportion of migrants has not grown significantly, the origin and direction of migration has changed: research by Hein de Haas and Mathias Czaika suggests that people are leaving a much wider range of countries than ever before, and they are heading to a much narrower range of destinations than ever before. They are going to the places where power and wealth have become concentrated.

Europe, and north-western Europe in particular, is one

of those places. Most of this migration takes place legally: an estimated nine out of ten migrants who enter Europe do so with permission. But wealthier countries are making increasingly severe efforts to keep out the uninvited, a significant number of whom are refugees fleeing war or persecution. In 1990, according to research by the geographer Reece Jones, twenty countries had walls or fences on their border; by the beginning of 2016, that number had risen to almost seventy.

The European Union, a political and economic alliance of – at the time of writing – twenty-eight nation states, plus neighbours such as Norway who take part in certain common agreements, has perhaps the world's most complex system to deter unwanted migrants. Since the 1990s, as borders have come down within Europe, giving most EU citizens free movement and passport-free travel, its external frontier has become increasingly militarized: Amnesty International estimates that, between 2007 and 2013, the EU spent almost two billion euros on fences, surveillance systems and patrols.

What happens to refugees who try to make it past these obstacles? Under the 1951 Refugee Convention, to which all EU members are signatories, states are obliged not to penalize people who cross their borders in search of asylum, or to force them back to territories where they would be in danger. Anybody who asks for asylum is entitled to due process, and to have their claim assessed on an individual basis; officials can't just declare a whole group of asylum seekers 'genuine' or 'bogus' at the stroke of a pen.

In reality, the EU has tried to prevent refugees from reaching its territory wherever possible – by closing down legal routes, such as the ability to claim asylum at overseas embassies; by introducing penalties for transport companies that allow people to travel into the EU without the correct documents; and by signing treaties with its neighbours that offer them trade incentives and easier travel for their own citizens in return for policing their borders with the EU more thoroughly. If refugees do make it into the EU, then an agreement known as the Dublin Regulation stipulates that it is the responsibility of the first EU country they set foot in to deal with their asylum claim. If they travel on to a second (or third, or fourth) country, they can be forcibly returned to their point of arrival, with the help of an EU-wide police fingerprint database known as Eurodac. This arguably places the greatest burden on EU members at the bloc's southern and eastern edges, which tend to be poorer and less well equipped to support new arrivals.

To give a sense of Europe's priorities, in the same period as it spent two billion euros on border security, the EU spent only an estimated 700 million on reception conditions for refugees. There are other kinds of costs, too: in November 2017, a coalition of human rights groups published a list of 33,293 people who had died since 1993 as a result of 'border militarization, asylum laws, detention policies and deportations' in Europe.

*

Border defences often produce or exacerbate the very problems they purport to solve, by forcing irregular migrants to take more dangerous routes, often with increasing reliance on people smugglers, which in turn encourages states to crack down further. Such a process has been at work in Europe in recent years.

According to the office of the UN High Commissioner for Refugees (UNHCR), there are sixty-five million people displaced by conflict in the world today. Of those, twenty-two million have fled their home countries, which makes them refugees under international definitions. The vast majority of these people – 86 per cent – are hosted in poorer parts of the world; indeed, this proportion has risen in the last decade. Since 2011, however, the number of people coming to Europe to seek asylum has risen sharply due to conflicts taking place beyond the EU's borders.

They have travelled by two principal routes: across the central Mediterranean from North Africa, and through south-eastern Europe via Turkey. The largest group by nationality to take these routes are Syrians; the war in Syria has caused one of the most acute refugee crises in recent memory, although most of the six million Syrian refugees are living in Turkey, Lebanon and Jordan. Those who have come to Europe to seek asylum are joined by people from Iraq, Afghanistan, Pakistan, Eritrea, Somalia, Sudan, Nigeria, Mali and elsewhere.

In the mid-2000s, according to the EU's statistics authority Eurostat, around 250,000 people a year were claiming asylum in the EU. From 2011, as numbers began to rise, Europe continued to make security its priority, rather than the protection of vulnerable people. In 2015, arrivals peaked when well over a million people came to Europe to seek asylum. This is still only a small fraction of the EU's total population of 508 million, but the manner of their arrival was chaotic. Thousands died in the attempt. Most of the migrants who arrived tried to continue their journeys to north-west Europe, and enforcement of the Dublin Regulation effectively collapsed.

You have probably heard this described as Europe's 'refugee crisis'. It might better be described as a border crisis. In the twenty-first century, a border is not just a line on a map; it is a system for filtering people that stretches from the edges of a territory into its heart. Asylum seekers are subject to particularly complex and often violent filtering. Once they cross Europe's frontiers, their movement is restricted; they are locked up or segregated in accommodation far from city centres. Their right to work or to access social security is denied or severely limited. While their claims are being assessed, often by a process that is opaque, hostile and inconsistent, they live with the threat that what freedoms they do have might be curtailed at any moment. The system tries to place them into categories – refugee or economic migrant, legal or illegal, deserving or undeserving – that do not always fit the reality of their lives. And if the system breaks down, then people are cast into a legal and moral grey zone that lasts for many months or even years.

This book investigates the effects of Europe's border crisis on the people caught up in it.

'Migrant' describes a person on the move for an unspecified reason.

'Refugee' has both a legal meaning, in that it describes a person who is eligible for asylum under international refugee law, and a colloquial meaning, in that it describes a person who has fled their home.

'Asylum seeker' describes a person who has come to a country in order to claim asylum, but whose claim has not yet been either accepted or rejected.

In many cases, there exists a more precise description of a person than any of the above.

CITY

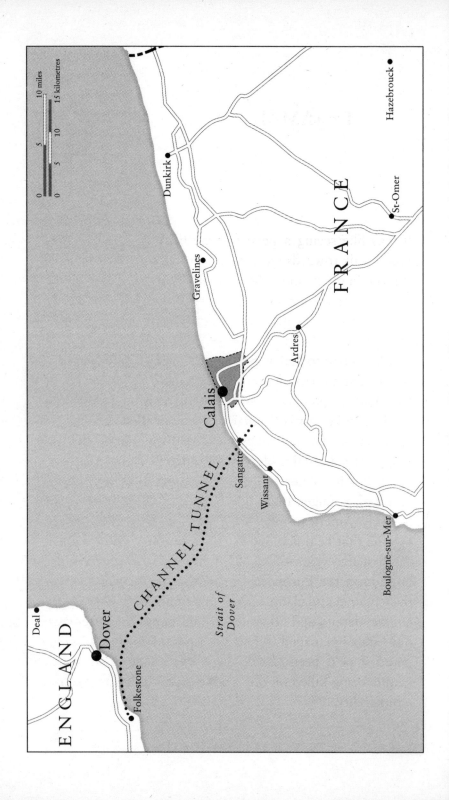

1 · JAMAL

It was like seeing a person come back to life, watching Jamal walk towards me across the town square outside the station. In my memory, he was the skinny, shivering young man I'd met in Calais in early 2014. Now, eighteen months later, there was a grin of recognition on his face as he hugged me.

I had gone to Calais because the city puzzled me: how was it that a crossing point between two European countries had become synonymous with refugees from thousands of miles away? Jamal was one of the first people I met; that winter day, he had emerged from a tent pitched underneath a canal bridge, into the drizzle. He was twenty-three, but his slight frame and loose crop of curls made him look younger. I had been struck by the way he spoke in lively, American-inflected English as he told me about his life: that he'd fled Sudan as a teenager; that he'd spent the first five years of his adult life living as an irregular migrant in the European Union; that he wanted to cross the Channel and claim asylum in Britain. We had swapped contact details, and I'd visited Calais many times after that, but I never managed to find him again. Sometimes I wondered if he'd been killed; there were enough stories of people being killed on the roads around Calais to make it a possibility.

But, after months of silence, Jamal had eventually sent me a message online saying he'd moved to a different part of northern Europe. I was surprised; he had been so set on the UK that he could already name the cities he wanted to visit and tell me where he wanted to go to college. What had made him give up?

It was the summer of 2015 when I came to visit Jamal in his new home town. We crossed the square and stopped at a supermarket to buy lunch. Jamal was as I'd remembered him: his laid-back walk, the way he would throw his arms open and widen his eyes when he wanted to heighten the drama of a story. He said he'd explain everything: how he'd ended up in Calais; what had gone wrong there; how he'd left. I said I wanted to know a lot, and that it might take several days of interviews. He was fine with that.

*

We reached Jamal's apartment, in a block for newly arrived refugees, on the outskirts of town. Inside, it looked like student halls of residence. He showed me to his corridor: five single bedrooms, all for men; a shared shower room, toilet and kitchen. We went into the kitchen, put the food onto plates and carried them into his room. It was big enough for a bed in one corner, a table and some cushions in the middle, and a desk with a laptop and a couple of Stephen King thrillers on it in the opposite corner. Jamal said he'd saved up for the laptop, a second-hand model, using the subsistence payments he'd received as he waited for his asylum claim to be processed. At the foot of the bed was a Hoover; the residents were expected to do their own cleaning.

As we ate, Jamal told me about his childhood in a

suburb of the Sudanese capital Khartoum, and about his parents: pious, working-class people who saw the Iraqi dictator Saddam Hussein as a hero because 'he stood up to the West'. Jamal described how his father had died when he was a baby, and how he'd grown up helping his mother and sister run a tea stall in the centre of town. He found school boring, and he liked to skip classes to play football with his friends, or watch the American television shows and movies beamed into his home by a Saudi satellite channel. He liked crime series the best: *CSI, NCS: Manhunt, Prison Break*. Or police comedies like *Bad Boys* ('I like Will Smith') or *White Chicks* ('It's about two cops impersonating their girls so they can see what's going on'). He'd been taught some English in school, but he became obsessed with these American shows, copying the accents of black American movie stars and trying them out on his family. 'They had a problem with me in the house because I was controlling the TV. My mum and my sister wanted to watch Arab series, but I would hide the remote. And when I was speaking with my sister, she would speak Arabic and I would annoy her by replying in English. They were asking me why, and I said, "Just because." I liked it.'

Khartoum was usually a peaceful city, but since 2003 the government had been waging war against rebel groups in Darfur, in the west of the country. Sudan is ruled by an Arabic-speaking elite based in the east, and the government had used militias to carry out a campaign of ethnic cleansing against the 'African' inhabitants of Darfur. In May 2008, when Jamal was seventeen, a rebel group raided Khartoum. The attack was swiftly repelled, and the following day Jamal set off by bus across the city to pay the satellite bill, like he did every month. His bus was stopped on a bridge that crossed the Nile, by soldiers who suspected fleeing rebels of disguising themselves as civilians. 'They searched us. Everyone who has ID, they let him go; anyone who hasn't, they stop him. I didn't have ID.'

Jamal was put in the back of a van. 'They beat us inside the vehicle and I was very scared. Back of the van, no windows. Many people there.' After a forty-minute drive to an unknown location, they were put into a cell. 'We didn't know what was going to happen. The people there, we were just ordinary people. The rebels all had their own vehicles and they had left the city already. For two weeks, we stayed there, and my mum was worrying because she didn't know where I was.' Every so often, the prisoners were called for questioning. If they refused to admit to being rebels, the soldiers beat them. 'With their hands, with a hose. Some people, with the guns. They didn't care; they wanted our answer to be what they said.' Jamal's left forearm was broken with the butt of a Kalashnikov. Even now, six years later, I could still see the scar. 'I had surgery, but in winter the pain is worse,' he said.

After two weeks, Jamal was released without charge. He went home. His mother hugged him, his sister teased him – 'Now, I suppose, I'm going to have to give you the remote control back' – and his life went back to its old routine: tea stall in the morning, television in the afternoon, football in the evening. But, as Jamal described it, a shadow had fallen over his life. 'The police told me I had to report to them for surveillance once a week. All the time, I'd go there: "You're still here?" "Yeah, I'm still here." It went on for a year, and after one year, I was like, "This is fucking bullshit; I didn't do anything and I'm still reporting, and for what?"' Before the arrest, Jamal had been happy to drift; afterwards, he said, his life felt like a dead end.

He started to pay attention to the stories his friends told about cousins, or friends of friends, who had left Sudan for Europe. 'We would be playing football, you see someone and he says, "My cousin is going to Britain, Mohammed's cousin is now in Greece," many things. We thought everybody who went had a better life.'

I asked Jamal what that phrase, 'a better life', had meant to them. 'When I'm saying I want to get my life better and better, I want it to have what I'm dreaming about. But in Sudan I cannot have it. Like, if I say I really want to marry, I want to have some shops. In Sudan, I cannot do it, because of limited things that I have. But if I get to Europe, I will finish my education and I will work there and I will start to get a better life and I will marry. But if I sit in Sudan, I will not do this. This is what I mean about better life. Some people, they have a dream to live. Some people, they want to die for something. Like, some people they say, "I want to go there to educate myself and I want to come back and change the system here." Some people say, "I want to change the government, I want to go there and see what they're doing and bring back the ideas to improve the country." We say this in Sudan: if you ain't found something to die for, you ain't fit to live.'

*

There are lots of reasons why young Sudanese might want to seek their fortunes elsewhere. Their country is rich in oil, gold and cotton, but a corrupt ruling elite and a crippling US trade embargo, imposed in the 1990s after Sudan was designated a state sponsor of terrorism, have hindered economic development. In 2015, a UN rapporteur found that the sanctions were having little impact on the elite, but had made life harder for ordinary people. The government's paranoid attitude towards its own citizens makes things harder still, especially for those who fall under suspicion, as Jamal did. Violent repression by the government of Omar al-Bashir has been forcing many Sudanese to leave since the 1990s.

The 1951 Convention on the Status of Refugees defines a refugee as a person who leaves their country with a 'well-founded fear of being persecuted for reasons of race, religion, nationality, membership of a particular social group or political opinion' and can't safely return home. The story Jamal told me – that his government regarded him as a subversive – was likely to place him in that category. In theory, this gave him the right to claim asylum in one of the 144 countries that have signed the Convention. But unless you're a political VIP – say, a senior North Korean official who wants to defect – it's almost impossible to claim asylum at an overseas embassy. Although some refugees come to Europe using their real ID documents, visas are hard to obtain for people from most parts of the world. Others who come to Europe to claim asylum do so with fake IDs, or via clandestine routes.

Jamal started to ask around. There was a route through North Africa, across the Sahara Desert, followed by a smuggler boat from Libya to Italy, but in 2008, when he first thought of leaving, migration was heavily policed by Muammar Gaddafi's regime. You could die in the desert, he was warned. One of Jamal's friends from football had a cousin who had taken an easier route, flying from Sudan to Turkey, then paying smugglers to take him across the border to Greece. Jamal got hold of his phone number and asked him for the contact of the smugglers in Turkey. First, though, he needed to get out of Sudan. He'd never had a passport, but he found a man in a bar who knew someone in the passport office, who said he could get a fake document for 2,000 euros. Jamal borrowed the money from his mother, although he didn't tell her what for.

'This is one of my rules,' Jamal said, as we sat on cushions in his room. 'If I want something, I will not say it's for me. I will say it's for someone else, so I can get something I need. Everything I want to do, this is how I do it.' Even his close friends didn't know what he was planning. 'Afterwards, when I get what I want, then they can know about it. If my friends knew, they would try and put things in my mind – this is dangerous, you will get caught – and it would confuse me.' It sounded crafty. 'Yeah,' Jamal said. 'Whenever I want to do something, I don't tell nobody. Just do it, whatever the consequences.'

Jamal's mum guessed what he was up to, though, and she thought it was a good idea. She helped him get a visa stamp for Turkey, via a friend who worked in the embassy, and lent him the money to pay smugglers there. Jamal booked a flight to Istanbul.

*

Jamal left Sudan in the spring of 2009; he remembered the date, he said, because a Champions League match was playing on the television at the airport in Khartoum. It was a few months after his eighteenth birthday, and this was the first time he'd ever crossed an international border – an unremarkable journey, if it hadn't been for the false documents.

On arrival in Istanbul, Jamal phoned the smugglers whose contact details he'd been given. Two Arabic-speaking men – he didn't know if they were Turkish or

Middle Eastern – came to pick him up. They took him to an apartment in the city, where he stayed overnight, and then drove him to Izmir, on Turkey's Aegean coast. There, he waited for a few days in an apartment with a dozen other people, from Sudan, Somalia, Egypt and elsewhere, who wanted to cross into Europe by boat. There were two false starts: one time, because the weather was bad; another, because a pregnant woman was part of the group and Jamal and some of the other men thought she might slow them down. On the third attempt, Jamal and the rest of his group were driven by minibus in the small hours to a deserted stretch of coastline a few hours from the city. By moonlight, the smugglers gave them a deflated dinghy and showed them how to blow it up. One of the group had been shown how to operate the motor. The journey took two hours, the crossing was calm and silent, and the group arrived on the shore of an island without incident. They destroyed the boat and threw the remains in the water, then set off inland to try to work out where they had landed. 'We didn't know where we were,' Jamal said. 'We started walking up the hill, then, after one or two hours, we saw an electricity pylon. An African guy with us knew some Greek letters, so he looked at it, saw the letter delta and said, "Fine, we're in Greece."' After several hours walking through the hills, Jamal's group encountered some police officers, who took them to their station, took their details and kept them overnight.

This was the second international border Jamal had crossed. But he hadn't only moved from one country to another; he had crossed the EU's external frontier. In 2009, according to statistics compiled by the EU border agency Frontex, there were 106,200 detections of unauthorized entry into the EU.

I asked Jamal if he'd had a plan for what to do next. 'No, just to Greece first of all. I didn't think it would be that difficult, so I just thought I would get to Greece and that's it. I will be safe in Europe, I said to myself. I know what I want to do there, in Europe. Turkey is not part of Europe, so they will not treat me the way that European people will treat me.'

The boat had landed on the island of Samos. There were now several sets of rules that potentially governed Jamal's movement. He had entered Greece without permission and without documents – he had ripped up his passport before leaving Turkey. The Greek authorities were within their rights to detain him and send him back to his home country, if they could determine where that was. But if he claimed asylum, then Greece would have to treat him in accordance with international and European agreements on refugees. Under the 1951 Convention, they would have to assess his claim on an individual basis. They were not allowed to punish him for entering the country illegally, and they were not allowed to send him back to Sudan, or any other country he had passed through where his safety was at risk. Under the Dublin system, it was Greece's responsibility to process Jamal's claim, since this was the first EU country he'd set foot in. But the Greek officials on Samos, knowing full well that most irregular migrants they encountered wanted to continue their journeys to elsewhere in Europe, or were willing to work on the black market in Greece, could neglect to ask if he wanted to claim asylum and send him on his way.

The police chose to let him go. They gave each person in Jamal's group a ferry ticket to Athens and a piece of paper saying they had to leave the country within a month.

In Athens, Jamal found his way to a Sudanese cafe, where the owners let him stay for a few days and advised him to go to Filiatra, a village in the Peloponnese, to find work. He went to Filiatra. He didn't like what he saw there – Sudanese men queuing up in the mornings to work on farms for twenty-five euros a day – so he asked the farm workers how to get out of Greece. They told him to go to Patras, a port in the west of the country, where ferries left for Italy. Greece is part of the Schengen zone of free movement, but it's cut off geographically from other EU member states by the Mediterranean, in one direction, and its Balkan neighbours, who aren't members, in another. At Patras, Jamal found some more Sudanese, living in abandoned train carriages on railway sidings near the port entrance. They told him that, since you needed ID to buy a ticket for the ferry, the only way to get into the port was by hiding underneath a lorry.

*

Lorries are like the red blood cells in our modern systems of distribution. They often mark the final stage of huge networks that span the globe, bringing food from industrial farms or consumer goods that arrive on container ships to local warehouses and shops. And to keep these systems working smoothly, the EU has invested heavily in removing the physical and legal barriers to trade. 'There is no single market without integrated transport networks,' a 2012 report from the European Commission declares. The report states that 44 per cent of goods in Europe are transported by road, and boasts of the funds deployed to improve roads, help drivers navigate using satellite technology and allow hauliers to pick up business in more than one member state. Lorry routes stretch across Europe and into Asia, and much like commercial passenger transport offers paying customers several classes of travel, the bulky vehicles offer a range of options to stowaways.

If you have the money and the contacts, you can pay a smuggling network to hide you among the cargo and take you, with the knowledge of the driver, from one destination to another. Otherwise, you need to hide yourself somewhere inside the lorry without being noticed. At ports and other freight-transport hubs, where large numbers of lorries have to park up or wait overnight, smugglers – or groups of migrants acting independently – might know how to unlock the back of a lorry and climb in while the driver is asleep, or away from the vehicle. It's riskier than the first option, and you don't necessarily know the lorry's destination, but at least you're inside. If you can't use either of these methods, because you don't have the money or you don't have access to the lorry parks, then you need to hide underneath, often while the lorry is in motion. This last method is the hardest and most dangerous. It rewards only the able bodied, and the migrants who try it are almost always men.

I'd spent a lot of time in Calais trying to find the spots where people did this, and a lot of time peering under lorries at home in London, trying to work out how exactly someone could hide themselves underneath, but I'd never quite understood it. I asked Jamal to explain.

'In Patras, there were traffic lights just before the port, and the lorries stopped there. They were in a big queue, waiting, with the smaller vehicles, so you go there and you run.' As he talked, I used the details to draw a diagram in my notebook. There was a road junction just before the traffic lights. Three of them, one acting as lookout, would hide around the corner. When the way was clear, the lookout would beckon the other two across and all three would run straight at the back of the vehicle, out of view of the driver's wing mirrors. Then they would crawl underneath, hoping that the driver behind wouldn't spot them, or wouldn't bother to alert the one in front.

I still didn't understand how they held on underneath, so I drew another diagram, of two wheels joined by an axle. 'You see the axle? You have to lay down here.' He pointed to the gap between the axle and the underside of the lorry container. 'You hold on above – to cables, or anything you find that isn't moving – then you're all ready to go.' I added a stick man with his head and feet resting on the wheel wells on opposite sides of the axle.

Jamal explained this with the confidence of a veteran, but when he first arrived in Patras, aged eighteen, he had been timid. And after a few days, the police caught him. This time, they asked Jamal if he wanted to claim asylum; he said yes, and they sent him to a camp for teenagers, outside Patras. Now, his movement was being governed by the Dublin system, the rules of which he had avoided on Samos. If he wanted to claim asylum in Europe, he would now have to do it in Greece.

But Greece, experiencing a severe economic crisis, was not what Jamal had expected of Europe. 'You arrive in Athens and you see people sleeping in the street, eating from the garbage, shops closed down. Then you go to Filiatra and they humiliate you there and give you twenty-five euros for a day's work. Then you go to Patras and you see how people like me are living: they're running from the police and the Greek community don't treat you well. So, all this makes you say you don't want to stay in Greece and you will try to leave.'

*

For the rest of 2009, Jamal used the camp as a base, taking trips back to Patras every few weeks to have another go at the lorries. He learned Greek and he bought a mobile phone with the money he earned doing odd jobs – painting and decorating, cooking – around the camp. This phone could play MP3s, and on the bus from the camp into town, he chatted to Greek teenagers about what music they listened to. 'I heard Rihanna in 2009 and I can't ever get tired of it,' Jamal said, explaining how he'd write down the names, then download the songs when he was back at the camp. 'I wanted to improve my English, so the more I listened to the music, the more I could speak.'

In 2010, he moved back to Patras, where he found a group of Sudanese men living in a disused factory near the port. There were about 200 in total, a few the same age as Jamal, but many who were older. Most of them came from Darfur, fleeing one of the worst massacres of the early twenty-first century; estimates of the death toll range from the tens of thousands to the hundreds of thousands. For a few years, the war was an object of global media scrutiny, after a campaign launched in 2006 by the Hollywood actor George Clooney. In 2009, Sudan's president, Omar al-Bashir, was indicted by the International Criminal Court for genocide, war crimes and crimes against humanity, but attention had already started to drift away from Darfur. Over two million people have been displaced by the conflict, a fraction of whom have sought asylum in Europe; most still live in camps in Sudan or in neighbouring Chad.

Like Jamal, the Darfuris had arrived in Europe with little money, and were relying on small networks of friends and contacts to help them make their journeys westwards. In the daytime, the inhabitants of the factory would go looking through the rubbish bins of Patras for food to eat, old electronic goods and clothes they could sell, or they would wait in supermarket car parks and offer to take back customers' trolleys in return for the one-euro deposit. In the evening, they would chase lorries that were queuing up for the ferry departures to Italy. The success rate was low, so most of the time the men would go back to the factory to cook dinner and spend the evening talking.

Jamal mainly spent time with people his own age, but in the evenings he would go and sit with the older men and listen to them talk politics. 'We couldn't be sitting around with these people in Sudan because we were too young and they wouldn't have allowed us to stay with them,' he said. 'But in Greece everyone was equal, if you're small or big, or you're poor or rich.' In Sudan, the older men had been doctors, engineers, teachers. Sometimes they talked about the corruption of the Sudanese government, or the persecution they'd suffered at the hands of paramilitaries and the security forces. Other times they'd talk about Sudanese music, or history. 'I was surrounded with people who had many experiences of life. Even the way they talked, I loved it so much. They would discuss politics in a fun way.'

Jamal had stopped going to school at fifteen because he couldn't be bothered to keep up the work, he told me, and he started to feel ashamed about his own lack of education. 'In Sudan, because of the way we were living, we didn't have time for searching what was going on in the news. We were working, making food, playing with friends, sleeping. In Greece, we had nothing to do; I was eighteen and my mind started to, like, catch everything around me. You start to realize what's going on there and make some questions. This is normal, every kid starts to do this, you know. The only difference is I was living in the factory. If I was in Sudan and I continue to the university, it will be much different. But these things came while I was surrounded with garbage and friends who were trying to cross to Italy and running from the police, so I didn't have the complete idea in my mind about everything. I was too upset, I was too disappointed and I was, like, "Why didn't I finish my school?"'

One of the elder men in particular helped Jamal broaden his horizons. He was a veterinarian who had been working in Darfur and was tortured by the government-aligned Janjaweed militia during the war. Jamal spent a lot of time talking with him. 'Every time we spoke, I felt happy, because he's a very funny man, and any topic you ask him about, he has ideas about it. When you speak with him, you benefit from him.'

This only strengthened Jamal's resolve to get out of Greece and reach a place where he could go back to school. The people around him had one destination in mind. 'Every time someone left, you would ask where he'd gone and he would be in Britain. We knew it was easier to claim asylum there. In some countries, you have to wait years, but in Britain, you'd only have to wait three or four months.' They hoped everyday life would be easier there, too. Some of the elders would say Britain was less racist than other parts of Europe because it had a lot of black people living there already. Others suggested that Britain would treat them better because Sudan had been a British colony. A 2006 report by the IOM claimed that

Britain had the oldest Sudanese diaspora in Europe, and estimated the size of the community there at between 23,000 and 53,000. Jamal decided that Britain was the place for him, too – he had better English than most of the Sudanese he knew; he'd be able to get on well at school there. Only the vet disagreed. He told Jamal the others were talking nonsense and that Norway was a much better place to aim for; their system treated the Sudanese more generously, he said.

Jamal lived in the factory at Patras for four years, following the same routine: living on what he could find from the streets; being picked up by police, pushed around and released; trying but not quite succeeding to get out of Greece. Once, he said, he saw a Sudanese man, someone he didn't know well, crushed to death under the wheels of a lorry. Another time, he clung onto the underside of a vehicle long enough to make it onto a ferry bound for Italy – but he was spotted on deck and sent straight back to Patras on the return journey.

At the end of January 2014, Jamal got lucky. He made it onto a ferry and stayed underneath the lorry so nobody would see him. He crawled around on the floor, scooping up water to drink from puddles when he got thirsty, listening to the grinding of the ship's engines and counting the hours of the journey. If it took twenty-four hours, he would be in Ancona. If it took thirty-six, he would be in Venice.

It took thirty-six.

2 · JAMAL

'After the phone comes the money, but the phone is most important because, without the phone, you cannot do anything.' We had met again the next day to resume our conversation, and Jamal was explaining how he'd made it from Venice to Calais. We'd got bored of the apartment, so had gone out into the city and found an art gallery to wander around. There was an exhibition of impressionist painting, which he was curious about. 'Can you tell me something? What is the point of painting like this?' he asked. He didn't seem convinced by my answer. We went outside and sat on the grass in front of the gallery to continue our interview.

It had been the middle of the night when he crawled out from underneath his lorry at a petrol station a few hours' drive from the port of Venice. He'd arrived with just two euros in his pocket and had ripped up his Greek asylum-seeker's identity card before leaving the boat, but it wouldn't have mattered in any case; in 2011, most EU countries had stopped returning people to Greece under the Dublin system, after the European Court of Human Rights ruled that conditions for asylum seekers there were inhumane. Jamal knew he had to get to Milan, where he could find other Sudanese migrants. He walked along the main road until dawn, when he met a Bangladeshi man who gave him directions to the nearest mosque. At the mosque, the imam told him to wait until after prayers, then held a collection for the price of a train ticket.

'I got the train to Milan the same day,' Jamal said. 'But I was too tired, I hadn't slept in two or three days, and I fell asleep in the train. It went past Milan and stopped in Turin.' Some teenage girls at the station in Turin showed him the way back. It was midnight when he arrived in Milan, and the station closed soon after, so he spent the night riding around on the city metro, trying to catch up on sleep. The next morning, he went back to the station and talked to strangers until he found a man who could show him to the neighbourhood where the Sudanese lived, so that he could ask someone to lend him money. The man Jamal met at the station was an Eritrean refugee called Mesfin. He had arrived in Milan from Greece via an over-land route through the Balkans, and was trying to get to Calais, too. The next day, a friend of Jamal's from Patras, Abdi, arrived in Milan, having stowed away on a ferry to Venice, so the three of them decided to travel together.

They took a train across the French–Italian border at Ventimiglia, before switching to an express to Paris, at Nice. This was the first time Jamal had passed over a land border within the Schengen zone. For EU citizens – and, usually, anyone who looks like an EU citizen – this is an open border. A group of American tourists, or a Dutch businessman, can drive along the coastal road from France to Italy, or take the train, without having their identity checked once, particularly if they're white. But France is allowed to return irregular migrants to Italy, if it catches them close to the border, under a provision of the Schengen Agreement. Given that there isn't a formal checkpoint at the French–Italian border, the only way officials can identify irregular migrants is by boarding the trains and checking people at random; or, as often happens in practice, checking black, Middle Eastern or Asian men and women who look like they might be irregular migrants.

In 2011, when many of the first migrants displaced by the Arab Spring – Tunisians, who had landed on the Italian island of Lampedusa – started making their way north, France temporarily reimposed controls on its border with Italy. Since then, the random checks had become more frequent. To avoid being caught, Jamal and his companions had bought copies of ID documents, in Milan, that belonged to people who had claimed asylum in France.

Abdi phoned a friend back in Patras, to get the number of another friend, who was already in Paris. At the Gare de Lyon, the friend came to meet the trio and took them to the La Chapelle district in the north of the city. At La Chapelle, a cosmopolitan neighbourhood, a metro line runs above ground, on a raised iron bridge, down the middle of the main road. Homeless people sleep under the bridge. Jamal and his friends joined them for a few nights, sleeping on top of the air vents from a second, subterranean metro line to keep out the winter cold, until they'd got hold of the numbers of some people in Calais. For the whole of the journey from Greece, Jamal said, aside from the clothes on his back, he'd only been carrying a jacket, his phone, headphones and a piece of paper with contact numbers written on it. They arrived in Calais on 12 February, two weeks after Jamal had reached Venice. His phone had run out of battery, so Mesfin called one of the numbers they'd been given.

*

Calais, which overlooks the narrowest point in the English Channel, is where the Schengen zone ends and the British border starts. For centuries, the port has provided the town with its livelihood. Today, it's the busiest crossing between the UK and mainland Europe, with ten million passengers taking the ferry route each year, and 17 per cent of the UK's imports and exports passing through the port. Another ten million passengers – and 1.4 million lorries – pass through the Channel Tunnel. The French entrance to the tunnel is at Coquelles, a few miles outside Calais. Much of the town was flattened by bombardment during the Second World War and, even today, the centre is marked by wide open spaces, punctuated by post-war blocks and a few surviving nineteenth-century buildings, including an imposing neo-Flemish town hall.

In the 1970s and 1980s, the industries that had supported the surrounding region – coal mining, steelworks and textile manufacturing – were all but destroyed as globalization made them less lucrative in France, but the port was given a boost by the growth of the EU. The removal of customs barriers brought more visitors from Britain, who took the short journey across the Channel to stock up on alcohol, which is taxed more lightly in France than the UK. But while Britain wanted the benefits of easier trade with Europe, it also wanted to keep its own border controls, so opted out of the Schengen Agreement. When the Channel Tunnel was dug in the early 1990s, a treaty between Britain and France created an arrangement known as juxtaposed controls, where Britain would be able to make its passport checks at the Eurostar terminal in France, and France would be able to do the same in Britain.

Within a few years, the tunnel entrance outside Calais

was attracting people who wanted to claim asylum in the UK. In 1999, the French government asked the Red Cross to open a reception centre in an old Channel Tunnel construction hangar at Sangatte, a village outside Calais, to house a growing number of refugees from the war in Kosovo, who were appearing destitute on the town's streets. They were joined by people from Iraq – including many Iraqi Kurds – as well as people from Iran and Afghanistan, and the population at Sangatte rose to over a thousand people. In 2002, under pressure from the British government, which in turn was under pressure from the tabloid press, the French government closed Sangatte. A year later, a new treaty between Britain and France extended the juxtaposed border controls to the ferry port at Calais and the port at Dover, on the English side of the Channel. The port and tunnel entrance were equipped with technology to catch stowaways: X-ray scanners, and monitors that detect carbon dioxide, noise or heat. Lorries were made part of the system, too. The UK Home Office threatens drivers and their employers with penalties of up to £2,000 for each 'clandestine entrant' discovered in a vehicle and provides a checklist on how to secure lorries with locks, padlocks, cords and straps.

After the closure of Sangatte, migrants continued to arrive at Calais in the hope of sneaking across to Britain, but the city council tried to discourage them. Most aid agencies were prevented by the city council from operating inside Calais, and the migrants were left to live in makeshift shelters, often hidden near motorways or lorry parks on the edge of town. Some camps were controlled by people smugglers, while those travelling independently would have to find their own places to shelter. These informal camps were dubbed 'jungles' – in local legend, a name coined by Afghans, derived from *dzhangal*, the Pashto word for forest. Whatever its origins, this is how most of the migrants referred to their camps. In 2009, police bulldozed the jungles, which had begun to attract unwelcome media attention, but they soon grew back.

By early 2014, there were around 200 to 300 migrants living in the town, according to local aid workers. Most came from Sudan, Eritrea or Afghanistan. Salam, a charity supported by volunteers, provided one hot meal a day and some basic aid. Shops and restaurants wouldn't let the migrants use their toilets or charge their phones unless they bought something; if they wanted to take a shower, they would have to wait for a place on a bus service run by the Red Cross, which took them to a day centre outside the city.

*

The first time I met Jamal was only a few days after he had arrived in Calais. I had been accompanying Yves, an elderly volunteer aid worker, on his morning round of the camps. Three times a week, he would load up his car with cartons of milk, packets of tissues and sugar, thermos flasks of tea, and out-of-date patisserie from a local super-market, and drive round Calais offering breakfast to the migrants. As we drove, Yves said he'd been a refugee as a child: when the Germans began their invasion of Calais, in 1940, his mother had thrown a few of the family's belongings into their car and driven the five-year-old Yves to relative safety, in the centre of France. We had stopped by a bridge that went over the canal that rings the city centre. On the towpath, beneath the bridge, about thirty men were camping in tents. As we approached, and Yves called out to announce he had tea, two men stood up from where they had been warming themselves around a fire made from wooden pallets, and came over to greet us. They introduced themselves as Eritreans. One was limping; he'd hurt his leg chasing after a lorry the night before. Then a third person, Jamal, greeted us from his tent. It was only a few degrees above zero, and Yves asked me to run back to the car and see if there was a coat for Jamal among the second-hand clothes he'd collected.

'I moved from there two nights after I met you,' Jamal said. In Calais, the migrants had separated themselves largely by nationality: the Sudanese had their own spot, and the Eritreans another. Jamal's contact in the Sudanese camp had told him and his two companions not to come until he'd got hold of a tent, so they'd asked a group of Eritreans under the bridge if they could stay with them.

Once Jamal had visited the aid workers at Salam and got hold of a tent, he moved to the Sudanese camp. Yves and I had visited this place the day we met Jamal at the bridge. It was on the edge of town, in a patch of scrubland between a supermarket car park and a motorway embankment. I remembered that, as we approached, it looked deserted, but once Yves started shouting 'Who wants tea? Sugar? Candles?' we started to see heads appear from behind bushes as the men began to climb out of their concealed tents and walk towards us.

'Did you realize why they were doing that?' Jamal asked me. 'Because they don't want the lorry drivers to see the tents. Or the police.' To find a good spot, Jamal said, you look for a bush or some long grass, you clear the ground of stones and broken bottles, then you put up your tent and make sure it can't be seen from the motorway. There were two camps, in fact: one by the supermarket, and one in a field on the other side of a little stream. In between the two was a shared kitchen – a low shelter, made out of wooden pallets and covered with tarpaulin, hidden by bushes. It had enough room for a fire and a large cooking pot, and shelves to store food.

None of the inhabitants knew how long this camp had been there, Jamal said. The only point of continuity was a set of rules, passed along by word of mouth: hide your tent carefully; don't invite people to stay if they're not Sudanese or if nobody else knows them; learn the places where you can hide in wait for the lorries and don't give away their locations.

Like in Patras, Jamal said, the Sudanese were using the cheapest and most difficult method to catch a lorry. The Eritreans had a different technique, squeezing themselves into a storage box beneath the trailer without the knowledge of the driver, but they did this at a lorry park outside of town and most of the Sudanese didn't have the 500 euros they would charge for access. There were more sophisticated smuggling networks, too, run by mafia from different parts of the world. These smugglers would keep their passengers in hidden encampments well outside the town centre and would charge large sums of money for passage to the UK. A trial in 2014 of eight smugglers of Egyptian and Tunisian origin revealed they were offering 'à la carte' services that ranged from a 'Classic Package' (a journey in the back of a lorry, for up to £2,000) to a 'VIP Service' (a trip in a car, with a willing driver, for up to £4,000). When drivers couldn't be bribed, the techniques for breaking into lorries were sophisticated: cutting around the lock on the back of the trailer, replacing it with a new one and sealing it back up again, or cutting through a padlock and gluing it back together so it didn't look tampered with.

Jamal said he'd met Kurdish and Afghan smugglers who could provide services like these, but even if he'd had the money, they were off-limits to him. 'The smugglers each have their own parking lots, but the Kurds or the Afghans cannot take a black male there. They can take Afghan or Arab people, because you can dress well and, if the drivers see you, they won't be suspicious. But if the drivers see them with a black man, they'll definitely know they're smugglers.'

The advantage of the Sudanese camp was that it bordered a lay-by where lorry drivers stopped before joining the motorway, which, in one direction, ran towards the Channel Tunnel entrance. There were three places to hide and lie in wait: underneath the motorway bridge; behind trees that lined the road leading up to the lay-by; or in a hole the migrants had dug in the ground and lined with mattresses, just next to the lay-by itself. The last place was the best spot, but to avoid being seen you had to go there at night and stay there until dawn, or until you successfully chased a lorry.

'I always chose the trees,' Jamal said, 'because I don't like staying up all night.' When a lorry pulled up and the driver got out to check through his or her papers before entering the Channel Tunnel, or to go to the toilet, the Sudanese would make a dash for it. 'It was easy to run and hide quickly because we'd done the same things in Greece,' Jamal said. Those migrants who hadn't been in Patras didn't know how to do it, so Jamal taught them.

If you managed to get underneath a lorry, Jamal said, you had to wait and see if it turned in the right direction, towards the tunnel. If not, you'd be heading north, towards Belgium, and you had to pick a safe moment to drop off and start walking back to Calais. If the lorry was heading in the right direction, you'd wait and see if you made it past the checkpoints at the tunnel entrance and onto the train. Two days after Jamal and his companions had arrived at the Sudanese jungle, the friend who had brought them there made it through. 'He was hiding in the hole, at night, and when we woke up, he had gone.' A week or so later, Abdi and Mesfin made it across the Channel as well.

The two friends who had accompanied Jamal from Milan to Calais had left him on his own – but, as Jamal explained it to me, that was normal. You team up, you help one another for as long as it's necessary, then you separate. 'When the lorry goes onto the train and the train starts to move, you ring your friends, say, "Yo, guys, I'm in the train, good luck for you, I'm going now."' Then, he said, you take the SIM card out of your phone, rip it up and throw the pieces on the floor so you can't be traced back to France.

3 · JAMAL

We walked back to Jamal's apartment. He asked if I wanted tea, and we went into the kitchen. He showed me how to make it Sudanese style, with the bags dropped directly into a pan of milk, heated on the stove, and heaped spoonfuls of sugar stirred in at the end.

This was the sort of tea Jamal had helped his mother sell in Khartoum. Did she know where he was now? I asked. 'No, she died when I was in Greece,' he said, in a way that suggested he didn't want to talk about it any further.

Back in his room, Jamal described how he had settled into a new routine at the Sudanese camp. He'd wake up at ten or eleven each morning, having spent half the night waiting and watching for lorries. First, he'd go to the kitchen to check if there was anything for breakfast, left by volunteers like Yves, who the Sudanese nicknamed 'Uncle Foolly' – Uncle Peanuts – because of the food he usually brought. At one o'clock, the camp residents would make lunch – usually assida, a stew with flour, plus whatever they could find to add to it. They'd discuss who'd found a lorry the night before, who'd ended up where. When lunch was finished, people would either head to the site, out of town, where they could take a shower, or go to a church in the centre of Calais that provided second-hand clothes, or try to find somewhere to charge their phones.

Most of the time, Jamal said, he went to a squat on the edge of the town centre. For the migrants, Calais in 2014 was a network of hidden self-built encampments and squatted buildings, often taken over with the help of activists from the No Borders network. The activists were mostly Europeans, from France, Germany, Britain and elsewhere, drawn together through a loose network of groups that support freedom of movement and oppose border controls. No Borders isn't an organization, as such, more a shared set of ideas and methods for activists to adopt. 'Borders are created by, and serve, capitalist elites,' reads a statement on the UK No Borders website. 'Borders are used to divide and rule us, for example to set "citizens" competing against "illegal" workers, and to impose the law of the market.' In Calais, it was their skills in occupying and claiming squatters' rights on empty buildings that brought them into close contact with the migrants. The squat Jamal used to visit was an old town house, which sheltered women refugees. All but the front room was off-limits to men.

Jamal liked hanging out in the front room there, its walls graffitied with anti-racist slogans, because he could charge his phone and talk to the people who passed through. Many of the people he spoke to were from Eritrea. In most parts of Calais, Jamal said, the Sudanese and the Eritreans kept away from one another, to avoid fighting. 'The Eritreans resent the Sudanese because, in Sudan, they are treated badly and can't talk back there.'

Eritrea, a former Italian colony in the Horn of Africa, taken over after the Second World War, first by the British, and then Ethiopia, won its independence in 1993. But the rebel leaders who formed the first government have kept their citizens on a paranoid war footing ever since, with indefinite military service compulsory for all adult men and women, and severe restrictions on communications. The government persecutes religious minorities and opposition activists, and treats people who leave as traitors. A diaspora of several hundred thousand Eritrean refugees has spread into Sudan and Ethiopia, while some have gone further afield. In 2014, according to the EU statistics authority Eurostat, over 36,000 Eritreans applied for asylum in Europe, one of the largest groups by nationality.

'In Calais,' Jamal continued, 'they can do what they like and there are more of them. And the Sudanese, who are used to ordering them around, get upset and angry at them. So that's why they don't get on with one another.' But the front room at the squat was a kind of neutral meeting point; those who entered were asked to leave their rivalries at the door.

At six p.m., the migrants of Calais would converge on one place: the food distribution point on an empty industrial site near the port entrance. Overlooked by the town's lighthouse, its beam sweeping through the dusk, they would be made to queue at a gate in the wire fence. When it was opened, the migrants would dash to queue for food or use a tap, which provided the only clean water many of them had access to. They'd be handed a box of stew or curry with rice, a boiled egg and a banana. Medical volunteers were on hand to treat them for minor ailments caused by the cold and the dirt and the hunt for lorries: sprains and scratches, infected cuts or teeth, headaches and stomach complaints. Police officers from the French riot squad, the CRS, would gather around the distribution point and monitor the migrants, which made them uneasy.

Jamal would usually take his food back to the camp and wait there for a few hours before going to his usual hiding place and waiting for the lorries to arrive.

Only once during this period did Jamal successfully manage to stow himself away. 'I got to the tunnel, but at the first checkpoint I was caught. Security staff brought dogs at random between the lorries, and one dog stopped beside me and started to bark.' The staff shone a torch under Jamal's lorry, told him to get out, and handed him over to the French police. 'The police came, they asked me how old I was, I gave a fake name, they said, "OK, it's not a problem, no big deal. Where are you from?" I said, "Sudan." They said, "OK, let's go," and they dropped me off near the train station.'

It almost sounded like a game. Another person I'd met had even described it in that way: 'We're the little mice and they're the cats, and they try to catch us.' It wasn't in anybody's interest to make more of a fuss; the French state wasn't in a hurry to accommodate the migrants, while the migrants wanted to pass through Calais as quickly and as quietly as possible. But the game took its toll. During one week, in March 2014, two people – one Eritrean, another unidentified – were killed by vehicles on the motorway at Calais, and an Ethiopian man was found dead in the canal.

Jamal said that, from time to time, aid workers and lawyers would visit the Sudanese camp and encourage the inhabitants to claim asylum in France. 'For us, this was not acceptable,' he said, 'because France is not like the UK or other countries. If you're living in tents, on the street, like we were, you have to stay in these conditions.' In 2014, over 64,000 people claimed asylum in France, compared with around 33,000 in Britain. But long delays in the French system, and a housing shortage – 15,000 people were on the waiting list for accommodation at the end of 2013 and only a third of asylum seekers were being housed, according to a report by Human Rights Watch – meant many people would stay homeless, even after they claimed asylum. 'Even if they do house you, it's in a place with rules, where you are woken up every morning and told to leave, and not allowed back in until eight p.m. So you spend all day on the streets, anyway.'

*

Throughout March 2014, the number of migrants arriving in Calais began to rise. This usually happened in spring; people would wait until the end of winter before travelling, and the number sleeping rough in the town would rise from a few hundred to over a thousand in the summer months. Aid volunteers told me that movement had followed this pattern since the mid-2000s. But in 2013 and 2014, Calais started to feel the tremors of a larger crisis around the edges of the European Union. In October 2013, a group of Syrians blocked the entrance to the ferry port, demanding access to Britain. Their protest was ignored, and most of them either made it to Britain as stowaways or went elsewhere in Europe, but the camp they set up stayed, and by the spring of 2014, it was inhabited by Afghan and Pakistani men. Other sites were springing up around the town: camps hidden on former industrial land on the far side of the port; derelict buildings occupied in the centre of town. The local council was encouraging residents to report these sites, via an anonymous tip-off hotline, whenever they emerged.

At Jamal's camp, people continued to arrive from Patras every few days, but they were joined by men who had taken the more dangerous route out of Sudan: across the Sahara Desert, through Libya and to Italy via smuggler boat. They had mostly been farmers in Darfur, who either lost their land to the fighting or were chased out by Janjaweed militia. Unlike the veterans of Patras, who had arrived in 2008 or 2009 and spent several years working their way across Europe, building up networks of trust, many of the new arrivals had come directly from Italy. The smuggler route from Libya had become more popular after the fall of the Gaddafi regime, and since October 2013, the Italian navy had been running a search-and-rescue operation in the central Mediterranean to bring migrants to dry land.

Jamal didn't get on as well with these new arrivals. They were older, in their thirties mainly, and they were strangers to him; they'd formed their own networks and relationships of trust during their journeys through Libya. Jamal didn't even like the music they listened to – traditional Sudanese crooners, like Mustafa Sid Ahmed and Mahmoud Abdel Aziz – so he often preferred to sit alone in his tent, or at the squatted town house, listening to Eminem on his headphones, while the newly arrived Sudanese sat in the camp kitchen together. Jamal missed his friend Abdi, he said. 'He's a very funny guy. We'd always be joking, sometimes cursing each other. But because of the age difference, I couldn't joke with the older guys in the same way.'

*

About a month into Jamal's stay, life for the Sudanese was disrupted when a Calais resident spotted the part of the camp located in the field across the stream, and reported it to the council. Police came to evict the inhabitants, making them tear down their shelters. When the police had gone, the evicted migrants came and pitched their tents in the scrubland behind the supermarket. Now, around forty people shared this small patch of ground next to the motorway, and there wasn't enough space to hide all of the tents. The atmosphere between the inhabitants became tense, and people started to blame Jamal for bringing strangers to the camp.

'Every three days, every four days, someone new would arrive from Patras and they would phone me to ask where they could stay.' This was normal, Jamal thought. When he had arrived, he'd had the knowledge passed on to him; now, he was the point of contact and he would pass it on to others. 'I felt like I was a part of the jungle, and my friends coming from Greece had known me for several years, so they wanted to stay with me.' But the others, the ones who had come through Libya, started asking him questions: Why are you bringing so many people here? Don't you know we'll get discovered? 'They were saying it in a nice way, but I realized they were angry. And every time I brought someone to the camp, and that person managed to cross the Channel, they'd get even more angry. Because they were still stuck in Calais.'

Some of the men started to make pointed comments about Jamal's appearance, too, playing on the physical differences between Arab and African Sudanese. 'They said I wasn't Sudanese, because of my skin colour, because of my hair.' They suggested he was Eritrean or Ethiopian, and just pretending to be Sudanese. 'Or they said I was European, because I had been in Europe so long.' Jamal explained to me that, because of the Sudanese government's abuses, there was a lot of resentment among Darfuris towards people like him, who came from the 'Arab' part of the country. 'I tried to explain to them, "Please do not bring this problem here, don't blame everybody, we are not the government."' But he couldn't argue too forcefully, he said, because he didn't want to lose his place in the camp.

One evening, a group of strangers arrived at the camp and tried to use the hiding places to watch for lorries. The men sitting around the kitchen fire got up and chased them away. Jamal watched this happen from his tent. Afterwards, one of the men from the kitchen came over to Jamal and accused him of having invited the strangers. 'He said, "You are the one who brought people here." He was older – like, forty-five or something – and he had big muscles and often acted crazy to scare people.' Jamal's accuser picked up an empty beer bottle from the ground. 'I knew he was going to throw it at me,' Jamal said, 'so I bent over and the bottle came, *whoosh*, over my hair.' He pulled a face to show how shocked he'd been. 'I ran, and everyone started to laugh at me. I was like, "It's become crazy here! He might get out of control."'

Afterwards, another of the Darfuris, one who was usually kind to Jamal, came to find him. 'He came and he told me, "This is happening because of what you are." It's racism, he said.' Jamal didn't go back to his tent that night. 'I went and found the No Borders, and asked if I could stay in one of their squats.' He went back to the camp the next day, but, as he said, he started staying up all night because he was too scared to sleep. 'If you feel uncomfortable there, you take every word as a threat to you. Sometimes they say ordinary words, but they sound like threats: "We're going to take you from here, if you bring another person here."' He started to spend as much time as he could with the No Borders activists, away from the other Sudanese. 'I needed someone to talk to, because

I couldn't take any more, and if I didn't speak to someone, I would explode. If I got angry, it would have given the others more reason to attack me.'

But the more Jamal stayed away from the camp, the harder it would be for him to get out of Calais.

4 · ZAINAB

In London, shortly after visiting Jamal, I arranged an interview with someone else who'd passed through Calais in 2014. Zainab had travelled from Iraq with her three children; they'd stayed in Calais for several months, where they'd met a friend of mine, before making it across to Britain. I'd spoken to her over Facebook and she said she'd be willing to tell me her story.

It was a Saturday afternoon when I went to meet Zainab. She welcomed me into her house, an ex-council flat in a South London suburb. She was a quiet thirty-year-old with a cautious demeanour; she had received her refugee status a month earlier, and was only just beginning to rebuild her life. We sat in her living room, which was filled with furniture bought from a car boot sale. A playlist of songs by the Lebanese singer Fairouz was cued up on the television. Around the TV were photos of Zainab and her husband Ahmed, on holiday in Turkey and Jordan. 'We took a lot of holidays before,' she explained. From the room next door, I could hear her three children – a girl, aged eight, and twin boys, aged seven – fighting over the PlayStation Portable. Zainab asked them to come into the room and meet me, and they lurked in the doorway, staring shyly, before running back to their game.

It wasn't easy for us to communicate during this first

meeting. My Arabic was limited to a few nouns; her rudimentary English wasn't enough to tell me her story in detail. She was waiting for term to start, so she could take up language lessons at the local college. We smiled politely at one another a lot, and pointed to things around the room. Zainab managed to tell me that she'd left Iraq in June 2014, when ISIS took over her home province.

The story someone might tell about their journey after they've had a few years to reflect on it, and make sense of the things that didn't make sense at the time, is different to the story someone might tell upon their moment of arrival. And a story mediated through a translator might be different still; the more people involved, the more like a formal inquiry it feels. Displaced people are asked repeatedly to tell their stories by journalists, government agencies and NGO workers, sometimes by a hostile or sceptical interviewer. Points on a list are ticked off and people are assigned to different categories: genuine refugee or bogus asylum-seeker; urgent case or one for the waiting list; newsworthy or easily forgotten. Our conversation lapsed into silence, partly because of the language barrier, but also because we didn't yet know what to make of one another. Perhaps she was uneasy talking to a man, or I was more hesitant to ask questions of a woman. I felt like Zainab wasn't sure whether I was someone who would help her or exploit her; this was a weighing-up process she must have been through more than once on her journey.

I wanted, as far as possible, to hear Zainab's story the way she wanted to tell it. So I suggested that I leave my Dictaphone with her and she record her story in Arabic. I could then get a friend to translate it.

A few weeks later, the recording was ready. 'I am Zainab ------, from the Diyala Governorate in Iraq,' her voice began. 'I have three children: a daughter and two sons. My husband is a military engineer. We were living in Iraq, despite the dangers and despite death – despite the fact that absolutely everything was dangerous, even the air we were breathing was dangerous – but we tried to live, we tried to protect ourselves, our house and our children as much as possible.' I wondered if I'd made the wrong decision, whether Zainab would be too distressed to tell her story. But the details that followed were clear and precise.

Zainab described a relatively comfortable family life, even amid the chaos of Iraq after the US-led invasion. Her father owned a regional chain of supermarkets; she taught maths at a high school and ran an ice-cream making business on the side. Their province, Diyala, was bordered by Iran to the east, and Iraqi Kurdistan to the north. Her hometown was mixed, and Zainab, who was Sunni Arab, spoke fluent Kurdish and a smattering of Farsi. Her husband, Ahmed, was a technician at a base close to Iran. During the occupation, he'd worked with American soldiers who were securing the border. Some of the soldiers had befriended the family, and Ahmed would sneak them off the base at night so they could take showers, or drink together, at his and Zainab's house. The couple knew that a lot of people in their town hated the occupying forces and saw any friendliness towards the soldiers as collaboration, so they kept it a secret from their neighbours. When the soldiers left, in 2007, Ahmed continued to work at the base, driving thirty miles each way every day.

*

In June 2014, ISIS swept through northern Iraq, exploiting the country's instability to seize territory from the panicked and retreating national army. In June, when groups of ISIS fighters arrived in Zainab's hometown, sympathizers tipped them off about potential enemies. Ahmed was targeted because he worked for the Iraqi army. 'They came to the house looking for my husband,' said Zainab on the recording. 'They left us threatening notes three times. The first two times, they knocked at the door and gave the notes to me. The third note they left in the garden. We found it at eight in the morning. It was left next to my daughter's dog. They had slaughtered the dog, having fed it poisoned food beforehand. The note said, "We will slaughter you like we have slaughtered this dog." I took the note, ran back inside the house and started shouting and crying. My husband asked me, "Tell me what's happening, why are you crying?" I told him I had found the threatening note and found our dog. My children were crying, especially my daughter, about the dog. But they didn't know about the note and what was written in it.'

Ahmed hugged Zainab and the children and told them not to worry. 'If they do kill me,' he said to Zainab, when they were alone, 'I won't let them do it in front of my children. I will go to work and will live there, so that I don't have to go back and forth between work and home.' Ahmed went to stay on the base. From then on, Zainab recalled, 'our relationship was maintained only through the phone.'

After a few weeks, ISIS fighters came back to the house. From their accents, Zainab could tell many weren't Iraqi. When she said she didn't know where her husband was, they attacked her. 'I wasn't wearing a hijab; they pulled me by the hair and dragged me outside. They said, "You are an infidel. What's this? Why aren't you wearing a hijab? You're an infidel! You're not a Muslim." I said I was

Muslim, but that I wasn't wearing a hijab because I was indoors, in my house, not outside. I tried convincing them. They said, "No, even if you're at home, you must cover your hair with a hijab. Why haven't you?"

'My children and I were sitting in the garden, and two people were guarding us. One was carrying a pistol and the other a rifle, and they were pointing them at us, so that, if we moved, they would shoot us.' The fighters smashed up the house and looted the family's jewellery, mobile phones and their two cars. After they left, Zainab hurriedly packed a few belongings and took the children to stay with her parents and sister, across town.

The family had been displaced, but they didn't officially count as refugees because they hadn't yet crossed an international border. Internally displaced persons, or IDPs, don't have any special rights under international law, even though they face the same threats as refugees and are often more vulnerable because they haven't necessarily left the zone of conflict. International organizations like the UNHCR might provide assistance, such as tent camps or food aid, but the national government is still officially responsible for the welfare of IDPs. In 2014, the progress of ISIS through northern Iraq displaced over two million people, adding to the two million already internally displaced by more than a decade of occupation and internal conflict.

Zainab thought she would be staying with her parents for a few weeks, until things settled down, but being forced from her home was only the first in a series of catastrophes that brought her, ultimately, to Europe. 'I didn't tell my husband about what had happened,' she continued. 'I used to call him at work and not tell him about ISIS's visit, about the fact they had destroyed the house, taken the money, the gold, that they had threatened us.' For a few days, from her parents' house, Zainab kept talking to Ahmed on the phone as if nothing had changed. Then she suddenly found his phone was switched off. This wasn't usual. 'I called my husband's friend, but he would not answer. I tried reaching another of his friends at work, and again his phone was switched off. Same thing for the third one I phoned. Only one of his friends' mobile phones was switched on, but he wasn't answering. I got really worried.

'I called one last time. Finally, this friend whose phone was switched on answered my call. His voice was loud and he was crying. I said, "I beg you, brother, just tell me what's happening. Why are you crying?" He said, "No, nothing's happening. I'll just tell you that Ahmed is alive." I asked again, "Please, tell me what's happening." He answered, "A group called Asaib Ahl al-Haq [League of the Righteous] broke in."' The Iraqi government's response to ISIS had been to arm a series of Shi'a militia groups, who fought alongside the regular army to take back the territory they had lost in June. But many of the Shi'a groups had a sectarian agenda of their own, and were abusing the Sunni populations in areas they liberated, kidnapping people and holding them for ransom. 'They killed some here, but they didn't kill Ahmed,' the friend told Zainab. 'I saw them take him.'

Zainab wasn't any safer at her parents' house, either. About a week after Ahmed was kidnapped, ISIS fighters reached her new neighbourhood. 'It was around seven in the morning. They made all the families get out of their houses and stand on the street. When we got out, there were seven or eight bodies lying there. We saw them – they were neighbours from my parents' street. They beat us and they broke into my parents' house.' As before, the fighters took anything of value. Then they asked Zainab's sister where her husband was.

'She answered, "My husband is not here; I'm divorced." She didn't really think. She said she was divorced because, for her, it's a normal thing. They said, "You're divorced?" She answered, "Yes." They said, "OK, you're coming with us." We all tried to defend my sister. They pushed me, they pushed my mother down the stairs in the garden and she broke her foot. They shot at my father twice – once at his chest and once at his foot. The shot in his chest didn't go near his heart. They took my sister and left. My father kept bleeding and bleeding for about seven hours, in my arms, until he passed away.'

On the recording, Zainab told these details in a flat, slightly quickened voice. Every now and then, she would ask a rhetorical question. 'What could I do? None of the neighbours could do anything, as everyone had to take care of a body or two in their own house.' She tried to return home, but found that the ISIS militants had demolished her house with explosives.

*

Zainab and her children moved again, to the house of one of Ahmed's friends in a neighbouring town. 'He was a businessman,' Zainab said. 'Two or three months before everything happened, we had lent him a sum of money. So, when everything happened, and we were left without anything, and my husband had gone, my father had gone, I called him and told him I needed the money. He said OK, but added, "Why give you the money when you and the children are in a bad situation? This money won't help. You are homeless, you are displaced. What are you going to do with this money? My advice is as follows: I have a friend who is a smuggler and who can help you reach Europe."'

At first, Zainab wasn't sure. She still couldn't get in touch with Ahmed; her calls would go straight to answerphone. She called his brother and his father, but they didn't know where he was either. Zainab later told me that they put pressure on her to marry Ahmed's brother so that he could bring up the children. She decided to leave for Europe.

In mid-August, the businessman took Zainab and the children to Zakho, a town in Iraqi Kurdistan, near the border with Turkey. Here, he introduced them to some of his contacts, who also worked as smugglers. 'As we didn't have passports –' Zainab hadn't had time to take the family's passports before they were forced out of their home – 'they made us take a lorry, and we crossed to Turkey.'

The lorry drove them west across Turkey to Izmir, the city from which Jamal had left for Greece five years earlier. Many refugees from Syria and Iraq had joined the route, and, in 2014, according to the UNHCR, over 43,000 people made the crossing from Turkey. Unlike when Jamal passed through Izmir, the smuggling trade was now being conducted openly. Izmir's downtown district was full of families trying to make contact with smugglers. Zainab approached strangers until she found a husband and wife, from Syria, who had already made contact with a smuggler. 'Come with us,' they said. The smuggler brought their group to a beach outside Izmir, where they were told to board an inflatable dinghy. 'My children and I climbed on the dinghy, crying. My children didn't know what was happening. They used to associate the sea and the beach with happiness. They didn't know this dinghy could lead to death.'

The boat started taking on water midway through the journey and the captain made all the passengers throw their bags overboard. Zainab lost all her family's clothes, except for what they were wearing. But they made it to Greece. On arrival, they were picked up by police and allowed to continue to Athens by ferry. Zainab had been given the number of a smuggler in Athens by the businessman who took her to Zakho. 'My smuggler friend, who was in Iraq, called this smuggler and said, "I don't want you to take them to Europe; I want you to take them to Great Britain." I said, "Any place, but it's important that it's safe for me and my children." My friend in Iraq said that the only safe place was Great Britain, and asked him to take us there.'

They were taken by boat – this time, a yacht – to Italy, with other refugees from Iraq and Syria, then hidden in the back of a lorry on a circuitous journey to France. Somewhere in Austria, they were made to change vehicles. After that, Zainab didn't know what route they took, but in Paris they transferred to a car, which took them the rest of the way to Calais.

Zainab had left home with about 30,000 dollars – the money the friend owed her – most of which was in 500-euro bills. The trip in the lorry from Iraq to Turkey had cost 5,000 dollars. The trip in the boat from Izmir to Greece had cost 7,000 dollars. The journey from Greece to France, in all its stages, had cost more than 11,000 dollars. By the time she and the children arrived in Calais, all Zainab had was her phone and enough money to pay for the final stage of the journey. Her businessman friend had been very insistent that they aim for Britain. 'He said that Britain was better because they had better human rights and the language is easier. The way he explained it to me is that I would arrive to France and the following day I would be in Great Britain. I didn't know what smuggling meant, anyway. But I never expected this. I thought the whole journey from Iraq to Britain would take, at most, a week.'

5 · JAMAL

It was my third day of interviews with Jamal and he suggested we meet at the train station, as we had before. He was late, and apologized when he arrived. He'd been waiting to meet someone who could send money back to Greece for him. Jamal explained that only one of his friends was still in Patras – a young man who was too fat and too timid to chase after the lorries. He wanted to borrow money to pay a smuggler to take him across the Balkans towards Germany. This was how people lent each other money, Jamal said: through trusted contacts. Or they transferred it via Western Union and got someone with a passport to go and collect it. Jamal told me that his sister had done the same thing for him a few times when he was on the road, sending a hundred euros or so, on the rare occasions she had it to spare.

It was hot, so we made our way down to the river that runs through the town, and bought ice creams. Jamal picked up his story where he'd left off the evening before.

Shortly after his clash with the Darfuris, at the beginning of April, the police started visiting the Sudanese camp behind the supermarket, taking photos and counting the number of people living there. At first, they left the inhabitants alone, but No Borders activists told Jamal and the others that the camp would be evicted soon. Activists with a connection in the local council managed to find out the date, in mid-April, that the eviction was scheduled for. To avoid being arrested, most of the camp residents left and went back to Paris, where they could sleep rough until it was safe to try Calais again. The day before the eviction, No Borders activists came to stay with Jamal and the few others who remained.

'I was trying the lorries that night,' he recalled. 'I came back at five or six in the morning, to sleep. At seven o'clock, I started to hear whistling.' The activists were trying to wake everyone up, to warn them that the police had arrived. 'We found we were surrounded – on both sides, from the motorway to the supermarket.' Officers from the CRS, France's riot police, were encircling the camp, dressed in protective vests and wearing helmets. 'I tried to run, but they caught me. They took me to my tent and told me to pack everything.' Jamal was tired and irritable, he said, and he argued back. 'They were taking pictures of everybody and I hid my face. One of the cops asked why I didn't want my picture taken and I said, "Do you want me to take your personal picture?" They started asking questions and I was acting like an arrogant boy. I didn't want to speak.' He was led to a police van and, once inside, one of the officers hit him. 'Like, "Now you listen to me and do exactly what I say."'

Jamal was taken to a police station near the port. He was asked to give his fingerprints, but he refused. 'They tried to question us: "Where are the rest of you in the camp?" "Who leaked the information that we are coming to you?" "If we let you go, where will you go?" I said I'd go anywhere. They tried to convince me that, if I claimed asylum in France, they could help me, but I refused.'

After five or six hours, the police let Jamal go. He

headed for a building that the No Borders activists had recently occupied: a disused office block near the canal that rings the town centre. 'They wanted refugees to come and stay there; it was a huge building in the middle of town, with two floors. It had a kitchen and a bathroom.' Jamal took possession of the upper floor.

'And here's the funny thing,' he said. 'I started to create my own group: only Sudanese people who came through Greece.' Each time a new person from Patras arrived in Calais, they would phone Jamal, and he would show them to the upstairs of the office building. 'A lot of people were coming from Greece, and nobody could tell me, "Don't bring them here," because the place belonged to no one now. The people from the jungle who had a problem with me stayed downstairs.'

Jamal started to feel confident again, he said, especially because he had a skill that was now in demand. His years in Patras had taught him how to find the best food from the town's rubbish bins. Jamal and his newly arrived friends on the upper floor of the office block set themselves challenges to see who could find the most food in a day. Soon, they had made a mental map of Calais, with all the best spots marked down. The bins of Carrefour, near the train station, were often stuffed with cheese and croissants. At the Match supermarket, you could find meat, although you had to check it hadn't gone green yet. The McDonald's tipped away buckets of uneaten French fries, while the out-of-town Lidl was good for bread. 'It kind of made me the leader,' Jamal said. 'I told my friends where to go, and they'd bring food back. I became the king of skipping, there.'

Even the people downstairs, the men who had threatened him at the old camp, started to change their attitude.

'They started to open their arms to me and laugh with me. They came and asked us for food. Even the guy who had thrown a bottle at me came upstairs and said, "Please, I know you've got more than you need, will you share it with us?" I thought, OK, I won't treat them the way they treated me, so I gave them what I had. I didn't forget what they'd done to me, but I didn't want to embarrass them in front of my friends.'

The new squat was further away from the motorway, so between them, upstairs and downstairs, the Sudanese made new rules about who could go to chase for lorries and when. 'We made four groups. Each had a day they could go to the old hiding places. We were still about thirty to forty people, but the squat was growing bigger because more people were arriving in Calais. We had a waiting list. If someone in a group managed to cross the Channel, then we replaced him with one of the people waiting.'

The new space became a centre for new activities. A local man, originally from Sudan himself, came to offer French and English lessons. He had been a teacher before coming to Europe, and liked to play up to the role: in a corduroy jacket, he would write out long lists of French and English proverbs on a whiteboard and get his class to repeat them in unison. The No Borders activists organized political meetings, inviting refugees and activists living elsewhere in Europe to come and share ideas. They talked with the migrants about how best to defend themselves from racist attacks. Since the start of 2014, an anti-immigration group calling itself Sauvons Calais ('Save Calais') had been trying to build support for its demonstrations, via Facebook. It was becoming increasingly common for migrants, as well as the volunteers who worked with them, to be intimidated or assaulted when walking around the town at night.

*

As the coastal spring weather softened, migrants were arriving in Calais with greater frequency. By early May, their estimated number had risen to over 800 and their presence began to attract the attention of international media. On 5 May, an Afghan man was rescued from the Channel after trying to sail to Britain on a boat made from wooden planks, with a bed sheet for a sail. At the end of the month, the local council announced that inhabitants of the Eritrean camp under the canal bridge and the 'Syrian' camp outside the port (which was now inhabited by people of different nationalities) had become infected with scabies, and their shelters needed to be demolished. In view of television cameras and reporters, riot police pushed out the inhabitants, before bulldozers moved in to tear down the tents. Council workers dressed in protective white suits, with white face masks, came last, to clear away the rubbish and sodden blankets.

With nowhere to go, several hundred of the displaced occupied the Salam food-distribution site. Jamal and the No Borders activists helped them to secure their new home. 'We blocked the gates with a big shield of wooden pallets, so the police couldn't come in,' Jamal said. 'And there was a lot of media that day, so the police couldn't beat anyone. They just warned us they'd be back to evict the site another time.' The occupiers, several hundred of them, encouraged by No Borders activists, held an open meeting where they discussed their aims. A few days later, they issued a letter, addressed to the Calais prefecture. *Mr Prefect,* it began. *We, the homeless migrants of Calais,*

*have occupied the food distribution centre. All of the com-
munities have come together and decided to unite to find
a solution for our situation. We do not want to live like
animals anymore, we want to live like normal human
beings and to have access to dignified living conditions, no
matter whether we have papers or not.* The letter went on
to demand housing with decent hygienic conditions, protection from harassment and eviction, and negotiations
between Britain and France to allow people to access
British territory. The response from officials restated their
position: migrants could claim asylum in France, but they
couldn't stay in Calais. The night-time harassment continued. On 11 June, two migrants were shot with an air
rifle, one in the arm and one in the back, as they were
walking near the port.

Jamal had no intention of staying. 'My plan was still to
get to Britain, claim asylum and find a place I could go to
school.' At night, he continued to hunt for lorries. The
approach to the Channel Tunnel was more difficult to
access now, because of the new rules the Sudanese had
agreed, about taking turns, but Jamal had found a spot to
hide at a junction on the road to the ferry port. His luck
hadn't improved, however. 'I'd get on the lorries and
sometimes I'd even pass through the first checkpoint
before the dogs would catch me.' Once, he said, he'd made
it onto a ship, but his phone fell out of his pocket and the
clang as it hit the metal deck gave him away. 'Next time,'
said the security guard who found him. 'They always say
that – "No luck today; try again tomorrow."' But, a lot of
the time, the lorries didn't even go towards the port –
they'd turn north, and Jamal would have to make the long
walk back to Calais.

Slowly, however, Jamal was losing his enthusiasm. It

crept up on him gradually, he said. 'I stopped trying to hide on the lorries every night. The more you fail, the more upsetting it is having to go back to Calais in the morning.' He started taking breaks: first a night off, then a few nights, then a week at a time. The conversations of the other Sudanese started to grate on him. 'It became annoying, hearing people saying, "My friend went to Britain, he got his bank account," and all these silly things about jobs and money. These people sounded ignorant to me; you've not been to Britain, so how do you know if you can have a good life there? Maybe your friend is lying to you. People get to Britain and take pictures of beautiful nature, or they're in the centre of the city, next to a car, and they post it on Facebook or Twitter. People see it and say, "This guy's got a good life," but I can't. I cannot speak about a country I've never been to. I can't believe.'

It was dangerous to lose hope. 'I've got friends who became crazy,' Jamal said. 'One died a few weeks ago, because of drinking. But it happened to me before, too.' He showed me marks on the insides of his elbows. 'When I was in the camp for teenagers, in Greece, I got depressed. A guard at the camp told me that there was an area of town where the mafia sold drugs, so I went there and they showed me how to inject cocaine by melting it in a spoon.' He quit, eventually, and he didn't want to go back. 'After all these years, though, it's not easy. You know, these thoughts come to your mind.'

Jamal knew something had to change, so he started to think about leaving Calais. He wasn't sure at first, but the final straw came in the middle of June, when another friend arrived from Patras. The vet who had told him he was stupid to want to go to Britain, and should try Norway instead, had changed his mind. Norway, he said, wasn't as open to Sudanese asylum-seekers as it had been in the past. The vet was only in Calais for a few days, and then he was gone, too, across the Channel. Jamal laughed as he told me. 'After that, I said, "OK, I give up. That's it."'

Jamal left Calais in mid-summer. When he'd arrived, in February, there were a couple of hundred migrants sleeping rough in the town. By the time he left, heading back to Paris on the train, the migrant population had grown to around 800, and international media were beginning to pay closer attention.

6 · ZAINAB

In late August 2014, Zainab and her children were brought from Paris to Calais by car. The number of irregular migrants arriving in Europe by sea had grown throughout the summer, and a minority of them were making their way to Calais, where an estimated 1,200 were now living rough. French police announced that, since January, they had apprehended twice as many people trying to cross the Channel as they had in the same period the year before, while the UK Home Office said they were finding more than 200 'lorry-drop suspects' – stowaways who had made it through to the UK – a month. The deputy mayor of Calais threatened to buy ferry tickets for the rest, 'so Britain understands how difficult the problem is'.

Zainab's family was met by another member of the smuggling network that had brought her to Europe. 'He told us, "I'm going to take you to a place where you can sleep. Just bear with me, this won't be very comfortable but just for a night or two before you can leave."'

The man took them to the same patch of scrubland, between the supermarket car park and the motorway, where Jamal had been living until the residents were evicted at the end of May. A group of Sudanese migrants had quietly reclaimed the area since the eviction, and Zainab was shocked to discover that she and her family were being asked to stay in a tent, hidden in the undergrowth. 'The children had never seen anything like it and they were crying the whole time. They were saying, "Didn't you say we would make it to France? Where are our bedrooms? Where is our house?"'

The police had continued with their programme of evictions. In July, the occupied Salam distribution site and the women-only squat had been closed down. The council had opened a centre for women and children outside the town, but it only had a limited number of spaces, and most migrants didn't want to make themselves known to officials. Instead, a large group of different nationalities were living at an abandoned chemicals factory, in the industrial zone, on the far side of the port. In early August, riot police were deployed to break up a fight over territory between more than a hundred Sudanese and Eritrean men. Police reinforcements were sent to the town and began a daily process of cordoning off the train station, checking the ID of anyone who looked like an irregular migrant and arresting those without documents.

Zainab waited with her children at the Sudanese camp for a week, but the smuggler didn't come back. She phoned her friend in Zakho and found out that her contact had been stabbed in a fight with a rival group, and had left Calais. Her Sudanese neighbours were sympathetic, but they said it was no good for her to stay with them. After a week, they showed her the way to another camp, run by a group of Iraqi Kurds. It was outside Calais, hidden behind a retail park, near the entrance to the Channel Tunnel.

There, she discovered a tent camp, with around a hundred inhabitants, all men, overseen by a dozen smugglers. Knowing there might be some animosity between Kurds and Arabs, Zainab used her language skills to conceal her identity. 'When I arrived at the Kurdish jungle,' Zainab recalled, 'I didn't speak Arabic at all, I just spoke Kurdish. I said, "I'm a Kurd from the north of Iraq and I came here so I could go to Great Britain."' To explain why her children spoke Arabic and not Kurdish, she invented a cover story: they were born in Baghdad and had grown up there.

*

One of the smugglers, who called himself Masoud – although, like with all of the smugglers Zainab had encountered, this was a pseudonym – said he could help the family get to Britain. 'He asked if I had any money and I said, "I don't have any." He said, "No, you can't have no money; you have to give me at least a certain sum." So, when he said this, I believed him very quickly. I said, "How much would you like?" He said, "Seven thousand dollars." So I said, "OK, here you go."'

Masoud promised he would get the family out of Calais within a day or two. 'But two days became two weeks. Every day, I would see him and say, "When are you taking me out?" And, every day, he would say, "Tomorrow."' As Zainab waited, she started to see how the camp – strewn with rubbish and pervaded by a smell of sweat, unwashed skin and urine – was run. She had travelled to Calais via a smuggling network whose contacts stretched, from Iraq, all the way across the European continent. This new group of smugglers was different. A dozen or so men were working as a single unit, making money by arranging short journeys across the Channel. Zainab noticed that many of them had European ID cards or passports. They carried weapons – guns and knives – and were paranoid about protecting their patch. Anybody whom they didn't know, was a spy; smugglers from other gangs were rivals, whom they would fight with. If the police came close to the camp, the smugglers would disappear, leaving the other inhabitants exposed.

People smuggling wasn't their only business. 'They were always drunk, or on drugs. I don't know what they were taking, but you could see it.' One day, Zainab saw one of the gang lift up a corner of her tent and take a package out. 'I said, "What is this?" He said, "Nothing; don't tell anyone." And then he gave that package to someone and the person gave him money.' Afterwards, one of the camp residents whom Zainab had befriended, a man from Egypt, told her what was going on. 'He asked me, "Why are you allowing them to put these drugs under your tent?"' Belongings went missing, too: food, cash, and Zainab's phone.

On the surface, the smugglers were friendly to Zainab. Thinking she was Kurdish, they would confide in her. 'There were two guys from Baghdad who had come to the Kurdish smugglers and asked them to smuggle them to Britain. They said, "Yeah, of course, no problem." And then the smugglers came to me and said, "Do you know what we did? We put them on a lorry that went to Spain."'

Zainab still had 2,000 dollars left of the money she had taken with her when she left Iraq. After making her wait for a month, Masoud told Zainab that he needed more money. 'He said the money I had given him was not enough, that he had distributed parts of it to different smugglers, but now he needed to buy a car so he could take us out to one of the lorry parks. Because of the hardships and the conditions of the living circumstances, I was ready to believe anything and everything. So I said, "OK, how much is the car?" He said, "Two thousand dollars."

So I gave 2,000 dollars to him. That was the last of my money. I didn't care I just wanted to get out of there.'

A few more weeks went by, and nothing changed. Zainab realized she had been duped. 'I told Masoud I could not take it anymore and asked him to give me my money back so I could find another smuggler. He said, "I'm not returning the money. You can do whatever you want, but I'm not returning the money." I started crying and asked him, "How can you do this?" He said, "What are you going to do about it? Complain to the authorities? Go on."'

*

Officials now estimated that 200 migrants were arriving in Calais every week; at the end of August, the British and French interior ministers had met to promise more security. British holidaymakers returning to the UK from their summer vacation found that their caravans and motorhomes were being targeted by stowaways as they queued on the roads leading to the port or the tunnel, and, on 3 September, around a hundred migrants climbed the fences of the port and tried to run onto the ferries at the dock. Police began using tear gas to repel groups of migrants on the motorway. On 7 September, Sauvons Calais invited representatives of several fascist fringe parties to address a rally of a few hundred supporters outside the town hall. Speakers described the migrants as filth and denounced those locals who helped them as *collabos*, slang for French citizens who collaborated with their Nazi occupiers during the Second World War. In the weeks that followed, Britain announced it would send to Calais the security fence from a recent NATO summit in Wales, and promised twelve million pounds in extra funding.

As the sense of political crisis grew, Zainab's own situation became more precarious. Her Egyptian friend had an argument with one of the smugglers, and the gang attacked him. 'The gang brought knives and they wanted to kill him. They told him, "You're a virus. We will kill you and get rid of your body here, and you will disappear."' Zainab had confided in him her true identity, and he yelled to her in Arabic to come and help.

'I came out and yelled at the Kurds in Kurdish, saying, "What are you doing? Let him go!" He was quite old. They asked, "Why are you defending this Arab?" I said, "I have children; I don't want them to witness blood and murder. He's just a filthy Arab, but let him live."' The smugglers let her friend go. 'When I came back to my tent, I closed the zip and started crying and thinking, if they ever found out that I was an Arab, I would go through the same thing as him, and it would be even worse because I don't have any man to stand up for me.'

She started taking her children to spend more time away from the camp. One of the aid volunteers, a French woman, let them visit her house to shower and change their clothes. Since Zainab's phone had been stolen, this provided her only means of communication with the world outside Calais. Zainab would borrow an iPad and make voice calls to family and friends on Facebook. She discovered that her sister had escaped her ISIS kidnappers, and was back with her mother. The two were hiding in northern Iraq, also pretending to be Kurdish to avoid attracting unwelcome attention. Her sister was severely traumatized, and her mother had stopped speaking altogether at the shock of seeing her husband murdered. Zainab told her sister that she and the children were fine, there was nothing to worry about.

Zainab still hadn't heard any news of her husband. During one of her visits to the house, she received a message from Ahmed's family, saying he'd been released. 'He's going to call you,' they said. A voice call, from Ahmed's Facebook account, popped up. 'Come back,' said the voice on the other end of the line. That's all it said – just, 'Come back,' three times over. Something sounded odd in Ahmed's voice. Zainab hung up. Then she called one of Ahmed's cousins, a relative who lived in Turkey and had remained friendly to her when she left Iraq. 'He told me Ahmed was still kidnapped. I realized it was Ahmed's brother, pretending to be him.' Zainab cut off contact with Ahmed's family.

At night, Zainab and her children would have to return to the camp, to ask the smugglers yet again if they'd help them get on a lorry to Britain. Masoud grew suspicious of Zainab's new French friend. 'He was angry at me for letting her come and check on us every day. He pretended that she was a spy and it was because of this that he couldn't take the risk of taking us out.' Zainab told her friend not to come and visit anymore. 'She said, "Fine, I won't come for now." But she was always telling me not to leave for the UK, and she said, "It's like death waiting for you at the end. It's really dangerous."'

Zainab paused in her monologue. 'What could I do in this situation?' she asked herself, again. 'I stayed quiet, and I stayed in the jungle, without being able to leave France. I couldn't stay in France, because my children became traumatized by anything to do with France. We stayed in the jungle for three months. Three months, during which I witnessed death, I saw things very difficult to accept.'

The children's behaviour had changed, too. On the journey to Europe, they had been noisy: crying when the journey was dangerous, playing and fighting with one another at moments of boredom. Now, in the camp outside Calais, they had become quiet. 'I was always telling them that we had bought a new house, far away, where there would not be any more bombings, any more explosions,' Zainab said. 'I said, "Do you want us to go back to Iraq? You saw what happened to our house – it was completely destroyed. Where are we going to go back to?" I was trying to really explain to them the situation. I treated them like adults. They said, "OK, Mama." All three, the same. They didn't argue with me. They didn't fight with one another. They listened to their mum because they didn't know anyone else and they didn't have any other choice.'

7 · JAMAL

Jamal had almost reached the end of his story, as we sat beside the river in the town he now called home. It was nearly evening, and he invited me back to his apartment one more time, to make dinner. In the kitchen, we made a potato stew, with onions, paprika and rice. 'We used to eat this in Calais,' he said. 'If we found meat, then we'd put meat in it, too.' Rihanna songs played from his phone as we chopped the vegetables. A lot of his Sudanese friends had got into R 'n' B and hip hop since they'd arrived in Europe, Jamal said. He laughed as he told me a story about a friend who was now in the UK. 'When he texts, he's always, like, "Yo, yo, yo." Why can't he just say "Hello" or "Hi"?'

I asked Jamal again about the sequence of events that had brought him from Calais to this northern European country. He didn't want to go into detail – he didn't yet feel secure enough in his new home – but I suggested he could tell me just enough so that my readers would understand the dysfunction in Europe's asylum system, to give them a sense of the gulf between the way states try to regulate movement, and the messy reality of life. He agreed to try.

'After my friend, the vet, crossed to England,' Jamal said, 'I started to become calm in my mind. And I said, "Let me try something while I'm taking a break from the lorries."' At the squatted town house, he had made friends with an Eritrean man. 'We would meet at the squat. Every time I went there to charge my phone, I would speak to him.' Jamal didn't want the other Sudanese to know he was meeting up with an Eritrean, 'because, if I get caught talking to him, people will say I'm causing problems again.'

The 'rule' Jamal was so proud of – don't tell anybody what you're doing until you do it – was in play. As he had done with the elders in Patras, Jamal used his new friendship to educate himself, learning the names of other places in Europe where a young man like him might get a better deal. After being rejected by many of the other Sudanese in Calais, Jamal wasn't as keen as he used to be to join the diaspora in the UK; perhaps he would fare better elsewhere. Based on what his new friend had told him, he chose another country.

Jamal left Calais and went back to La Chapelle, in Paris. He was taken aback to see how many more people there were sleeping rough under the railway track. 'In February, there were only thirty of us; now, it was around a hundred.' He spent three days at La Chapelle, mainly in internet cafes, researching his new destination, while he waited for his sister to wire him some money.

On the third day in La Chapelle, Jamal phoned a contact who said he could arrange transport for a few hundred euros. Jamal made a playlist for the journey, on his phone: Sean Paul, Jennifer Lopez, Rihanna and 'a lot of English rappers, since I was going away from England.' At La Chapelle, the Sudanese contact met him and took him to a Paris train station. There, he was shown to a waiting car. One man sat in the driver's seat; two men, who spoke Syrian Arabic, sat in the back. 'The driver wasn't Sudanese;

he wasn't French either, but I don't know where he was from, because he didn't speak to me at all during the journey.' When the driver stopped for a break, he would write out a note in English on the dashboard, telling the passengers how long they could get out of the car for. After some time, the car stopped and the two Syrian men got out. Then Jamal and his driver continued, still without speaking. Jamal had his playlist. 'I kept listening to Lowkey's "Dear England". Do you know that song?'

I didn't, so I asked him to play it to me. He paused Rihanna, midway through 'American Oxygen', and switched to 'Dear England'. It was a melancholy track with lyrics about police brutality, about military intervention overseas and treasures looted from the empire and displayed in the British Museum.

When Jamal reached his destination, he wandered around until he found some police officers who could tell him where the nearest asylum reception centre was. 'I got there, they took all my details, my date of birth, my nationality. I stayed there three or four days, then they sent me to a camp.' At the reception centre, he applied for asylum. He was interviewed. The interviewers asked him questions about his home country, his reasons for leaving, why he hadn't stayed put elsewhere. He answered their questions, hoping they would satisfy criteria his interviewers did not let him see. They called him in for a second interview and asked him all the same questions again. He answered them again. Then Jamal received a letter saying his application had been accepted.

'The last time I had a passport was when I was in Sudan, and that was a false passport so I could get out of Sudan,' Jamal said. 'That was the first passport I ever got. Now, I will have a real one – my passport here will be my first real one – I will not be afraid of everything in my head.'

*

I hardly knew Jamal, and yet he'd told me his story in such detail. His whole adult life up to this point had been shaped by systems – for protection, for deciding who deserves which resources, and where – that weren't working as they should. Instead, he'd had to build small networks of friends, or acquaintances with whom he shared temporary goals, and use those to survive. Why did he trust me, and why did I trust him back?

While we were waiting for the stew to finish cooking, Jamal described how, in the evenings, at the Sudanese camp behind the supermarket, in Calais, men would sit around the fire and try to burn off their fingerprints. They were mutilating themselves to avoid detection by the Eurodac police database, so that they could make an asylum claim in France while trying to reach the UK at the same time. 'You put one end of a metal pole in the fire,' Jamal said, 'and wait for it to go red-hot.' Then you take it out and run your fingertips along the glowing end, one by one, for an hour or two, until they're too blistered to be recognized by a scanning machine.

'Like this,' he said, grabbing my hand and pressing it into the handle of the fridge door. He pushed my index finger into the metal and ran it downwards, firmly, two or three times.

8 · ZAINAB

Throughout October 2014, Zainab stayed with her children in the camp outside Calais, trying to avoid Masoud and his gang. She was still determined to make it to Britain, and when she was away from the camp, she would ask the other migrants she met if they could put her in touch with a reliable smuggler. By now, there were over 2,500 migrants in Calais. In evidence given to a UK parliament committee hearing that autumn, the town's deputy mayor estimated that around forty were making it across the Channel each night. Britain announced it was investing in extra security at the port, including thermo-detection cameras and more vehicle-scanning equipment. Interviews conducted by Human Rights Watch around that time recorded numerous accounts of migrants having been beaten or pepper-sprayed by police as they walked in the street or hid in lorries; the police denied these claims.

In the late autumn, Zainab said, she found a smuggler, 'a respected man', who took pity on her family. 'He said, "Sister, you have been here for months. Poor you, you haven't left yet." I asked what I could do and told him that the previous smuggler had taken my money and that I didn't have anything left. He said he would help me without asking for money.'

One night, Zainab and the children went to meet him

and he drove them by car to a lorry park, outside Calais. He took them to a parked lorry, which an associate had opened up at the back, and told them to get in. A dozen other men and women were waiting near the lorry, and they boarded, too.

'We were on board a refrigerated lorry, but the fridge was turned off. It was transporting vegetables, broccoli and cauliflower. We climbed inside the fridge. We had to lie down on top of the merchandise because there wasn't space to sit. Between the ceiling of the car and us, there was only a centimetre. You couldn't even lift your head.' The lorry stayed parked. After three or four hours, the oxygen started to run out. 'We started banging on the door in the night, at three a.m. And we begged the driver to open the door. He wouldn't open it. We were crying and shouting that people were suffocating; he still didn't want to open the door. He said, shouting from the outside, that he wouldn't open the door and that he didn't care about whatever was happening.'

Some of the passengers began to lose consciousness. 'There was an Iranian man in the car, lying near me. He was pulling my hair and hitting me with his foot because there was no oxygen; he was suffocating. He was hitting me without knowing what he was doing. I begged him not to hit me, and told him I didn't want to die. He couldn't take it. We called the French police. They asked us, "What do you want?"'

'There was an Egyptian woman who used to be a teacher in Egypt and knew English fluently. On the phone with the police, she asked to speak to someone who knew English. They brought her an English speaker and asked her what she wanted. She said, "Please, we are parked in an area in Calais, we are sitting in a white lorry carrying vegetables. We are suffocating. There isn't any oxygen left. Please, come and let us out. We're knocking on the door, but the driver doesn't want to let us out." They said, "OK, stay there; we will be there within half an hour or an hour." She said, "Please, there are children." And the police could hear our voices, as we were shouting and crying; the children were crying, and so were the women. They said, "OK," and hung up the phone. We called back; they wouldn't pick up the phone. We thought the French police wanted us to die in the truck.

'Half an hour later, the police came and they opened the door. When they opened the door and oxygen got inside the truck, my children, myself and the rest of the people came back to life. I couldn't get out of the truck; I felt drugged, my children felt drugged; they fell, they couldn't leave the truck. I couldn't leave the truck.

'By the time we got out, it was four a.m. It was a very remote area from the tents, about twenty minutes by car, meaning an hour and a half by foot. The police told us, "Go on, get lost." We said, "How can we get back?" and asked the police to at least give a ride back to the children and women. They said, "We don't have to. Get out of our sight. Just go, don't stand around." So we walked and walked, and got back to Calais and to the tents. We rested a bit in the tents.'

On the recording, Zainab seemed to wrestle with her memories. 'We had to leave. I was fed up with the suffering and I just wanted us to settle down.' Back at the tents, she told the children that they would have to try again, and they would have to be quiet again, if they wanted to get to Britain. Again, the children said, 'OK, Mama.'

'Two or three days later, we called the smuggler so he could come and see us. He came and I told him how we had suffocated in the lorry, and asked him why this had happened. He said there wasn't anything he could do about it, that it wasn't up to him. He said that he could only help by putting us in a lorry. But that what would happen once we were in the lorry was not his problem, that it was up to the driver. He said that whether the driver would agree to let us out or not was not his problem, that we had wanted to take the lorry and that he had fulfilled his promise.

'Three days later, he made us take a lorry from an area near Calais, at night. Again, it was refrigerated, but the fridge was working. A fridge that's working is better than one that's not, because it renews the air inside. It was a fridge full of boxes of fruit.

'It was midnight when we got on the lorry, and drivers usually leave at four a.m. or five a.m. Sometimes, they leave at six a.m. We were approximately seventeen. We were lying down on the boxes of fruit and the fridge was not very cold, because they don't turn it on twenty-four hours for the quality of the fruit. He would turn it on for five minutes and then off for half an hour. Anyway, from midnight till six a.m., the driver hadn't made a move. At eight a.m., he still hadn't left. At ten a.m., he still hadn't left. We kept waiting and waiting until the afternoon. At sunset the next day, he finally made a move – around four p.m. As soon as he took the road, we thanked God.

'We reached the port in Calais. We heard the voices at the first checkpoint. We were sure that the driver knew we were there, because we had been inside the lorry for hours; the lorry was full of children, so we had moved around and made noise. But the driver didn't report us. At the second checkpoint, they brought a dog. We made it through. We thought it was incredible that the driver didn't hand us to the police, because he had certainly heard our voices. We continued and went through at the British checkpoint, which was situated just before cars boarded the boat. We thought, The lorry has made it onto the boat! The driver turned the engine off, and left the vehicle.

'Ten minutes later, we felt the boat moving. I had travelled by car on a boat previously, with my husband, so I knew what it felt like. I told everyone, "We are on the boat, and it's moving." They said, "No, it's not possible." I said, "I assure you. Can't you feel the boat moving?" After an hour and a half, we reached Dover. It was like Paradise in the Book. Everyone was congratulating each other.

'Of course, since the driver had turned the engine off, the fridge had not worked from the moment we made it to the boat. But even after we left the boat, and an hour later, the driver hadn't turned the fridge back on. So, again, we started suffocating and there was no oxygen left.

'We kept knocking at the door and shouting for the driver to let us out, now that we had reached Great Britain and knew we could surrender to the police. But he wouldn't open the door, no matter how hard we knocked. One of my sons fainted, and not only my son – all the families were suffocating. At ten thirty, the driver stopped and he opened the door. We got out. And this was our journey.'

Zainab pressed *stop* and the recording ended.

9 · ZAINAB

It had taken Zainab and her children nearly six months to reach a place where she felt they would be safe. After they were discovered in the lorry, somewhere outside Dover, the driver called the police, who took charge of the passengers, before handing them over to Home Office staff. Zainab claimed asylum and, in line with Britain's policy of dispersing asylum seekers around the country, she and the children were sent to live in state-supported housing in the English Midlands while their claim was being assessed. They moved to London with the help of a friend once their papers came through.

In January 2015, while Zainab waited in Britain, the Calais city council opened a day centre at a site six kilometres outside the town centre and announced that it would tolerate encampments in the surrounding wasteland. A thousand people were offered accommodation in shipping containers, repurposed from transporting goods to housing people. Throughout the spring, the migrant population grew, from an estimated 2,500 at the end of 2014, to over 4,000 in June.

Increased security and increased demand led to a boom in people smuggling. In June 2015, a French prosecutor claimed that one in four people they convicted for smuggling were British citizens. Some were well-wishers, acting

of their own accord; others were part of smuggling networks, or being paid by those who were. Lorry drivers
also complained of the impact the situation at Calais was
having on their work. In evidence to the UK parliament,
in July 2015, Britain's Road Haulage Association presented reports of damage to vehicles and the goods they
carried, urination and defecation inside the vehicle, intimidation of drivers, delays and extra costs for businesses.
'In 30 years of international driving I have experienced
fishermen's blockades, drivers' strikes, and even the fall of
communism in Eastern Europe but nothing, and I repeat
nothing has knocked my confidence as much as this last
experience which has led me to re-evaluate my future,'
wrote one lorry driver in his submission to the committee,
after describing a group of men climbing over his vehicle
and hanging from the wing mirrors as it waited in traffic
on the motorway outside Calais.

*

In May 2015, Zainab received her first news of Ahmed.
His family had paid a ransom to the gang that kidnapped
him, and he had been released. In August, he came to
Europe via a refugee route through Turkey and Greece
that was now being used by an unprecedented number of
people, mainly because of the war in Syria, but also because of ongoing turmoil in other countries, including Iraq.
That year, according to the UNHCR, 850,000 migrants
crossed the Aegean Sea; Ahmed was one of them.

Ahmed made his way from Greece to Calais, arriving
in September. At the new camp, dubbed the 'new jungle',
the once-hidden encampments had emerged into full view:
a shanty town, with its own makeshift streets and shops,
had grown up. Volunteer aid workers, whom Zainab put

Ahmed in touch with, helped him apply for permission to join his family in Britain. Helping close relatives reunite with one another is a crucial part of refugee law and Ahmed's application took two months, a relatively quick turnaround, because his case was simple. But delays in the French system, and the unwillingness of the British government to intervene in the process, have left many others, including unaccompanied children, stranded in Calais. In November, a year after Zainab had arrived in the UK, Ahmed was issued with a laissez-passer travel document, and he flew to Heathrow.

*

In April 2016, I went back to visit Zainab, this time with a friend who could translate for us. It was a Saturday afternoon; Ahmed was out at work, at a car mechanic's a few miles away. The children were running in and out of the living room excitedly and I could hear that, within a few months of enrolling at the nearby primary school, they were speaking English with a London accent. Zainab seemed more settled, too; she told us, a little shamefacedly, how they wanted to move to a neighbourhood with fewer immigrants in it. This didn't feel like the real London, she said. I got the impression she wanted to bring her children up in similar middle-class circumstances to the ones they'd enjoyed, for a time, in Iraq. But the children seemed to be happy here; their lives were taken up by school and new friends. Only the adults talked about the circumstances that had brought them to Britain. Zainab sent the children out of the living room, so she could explain how she'd re-established contact with her husband.

Zainab's first news of Ahmed, the previous summer, had come via a call from his cousin in Turkey. 'He said,

"Look, I'm going to tell you something, but don't get too excited. The gang have got in touch with Ahmed's family and they've negotiated a ransom of 30,000 dollars."' The exchange was due to take place on the day the cousin called, but he warned Zainab not to get her hopes up, because there was no guarantee the kidnap gang would hand Ahmed over alive.

Later that day, the cousin phoned, using the internet voice-service Viber, to say the exchange had taken place. He told her to stay silent while he opened another call window and connected to Ahmed's family. 'At the last minute, when Ahmed was on the line, he added me. Ahmed didn't know I was there.' Zainab heard her husband's voice for the first time in a year.

'I got in touch with Ahmed three weeks later. He couldn't get in touch with me because he was very ill and he had a lot of health problems after the kidnapping. He would ask about me and the children, and his family didn't tell him that we had gone abroad. They told him I was in another place. They told him, "Forget about her, she doesn't deserve you. She's not someone you can trust."'

Zainab told Ahmed that she and the children were in Britain; he insisted on coming to join them. 'Ahmed spoke to me two days before he left and I told him, "Don't leave; just stay where you are. I have the right to bring you over." But he said, "No, but you don't know the conditions I'm living in. My parents keep saying, 'We're not going to help you go to this woman who we don't even recognize.'" So he went to Turkey. He said, "You can apply for family reunion, but I can't wait for two months." He was just trying to get closer and closer.'

Now, nearly two years after Zainab left Iraq, the family was back together. I wanted to know if she would have made that journey with her children, had she known how dangerous it was going to be.

'No,' Zainab replied.

What would she have done instead?

'I don't know. I don't let myself think about that. I don't wish it upon anyone, this kind of journey.'

I asked if there was anything else Zainab wanted people to know.

'I'm always surprised when people ask, "Why are refugees coming to the UK?" I would like to answer back, "Hasn't Iraq been occupied by Britain and America?" I want people to see the suffering that the populations from these places have gone through. I really wish for people to see the connection.'

*

In October 2016, the French authorities dismantled the 'new jungle', which had become home to an estimated 8,000 people. The makeshift streets, shops, homes and social centres were destroyed, and people's social and support networks were scattered as thousands of migrants were bussed to reception centres elsewhere in France. Many more retreated into hiding, and smaller, less visible camps have returned to Calais and the northern French coast.

On one of my earlier visits to Calais, I cut through a park opposite the town hall. A squat concrete building sat incongruously in the middle of the landscaped gardens; on closer inspection, it turned out to be the Second World War museum. I had been struck by how often the traces of siege and invasion were visible in Calais. The effect of Second World War bombardment is apparent almost everywhere; the town centre has the empty spaces and piecemeal architecture to show for it. The canals that surround the centre trace the outline of the medieval city walls. One side of the port is made up of a remnant of defences built by Napoleon, as he dithered over invading England. Outside the town hall itself, a statue by Rodin commemorates the local legend: as the English besieged Calais in the fourteenth century, six of its wealthiest citizens gave themselves up to spare the lives of others. Rodin's figures stand emaciated, with ragged clothes and ropes around their necks, looking down on passers-by.

There is no comprehensive record of the people who've passed through the Calais camps in recent years, but a survey of 870 inhabitants by the Refugee Rights Data Project in February 2016 gives us some sense of who was there. Most people had come from some of the world's top refugee-producing countries: Afghanistan, Eritrea, Somalia, Syria, Iraq and Sudan. In their previous lives, they had been technicians, carpenters, cleaners, porters, farmers, business owners, doctors, lawyers, pharmacists, soldiers and unemployed. Their ages ranged from twelve to sixty-five, with most being in their twenties. Around 15 per cent were children. The majority interviewed – 97 per cent – were male, but this was partly because women refugees often have to hide themselves away for safety, or they rely on smugglers who keep them hidden. Forty per cent said they wanted to go to the UK because they had friends or family there, 23 per cent because they spoke English, and 14 per cent because they thought the UK's asylum system would treat them better than the French one. Fewer than 4 per cent of those surveyed spoke good French.

I had some time to spare, so I visited the museum. It was an old German command bunker, now full of displays of rusting guns and aircraft machinery salvaged from the mud and the sand around Calais. I walked past recruitment posters for troops from the French colonies, and propaganda that declared, *Without wheat from North Africa, industry in France wouldn't be possible.* One room was dedicated to the resistance members who had smuggled Jews and British soldiers out of occupied France. A giant map took up one wall of the room, traced with dotted lines that showed how the clandestine routes crossed France and branched out into Spain and across the Mediterranean. A portrait gallery sat on the wall opposite, showing the members of the resistance network, mainly women, who had survived into old age.

On my way back out, I noticed that the other end of the park was inhabited by men from East Africa. We were midway between the train station and the port, and it looked like they had recently arrived. They had travelled via routes of their own, ones that were not as likely to be memorialized, or regarded as heroic, by the municipality. Some of the men were lying on the grass, sleeping, while others sat on the benches and chatted, or stared into the distance. One man was shaving, looking at his face reflected in the shiny surface of his phone.

COUNTRY

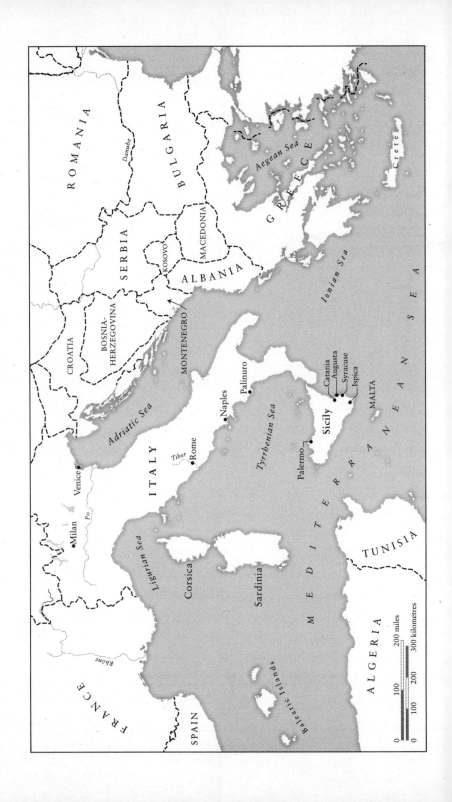

10 · THE PORT

Bright yellow grains crunch underfoot as the passengers take their first steps on Italian land. It's sulphur, scattered everywhere on the quayside: in the cracked tarmac, on the bonnets of cars parked along the dock, among the rusting piles of metal in a nearby scrapyard, raked over idly by a crane. When a breeze blows in from the sea, a fine dust lifts into the air, stinging the eyes and the backs of the throats of the passengers, sending many towards the medical tents for soothing eye baths and mouthwashes.

Until recently, sulphur was the main cargo that passed through this dock at Augusta, an industrial port on the east coast of Sicily. A by-product of the oil refineries that line the wide, hazy bay, it's what's left over after all of the more valuable parts of crude oil are separated, stored, priced and shipped off to their customers. Sulphur powder has little value attached to it, and is shovelled onto cargo ships at the dock in huge piles before being taken away for sale elsewhere.

Since the autumn of 2013, as sulphur has left the port, people have been arriving, from navy ships and commercial freighters that rescue them from the middle of the Mediterranean. As they arrive, and take their first look at the low hills in the distance and the tumbling pink bougainvillea that surrounds the port, the sorting begins.

Before the passengers are allowed to disembark, the ship's gangplank is surrounded by officials and volunteers whose shirts are branded with an array of titles and acronyms: UNHCR, IOM, Save the Children, Médecins Sans Frontières, Croce Rossa, Emergency, Carabinieri, Frontex, Protezione Civile, Guardia Costiera, Polizia Scientifica. The names evoke a bewildering mix of humanitarian disaster and security threat. Police officers in stab vests stand in a group, while health officials in protective white suits and masks board the vessel and inspect the passengers, who are being made to sit silently in rows on deck. When the inspectors are satisfied, the passengers begin to disembark, urgent cases first. A young black man who has fainted is carried on the shoulders of two doctors. A middle-aged Arab man, his legs paralysed from polio, is brought down in a wheelchair.

Then the rest of the passengers start to walk down the gangplank. Most are without luggage, wearing the kind of mass-produced, globally distributed checked shirts, T-shirts and distressed denim you'd find in European high-street shops. A few have bags, and one young man strides down the gangplank wearing a shirt and trousers and carrying a laptop case, as if he's commuting to work. A group of teenage girls from East Africa, wearing black hijab marked by white sweat lines, walk down in a huddle.

Once they've disembarked, the group of several hundred are made to wait on the quayside by police officers barking instructions in Italian, before being directed to a giant white tent further inland. As they set off, the captain of the ship is telling a local TV news crew that they rescued a boat that had got into navigational difficulties a few hundred miles off Sicily. 'Syrian, Sudanese, Somali, Palestinian,' he is saying. Of just over three hundred, forty-six are women and twenty-one are under eighteen. 'We're used to making rescues; it's something all sailors do.'

The passengers are marched to the giant white tent. It's largely silent, except for the crunching of the sulphur and tarmac. 'Dehydration,' one man says to me, mock panting. 'Do you have a cigarette?' asks another. Some people have no idea where they are going. Others are already making phone calls. 'Yes, I'm alive. First the camp, then Milano, then Germania.'

*

In the space of a few years, Italy went from trying to force undocumented migrants back to Libya, to sailing out into international waters and bringing them to European shores. As in other places along the coast of North Africa, a people-smuggling trade had existed in Libya for several decades. After Colonel Gaddafi destroyed his country's chemical weapons and international sanctions were lifted in 2003, the EU sent missions to Libya to advise on ways of stopping irregular migrants, largely from sub-Saharan Africa, passing through the country. Italy, the former colonial power in Libya and a keen customer for Libyan oil and gas, often took the lead in these efforts. The Gaddafi regime had built a network of detention centres in which to keep unwanted migrants captive; an Italian parliamentary committee heard evidence that inmates were being locked up 'like dogs'. In 2008, Italy signed a 'friendship pact' with Libya, and a year later, the two countries began joint naval patrols in Libyan waters. The arrangement, which led to a dramatic fall in the number of migrants making crossings from Libya to Europe, was criticized by human rights organizations; Italy was sending boatloads of people back to a country that had not signed up to the Refugee Convention, without first checking if any of the passengers were in need of asylum. In 2010, Gaddafi demanded five billion euros from Brussels to further combat irregular migration, or else, he threatened, 'Europe will turn black'.

In early 2011, protests against the Libyan government became an armed uprising, NATO intervened with air strikes, and the dictator was toppled. During his three decades in power, Gaddafi had controlled and manipulated various smuggling trades in Libya, allowing favoured elites to trade in weapons, drugs, contraband goods and people. His fall led to a power vacuum and competition for business increased, at just the moment when demand increased, too. In 2012, tens of thousands of refugees from the war in Syria started to arrive in Libya, by air from Lebanon and Jordan, or overland from Egypt, hoping to find a route to Europe. Relatively affluent, their money and determination to reach Europe led to a smuggling boom along Libya's long Mediterranean coastline. The smugglers started to send them out in large fishing vessels, towards Malta or the Italian island of Lampedusa; to make the trips profitable, they would encourage poorer migrants, mainly those from sub-Saharan Africa, to take up less comfortable places on the boats for knock-down prices. For 2,000 dollars, you could get a spot on deck, with a life jacket and the right to carry some luggage; for as little as 800 dollars, you would be packed in below, and often locked into the hold. If the boat sank, you would be more likely to drown.

At first, the smugglers used relatively seaworthy vessels, but these were scarce and expensive to lose, so they started to put people to sea in rickety wooden boats instead. Deaths by drowning became more common, and in October 2013, after two shipwrecks, in which close to 400 people died, Italy launched a major naval operation to search for boats in distress and rescue people from international waters as well as its own. They called it Mare Nostrum, Latin for 'our sea', the Roman name for the Mediterranean. In 2013, 42,495 rescued migrants arrived in Italy, according to the UNHCR; in 2014, more than 170,000 arrived. Most of the boats came from Libya, with a smaller number launched by smuggling networks in Egypt. Despite the rescue efforts, thousands of people drowned. In 2014, the death toll in the central Mediterranean was estimated by the IOM to be over 3,200. It continues to be the world's deadliest migration route.

Those who survived would be brought to Italian ports, most of them in Sicily. During the summer of 2014, aid workers at Augusta told me they were receiving ships with a hundred or more migrants on board every one or two days.

*

The passengers' needs are only attended to after they've been screened for risks. They're made to stop outside the giant white tent, which is lined inside with camp beds that they'll sleep on for a night or two, until they're moved elsewhere. As they sit on the ground in the sun, aid workers hand out bottles of water, cheese sandwiches and apples. The police call people up to a desk, one by one, and take down their details. A medical tent nearby receives people with health problems, most of which are related to their journeys through Libya: cuts and bruises from being beaten; skin burns from the sun or from engine oil in the boats; scabies, respiratory infections and stomach conditions caused by overcrowding and poor hygiene; complications arising from pregnancy or from sexual assault; leg and foot injuries consistent with being thrown from buildings; severe psychological trauma.

Once the passengers are registered and rested, their journeys will continue – and so will the filtering. They'll be sent to reception centres around Italy, where they'll be asked if they want to claim asylum. Those with enough money and the necessary contacts will continue their journeys to other parts of Europe. At this point, in 2014, it costs 800 euros for a taxi from Augusta to Milan, if you can afford it. Many of those who arrive at Augusta – particularly the Syrians and the Eritreans – will disappear from their reception centres in a few days and end up in northern Europe to claim asylum there. Some will have relatively easy journeys, travelling mainly on public transport. Others – young Eritreans, in particular – will be taken by smuggling networks who sometimes abuse and extort money from them. At busy times, according to some of the aid workers at the port, police have been allowing new arrivals to leave without being registered, not wanting to overburden the Italian asylum system.

But those who don't have money – or don't have contacts, or don't have any idea about where to go – they stay and wait to see what happens next.

11 · OUSMANE

Three skinny boys dressed in polo shirts, shorts and flip-flops approached me. I was on the first floor of a derelict school in Augusta's old town, looking out of a window into the courtyard. The building was full of boys like them: teenagers from West Africa, mostly. One said, '*Ciao*,' and tried a few words of broken Italian.

'Where are you from?' I asked in English, and he said, 'Mali.'

'*Alors vous parlez français . . .*' I tried, and they nodded.

The boy from Mali, the tallest of the three, told me his name was Boubacar. The second, shorter and stockier, said he was called Ousmane and that he came from Guinea-Conakry. They both said they were seventeen. The third, who looked younger and more timid, was Mamadou, from Senegal. He was fifteen.

They wanted to know where I was from and if I knew what was going to happen to them here. 'We want to get out of here,' Boubacar said. 'I've been here four months, no money, no clothes.'

'Mosquitoes bite us all the time,' Ousmane added.

'What do you want to do?' I asked.

'We want to study Italian, study business, find work,' Boubacar said. 'But we need our papers.'

'Do you know where I should go?' asked Mamadou.

'I was living in Côte d'Ivoire with my friend, but we ran away because of the war. We were in Libya for three years and my friend was killed, so I got on a boat to Italy.'

All three of them stared at me. Mamadou looked like he was trying to make himself cry. I didn't know what to say, so I looked out of the window. In the schoolyard below, one group of boys was playing football against a wall, while another group was praying on mats pointed east. A portable blackboard, with Italian vocabulary written out on it, stood in the shade. In the few hours I'd spent at the school, I'd come to recognize the look the boys were giving me: sad and vulnerable, in the hope that I'd do something to improve their situation.

The school had been pressed into service by the local council to house boys who'd been rescued from the sea without their parents. Over a hundred were living there when I visited, after asking permission from the local council, in October 2014. It was a year since Italy had launched Mare Nostrum. In mid-2014, the number of people leaving Libya rose sharply; after a few years of relative stability, clashes between Libya's tentative new government and Islamist militias escalated into civil war.

A significant minority of the migrants – 14 per cent, according to the UNHCR – were under eighteen, and half of these were travelling alone. Over 4,000 unaccompanied children had passed through the port of Augusta alone, according to the local council. While adults and families could be accommodated in other parts of the country, Italian law made these lone children the responsibility of the *comune*, the local council where they first arrived in Italy. Augusta, a town of 35,000 people, was struggling to cope with them. Local officials couldn't even tell me exactly how many boys were accommodated at the school; people went missing often. That autumn, Italy's interior ministry listed 1,213 missing migrant children, although officials privately admitted to a reporter from the *Wall Street Journal* that the real number was much higher, because many children left before they were registered.

I'd spent the morning at the school, talking to the boys who lived there. 'We know some are lying about their age,' an Italian official had told me. 'The smugglers tell them to say their date of birth is 1 January 1997 when they arrive at the port.' But most of the boys were clearly children. The majority came from West Africa, a few were from Bangladesh and there was a group of younger teenagers from Egypt. Some had been here for months; they were waiting for their asylum claims to be registered so they could be transferred to other, better equipped centres around Italy.

All those who were in Libya had either travelled there to look for work, then been forced to flee, or had gone to the country with the aim of reaching Europe. They'd told me snatches of stories about life there, and their journeys to Italy. 'In Libya, kids hit you and, if you hit them back, they come and kill you with a knife or a gun; they don't see you as a human being,' one boy told me, describing the 'Asma Boys', armed gangs of youths who terrorized non-Arab migrants in Tripoli. 'I went by car, across Niger, to Libya,' another said. 'The journey was terrible.' A group of young men from Bangladesh told me they'd been doing construction work in Libya, but had run away when a missile hit their apartment. Others had stories about the smuggler boats. 'The waves go so high, they come into the boat,' a boy from Nigeria said. 'Mine capsized and I had to swim.'

Inside the school, which was known locally as the

scuola verde because of the green paint peeling from its outside walls, the boys were sleeping between eight and ten to a room, in former classrooms. Two showers served the whole building. I asked Boubacar, Ousmane and Mamadou to show me their room; they were staying together, on the upstairs floor. They showed me into a room lined with camp beds. On the door, someone had written *VIP ROOM* in felt tip. There was more graffiti on the walls above the beds: *ROME*; *MILAN*; *GOD'S CHOSEN ONES*; *BALOTELLI*. At the far end of the room, a group of boys were playing cards next to a stereo that blared out hip hop. They looked up at us, and then went back to their game. Like other boys at the school, Ousmane, Boubacar and Mamadou had made friends and formed a tight little group. You could see them walking down the corridors or sitting outside together. The building was only staffed Monday to Friday, during working hours. Otherwise, the children were left to themselves. Fights had broken out in the summer and a police van was now permanently stationed on the street outside. As I walked through the school, I noticed a lot of the children had bruises and scratches on their arms and their faces.

*

The boys wanted to talk more, but I had an appointment across town. The old part of Augusta sits on a narrow peninsula at one end of the huge bay, about ten kilometres from the port. Long, straight roads run in parallel from one end to the other. When you reach an intersection, whichever way you look, you see the sea. The modern part of the town sprawls inland, but here felt hemmed in. Unlike Siracusa, further south along Sicily's east coast, Augusta isn't a tourist destination, and the only visitors it usually gets are sailors venturing into town for an evening meal. In the quiet of the afternoon, you can hear the grinding of machinery and smell petrol drifting over the breeze from the port, mixed with perfume coming from a row of fashion boutiques on the main street.

At the town hall, I was ushered into the mayor's office and introduced to Maria, a civil servant in her fifties who was running the town on behalf of a state-appointed commission while a corruption investigation took place.

'Tell me honestly,' she said, 'what did you think of the *scuola verde* when you visited?' I said I thought it looked terrible and that I couldn't believe children were being housed in such circumstances. Maria had an air of grim satisfaction as she reeled off the problems Augusta faced. Aside from the corruption investigation, the town was sixty million euros in debt. Since October 2013, when Augusta's port was first used by Mare Nostrum, around 4,000 unaccompanied minors had passed through the town. There were roughly one hundred boys to every ten girls. 'Where do we put them?' she asked. Some were housed in outlying suburbs. Others had been put in sports halls, but then the residents protested because nobody could play sport. The *scuola verde*, taken out of use a few years previously because the building wasn't safe, was their last resort. Children were meant to stay there for a few nights before being transferred to official reception centres, but some had been there for up to four months. The ministry of labour and social security was providing thirty-five euros per child, per day, but that wasn't enough. No money was being provided by the EU. 'The EU says it's a problem for Italy, Italy says it's a problem for Sicily, Sicily says it's a problem for the *comune*,' Maria finished.

By the time I left the town hall, it was the early evening

and shops were reopening. The local residents I had spoken to were ambivalent about the new arrivals in their town, switching between apprehension and pride at Sicily's historical role as a crossroads between cultures. Talking to people in bars and cafes, you'd hear one customer start up with, 'It's an invasion,' or, 'We're not racist, but . . .' and then another cut in with, 'Everyone's been to Sicily: Normans, French, Spanish, Arabs, Greeks. It's the north of Italy where they don't like immigrants.' A fascist group had tried to hold a rally in Augusta that summer, but few had attended. One of their placards, denouncing 'Mare Monstrum', was still chained to a lamp post; the chain suggested they were not confident of local support.

I took a walk around the peninsula and I could see boys from the school, walking up and down the streets in little groups. They gathered on benches in a park at the top of the peninsula, killing time. The park had been quite grand, once; it looked like it had been laid out in the 1920s or 1930s, when Mussolini had dreamt of southern Italy being the gateway to colonies in Africa. At one end, surrounded by palm trees, was a statue of a soldier in a pith helmet. At the other was a bust of King Umberto I, who had presided over Italy's first imperial expansion, in the late nineteenth century.

The boys were leaving the park in little groups, fanning out into the shopping streets of Augusta. I followed some of them and saw that they were begging outside the mini markets and cafes, holding out paper cups to people entering and leaving. One group had found a discarded mattress by some rubbish bins and they were carrying it, like pall-bearers, back towards the school.

I made my way back there, too, because I wanted to find the three boys I'd met that morning. By the time I arrived, the sun was slipping behind the hills on the other side of the bay, silhouetting the chimneys of the oil refineries. Outside the school, boys had brought out the infant-sized plastic chairs from the classrooms, and were sitting, hunched in a row, facing a pizza parlour on the opposite side of the street. Most of them were poring over phones, two or three to one handset. I found Boubacar, Ousmane and Mamadou there. They told me the pizza shop let them use its Wi-Fi for free; early evening, when it opened, was the best time to get online and talk to friends and family. They had bought the phones with the money they made from begging. On a good day, you could get twenty or thirty euros. They were talking to people on Facebook, so I asked if we could swap contacts.

12 · OUSMANE AND CAESAR

I stayed in touch with the boys from the school. In the weeks after I left Augusta, the pictures and comments they posted on Facebook gave me a glimpse into their lives. They liked to pose: they took photos of one another standing by parked cars in the street, resting a hand on the bonnet to suggest ownership, or browsing CDs and clothes in the town's shops. They'd post a photo, then tag twenty or thirty of their friends in it, fishing for compliments, which would appear in the thread below, in French fashion slang: *Trop cool*, *Trop swag*, *#bcbg*.

To me, it looked like a game, an in-joke for those who had made the journey to Europe, bragging for the benefit of those who hadn't. Only the occasional comment from a friend would refer to the circumstances in which they'd arrived:

- You're still alive?
- Yeah, I'm in Italy now
- Wow
- *mon petit*, you have become an ITALIAN, stay there, we'll join you there because there's nothing but poverty in Mali ok
- kid, you're one of the heroes after this heroic journey that you made. But know that the struggle isn't

finished. You've still got lots to do before you reach your final goal. Good luck to you and your companions. Thank you!

- I'm proud of you my friend

Every few days, usually in the evening, when the pizza shop with the Wi-Fi had opened for business, the boys would send me messages. Ousmane was the most persistent, although he didn't often write much, just *Sava?* (French text-speak for 'How are you?'), or he'd ask me if I was at work or what London was like. During one of our conversations, I asked him a bit about his life before the journey.

He'd grown up in Lélouma, in the west of Guinea, but his parents had sent him to Senegal for school, before they'd run out of money to keep up his education. At fifteen, he'd trained as a tailor, but quit after a year because he didn't like the work. After that, he'd laid floor tiles for a bit, but the jobs dried up and he travelled north, to Mauritania, in search of work. Finding work in Mauritania didn't go any better for Ousmane, but some friends had told him there were jobs in Libya, so they went there together.

As a 2015 report by the International Centre for Migration Policy Development indicates, most migration in West Africa takes place within the region, not to Europe. Boubacar and Mamadou described similar experiences of looking for work in various parts of West and North Africa. Unlike Ousmane, they'd both been displaced by civil wars. Mamadou, originally from Senegal, had been living and working in Côte d'Ivoire when fighting broke out there in 2011; Boubacar had fled a war in northern Mali that started the following year. Most of the several hundred thousand refugees from these conflicts were hosted by neighbouring countries in West Africa; a few, like Mamadou and Boubacar, had gone to Libya.

While I exchanged messages with Ousmane, I read up on Guinea-Conakry. A former French colony whose independence leader in the 1950s declared, 'We would rather have poverty in freedom than riches in slavery,' it was punished for its defiance by France withdrawing assistance and carrying out sabotage after colonial rule ended. The country has abundant mineral resources, especially aluminium ore, which is essential for the planes, trains and cars by which people travel around the world. Guinea is one of the world's poorest countries, with half the population living below the poverty line; it's not a major source of emigration in general, according to the IOM, although many of those people who do leave travel as irregular migrants because they lack the money or contacts for visas. In the last decade, Guinea has played host to refugees from Sierra Leone, Liberia and Côte d'Ivoire, all of which share a border with Guinea.

I asked Ousmane why he'd left Guinea in the first place.

'Life there's not very stable, you know what I mean?'

At the end of 2014, the Italian government modified its asylum system, commissioning a new network of reception centres. Unlike the existing ones, which were managed by central government, these 'extraordinary reception centres' were commissioned by regional administrations. Charities, NGOs, church groups and business owners could bid for contracts, and empty hotels, schools, private houses and youth hostels were pressed into service. The government also changed the rule that made unaccompanied minors the responsibility of the local council where they first arrived, allowing them to be housed across the country. In December, the *scuola verde* was closed down and its inhabitants transferred to official reception centres.

The boys were moved to a centre outside Siracusa, the provincial capital, and I could see a change in the photos they posted. They seemed to be better dressed, showing off baseball caps and new T-shirts, and in some of the photos they were posing with young women. That winter, they carried on sending me messages – 'What news from London?' – and I started to get new friend requests. They came from people I'd never met in person, friends of friends who were in other reception centres around Italy. It became routine: most would add me, maybe send me a message saying *Sava?* Then they would disappear into the digital ether. I got used to seeing their posts – photos of them posing in the side streets of Italian towns, political memes from their home countries, inspirational quotes superimposed over pictures of African footballers – among the daily feed of my European friends' jokes, new jobs, new babies.

*

In March 2015, someone new sent me a friend request, and the name – Caesar – caught my attention. He started sending me messages almost as soon as I accepted: he was a cousin of Boubacar and he also came from Mali, but now lived in a reception centre somewhere outside Milan.

'What do you think of the situation for refugees in Italy?' he asked me.

I replied that I thought it was very difficult at the moment, because Italy was struggling to support the number of people who had been arriving during 2015. The EU didn't seem to be helping much either. Mare Nostrum had been officially wound down at the end of 2014 because the Italian government was spending nine million euros a month on the operation, with no contribution from its European counterparts. The only other rescue operation was a private initiative run by a billionaire couple based in Malta, and later supported by Médecins Sans Frontières. The EU's answer to Mare Nostrum was Triton, a smaller operation run by Frontex. Operation Triton's primary function was to patrol borders, not save lives, and it only covered European territorial waters, a much smaller area of sea, much further away from the international waters where most of the boats leaving Libya got into trouble. Some EU members didn't even want to contribute to this: Britain initially declined to support Triton at all, claiming that search-and-rescue operations only created a 'pull factor', encouraging more migrants to make the journey.

'I don't understand the EU,' Caesar wrote back. 'It feels like we're not being protected by the [Refugee] Convention.'

I said I thought there was a lot of fear around immigration in Europe at the moment, and that was making the situation worse. In March, a proposal by Italy to let migrants claim asylum at embassies and EU offices outside of Europe, and to reform the Dublin system, had been strongly resisted by France, Germany and other member states.

'It's a bit late for that,' Caesar retorted, at the mention of fear. 'They sowed chaos in African countries and if it wasn't for that we wouldn't have had to flee for our lives.'

A few seconds later, my phone started ringing. He was making a voice call on the Messenger app and wanted to tell me directly how angry he was. Caesar had been caught up in the 2012 war in Mali, and his flight from the violence there had led him, eventually, to this reception centre outside Milan. In October 2014, he arrived in Italy. He'd been waiting for five months without any progress on his asylum claim and with little information about what was happening. He thought that, seeing as European countries had intervened militarily in both Mali and Libya, they had a duty to protect the migrants fleeing the violence there. Caesar was keen to know what decisions were being made by European politicians about his situation, but he had trouble accessing information. The €2.50 a day 'pocket money' given to asylum seekers by the Italian government was only enough to afford a phone deal with limited internet access. It was enough for messaging, but not enough to browse the web and read news reports. Caesar asked me if I'd send him updates; I said I would.

In early 2015, around the time Caesar first contacted me, smuggler boats had begun to leave Libya again in greater numbers. The scaling back of search-and-rescue operations had made little difference to the smuggling trade: in April, when the weather was more favourable, attempted crossings took place more frequently than in the same month in 2014.

During the week of 13 April, two huge shipwrecks near the Libyan coast killed over 1,000 people within the space of a few days. The first boat, on 13 April, sank close to Libya with 550 people on board; over 400 of them drowned. The second, on 19 April, sank during an improvised rescue attempt. Over 800 people were on board and many of them had run to one side of the boat when they saw a merchant ship approaching, which caused their vessel to capsize; as many as 700 died. According to the survivors, most of the passengers on the boats had come from Eritrea and Senegal, with smaller numbers from

Syria, Somalia, Sierra Leone, Mali, Gambia, Côte d'Ivoire and Ethiopia. A study by academics at Goldsmiths, University of London later argued that EU policy had contributed to these deaths: by abandoning search-and-rescue operations in international waters, they had left the task to commercial ships that were less well equipped to do the job.

The scale of these disasters provoked widespread public disgust and a political crisis in Europe. The European Council, which is composed of European heads of state, plus senior EU officials, declared itself 'chagrined' by the loss of life, and emphasized Europe's 'moral and humanitarian obligation to act'. On 23 April, the Council held an emergency summit. Caesar phoned me the day after, wanting to know what they'd decided. I sent him their conclusions, which stated that the most immediate way to protect life was 'to fight the traffickers, prevent illegal migration flows and to reinforce internal solidarity and responsibility'. The Council resolved to reinforce Operation Triton, along with a similar operation, Poseidon, in the Aegean Sea. It also promised to launch development programmes in Africa to tackle the 'root causes' of migration, and to deploy more resources to frontline EU states to help them accommodate and process the asylum claims of new arrivals.

'Did they mention a project to protect refugees and asylum seekers here in Italy?' he asked. I looked, but all I could see was the promise of more resources, plus a mention of a 'pilot project' to resettle refugees across the EU. 'Someone told me there's an internal project for asylum seekers and refugees, called SPRAR,' he said. Caesar was insistent I find out more about it for him. 'We're still here, we're still waiting, but things aren't easy and nothing's moving.'

The week of the EU summit, I noticed a meme on Facebook that spanned my different social worlds. A sombre gathering of world leaders – the photo call from the memorial march in Paris after the *Charlie Hebdo* terrorist attacks in January – had been cut and pasted into the centre of an inflatable boat, photographed mid-ocean.

13 · CAESAR

I visited Sicily a second time in May 2015. My first appointment was in Catania, a city north of Augusta that sits at the foot of the volcano Mount Etna. It was evening when I arrived and made my way to a crowded suburb near the football stadium. The narrow streets were lined with a jumble of weathered one-storey homes and apartment blocks, markedly different from the old town's dark baroque buildings carved from black volcanic rock. Grocery shops run by Romanian immigrants nestled among the Sicilian sandwich bars and jewellery shops. I checked the address I'd been given, and found an alleyway. A nineteenth-century town-house jutted out from the other buildings, and on the porch, lit by the glow of a street lamp, I could see a figure waiting. It was Caesar.

For many of the rescued migrants who pass through Sicily, Catania is a last stop before the Italian mainland. Every evening, around seven, in a windswept car park near the central train station, a queue of mainly young men and women, from Africa and the Middle East, assembles to take the coach to Rome. They arrive here by bus or by taxi, from reception centres across the island, to make their transfers to centres elsewhere in Italy, or to continue their journeys, by whatever means, to other destinations in Europe. But Caesar had come in the opposite direction: a few days before I'd arrived, he'd been transferred here from Milan. For nearly two months, I'd known him as a username, a blurry avatar that didn't show his face, and a deep voice with rolled *r*s and stuttered out *t*s, especially when he was angry. As I walked towards him, I could see he was wearing an orange polo shirt and that a headphone wire trailed from one ear into his mobile phone. He seemed agitated, rubbing his hands together and looking up and down the alleyway.

'I arrived the night before last and I didn't sleep at all,' Caesar said, after shaking my hand and giving me a nod. 'I was five months away from getting my documents in Milan and they told me to come here and said it was better, and when I arrived, they told me I'd have to wait another fourteen months. I asked to go back, but they said I couldn't.'

Now I understood why Caesar had been so eager to gather information about the Italian asylum system. He'd been looking for a way to get out of his reception centre in Milan, where he'd lived in a barracks-style settlement with hundreds of other inhabitants. It had been a primary reception centre: basic accommodation in which asylum seekers are supposed to be kept for a few weeks before being transferred to secondary centres, where they receive training and advice to help integrate with their new communities. In practice, because of the increased demand, the Italian government was putting people wherever they had space, for indefinite periods. In 2014, 66,000 people were living in Italy's primary and secondary reception centres, according to figures from the interior ministry; in 2015, this rose to over 100,000.

Caesar had been offered a place at a secondary reception centre – part of the SPRAR system, the *Sistema di*

Protezione per Richiedenti Asilo e Rifugiati, he'd asked me about – in Catania. But he hadn't been told that moving from one region to another would mean starting his asylum claim over again. In Italy, a claim often has to pass through several stages before a final decision is reached. First, you're interviewed by a commission: a panel of local officials who quiz you about your reasons for coming to Italy. Most of the time, they turn down the request for asylum, and it's passed on to a tribunal, where the case is heard in front of a judge. The majority of asylum decisions are reversed at this stage, and a successful claimant receives some form of refugee status. If not, there are then two more appeal stages. Even before 2011, the whole process could take years; now, there weren't enough judges and lawyers to deal with the volume of new cases. Caesar had been waiting six months and had yet to be given a date for his commission hearing. He'd just found out from his lawyer that the hearing wouldn't be for at least another fourteen months.

We were still standing on the doorstep of his new home as he told me this. The house looked like it had been quite grand; perhaps it had been built overlooking fields long since swallowed up by Catania's urban sprawl. The street was quiet and the evening air was warm. At one point, another lodger in the house – a man from Togo – stuck his head out of the door to say hello, but otherwise we were undisturbed. Caesar was upset by the bad news from his lawyer, and his words came out fast. '*C'est très compliqué*,' he'd say every now and then, in staccato. '*Très, très, très compliqué.*'

I asked him about his life before Europe. He told me that he was from southern Mali, but he'd been living in the north when war broke out. He'd fled to Algeria first, discovered they treated black Africans 'like slaves' there, so moved on to Libya in early 2014. The fighting in Libya had died down after the fall of Gaddafi, so he thought it would be safe, but it turned out to be *'une piège'*, a trap. Eventually, he'd escaped by boat to Italy. I wanted to know more about this journey, but our first meeting didn't seem the right time to ask – not least because Caesar's mind was focused on his current situation.

'They say Europe is the place of liberty,' he declared, 'but when you arrive, you feel like a foreigner – they make you feel the colour of your skin.' Caesar told me a story about two cafes near his old reception centre. Both had Wi-Fi, but the owner of one chased Caesar and his companions away because he didn't want blacks congregating there. They moved to the other cafe, where they were tolerated, and the second owner started doing more business. Caesar laughed at the absurdity of the story, exposing a flash of gold enamel on his upper row of teeth.

His main problem was that, without documents, even the temporary ones that were issued after making an asylum claim, he didn't have the right to work. It was obvious that he hated living in this limbo. 'They're treating us like ping-pong in the system, just so people can make a profit off us.' Since 2011, Italy had spent around two billion euros accommodating asylum seekers, according to government statistics. 'If they let us work, we'd be taxable.' He said he was thinking of leaving Italy altogether, even though he didn't have permission. 'Italians say to me, "Why don't you go to France, since you speak French?" It started on the rescue boat. An Italian sailor, the guy who was fishing people out of the water, was of Senegalese origin and could speak a bit of French, and he said to me, "You'll be better off in France." Even on the boat.'

I could see he needed to calm down. 'I had hope,' Caesar said as we parted company that evening. 'Now, everything has *basculé*, overturned. When we talked on Facebook, I wasn't telling you I wanted to leave Italy, was I? But fourteen months . . . *très, très, très compliqué*.'

*

That week, I visited Caesar several times. We'd meet on his doorstep, or he'd come over to where I'd parked my car, in front of the football stadium. Caesar would want to talk politics. 'I've been reading about Britain's elections in the papers; I was very disappointed the *travaillistes* didn't win,' he told me one evening. 'Did your minister really say she wanted to build detention centres in North Africa? Are they mad?'

His frustration was evident. It turned out that Caesar's new centre didn't offer anything beyond a few hours of Italian language lessons each week. The national SPRAR website, when I looked at it for him, had said there would be skills training, job advice and help integrating with the local community and services. He'd started to notice that Catania didn't offer many prospects for work, anyway. Sicily, poorer than the north of Italy, has an unemployment rate of around 20 per cent. After the financial crisis, many of the island's young were following earlier generations of Sicilians and leaving for northern Europe in search of work. Caesar was starting to rationalize his situation. 'Maybe I'll go back to north Italy,' he announced one evening. 'People don't like blacks, but they'll have to get used to it; you can't reverse the situation now; we've become part of the landscape.' Italians just needed to understand what made people like him come to Italy in the first place, he said. Milan hadn't been all bad; there was a priest who had come to his centre and got them to do the Stations of the Cross at Easter. 'Me, I'm Muslim, but there's nothing wrong with a bit of diversity,' he joked.

I still didn't know much about what had made Caesar come to Italy. If I asked directly, he didn't avoid the question, but he would only tell me the briefest of details before switching subjects. Every now and then, however, when we'd run out of things to say, a vivid detail would surface, almost unbidden. 'You know,' he once said, 'by the time you get to the boats, you can't turn back. You don't know if you're heading to Europe or not; you just get in and head off.' Another evening, he told me he'd spent three days walking through the Sahara Desert. 'It's too hot to travel in the daytime, so you go at night, and you navigate by cities in the distance. The light travels very far because the desert is empty. So you keep your eyes on the lights in the distance.'

In Mali, Caesar said, he had been an electrician. He had run a repair shop in the town where he lived. It sounded like everyone in town used it at one point or another, and Caesar said it was a place where people would drop in to gossip and talk politics. Although I hardly knew him, I could picture him at the centre of that world, receiving visitors, talking politics and philosophizing – like he was doing with me, in his new home by the football stadium in Catania.

'I left home to save my life,' Caesar said. 'Now, I just want to live and forget about the past.'

He didn't want to forget everything. Before I left, Caesar showed me a picture on his phone of his wife and baby son. He had been forced to leave them behind in Mali.

14 · OUSMANE

One morning in May, I drove inland from Catania, through wide fields of maize and fruit trees, framed by distant mountains. I was on my way to see Ousmane, the teenager from Guinea, who had been transferred to another home. First, though, I wanted to visit the largest reception centre in Sicily, to get an idea of what other rescued migrants experienced. Two hours' drive from Catania, close to the town of Mineo, I started to see African men making their way along the side of the road by bike or on foot. Then a row of buildings appeared on the horizon – identical orange apartment blocks – as if a suburban development had been dropped into the middle of the countryside. It was a former US military residential base, now used as a primary reception centre. More than 3,000 people were living there, even though the official capacity was 2,000. Its inhabitants came from the Middle East, Asia and Africa. Men, women and children slept as many as eight to a room. The private consortium that ran the centre was being investigated for allegedly committing bribery during the bidding process for its contract; although the company denied doing anything wrong, a trial was on-going in late 2017.

There was no chance of my getting inside; the prefecture in Catania hadn't responded to my request for a visit, and the gates were guarded by soldiers with guns. Along the road outside, small groups of people gathered. Many of them were loading bags into people carriers and haggling with taxi drivers for trips to Catania, or Rome, or Milan. Others were phoning people inside the camp, asking them to come and meet outside. I said hello to a couple of men who were leaning against a low wall opposite the entrance. They were Eritrean, and one said he'd moved out of Mineo when he'd been given refugee status. He worked at a car park in a town a few hours' drive away, he said, but the money he earned wasn't enough to live off, so he came back to Mineo, where his friends would sneak him inside the camp and share their food with him.

I carried on driving, towards Ispica, a town on a rocky plateau near Sicily's south coast. Ousmane lived here now, on a quiet residential street near the town centre. When I arrived, I discovered he'd been put in another school building. This one was smaller and in better condition – a one-storey former infants' school, with a small courtyard out the front and rooms inside arranged around a central hall. The centre, a SPRAR, was run by a local Catholic cooperative. Ousmane greeted me at the gate; he seemed more relaxed, less shy than when I'd met him the previous October. This was his home now and he was happy to have a visitor to show around. Ousmane took me through to the dining room, at the back of the building. There were twenty or so people living at the school, all young men and boys from West Africa. A few sat watching an Italian police drama on the television in the dining room; others were making lunch in the kitchen – Ousmane told me that they cooked in groups of three, on a strict rota – and a few more were kicking a football round in the backyard. As people walked in and out of the dining room, I heard

Ousmane switch confidently between languages: Pular, his mother tongue, with another boy from Guinea; Wolof with a friend from Senegal; French with some of the other boys; and a mix of broken English and Italian with the rest.

Ousmane told me he was comfortable, but bored. His claim for asylum had been turned down and he was waiting for his chance to appeal. He took out his phone and showed me a photo: him, Mamadou, Boubacar and another friend, Adam, were posing together in a corridor. They looked cheerful, as if they were being photographed on the last day of school term. It had been taken at the reception centre outside Siracusa, where they'd been transferred after the *scuola verde* was closed down. This was one of the last times the friends had been together. Shortly after the photo was taken, in early 2015, Ousmane had come to Ispica.

I asked Ousmane if he'd had any news from his friends. Boubacar had been transferred to the Italian mainland, near Naples, he said. Boubacar's main worry, as he waited for a decision on his asylum claim, was how to restart his football career – before leaving Mali, he'd played for the country's national youth team. Mamadou was still in Siracusa; he'd got a girlfriend, who was somehow making money and buying him flashy new clothes from the town's Chinese-run bargain stores. Adam, the fourth friend – fifteen years old and from Côte d'Ivoire – had been moved to another rural town in Sicily, but had run away when one of the reception-centre staff told him he'd have to pick oranges to earn his keep. He'd borrowed money from friends, taken the bus to Catania and then made his way from Sicily to Paris.

Ousmane introduced one of his housemates, who came

over and joined us at the table. Alimamo was a heavily built man, wearing a yellow LA Lakers basketball shirt. He told me he came from Kwinella, in Gambia; he was thirty years old and with a wife and two children to support back at home. 'I've been waiting a year and three months for documents, that's my problem,' Alimamo said. He'd found some work for the time being: the Italian asylum system allows people to take up temporary 'work experience' contracts while they're waiting for their claims to be processed. Alimamo had a contract with a shop in Ispica, and was earning 250 euros a month, well below the Italian minimum wage. As soon as he'd started earning, the reception centre had stopped his pocket-money allowance. 'I'm a family man,' Alimamo said. 'I came to Europe to find work. I knew the journey was dangerous, but I did it anyway because my family is not very strong and I'm the first son of my father. Now I'm having trouble sleeping at night because I don't know where I'll go.' Gambia, a poor country whose beaches are popular with European tourists, has been a significant source of migrants travelling via Libya. At home, Alimamo had sold potatoes and worked as a welder.

'Didn't those jobs pay?' I asked.

'They pay, they pay, but it's not the same.' He fell silent and looked at the floor for a few seconds.

Alimamo, who had been helping to get lunch ready, went back to the kitchen. Ousmane asked me if I wanted a drink, and brought over a carton of milk and a tub of sugar. Sweet milk was their favourite drink, he said. I asked Ousmane if he'd heard the news about the two huge shipwrecks of that April. Of course he had, he said; he was shocked to learn of it. Ousmane shook his head and looked grave. '*C'est pas facile*; I was four days at sea.'

I asked him what he thought of the distinctions European politicians were making between refugees and 'economic migrants'. He had left Guinea to look for work, so he didn't really have a case for asylum in Europe. 'They're right, but they're wrong,' he said, screwing up his face. 'There are many reasons people leave their countries. Politics, poverty, wars . . .'

Ousmane picked up his phone again. 'Do you want to see how I travelled across the Sahara?' he asked. He showed me another photo. 'This is the vehicle I travelled on.' The photo, taken from a news report, showed a flatbed truck, so heavily laden with water containers and sleeping bags that they poked out like the spikes of a hedgehog. A crowd of people sat on top of the truck, their faces covered by hoodies and scarves to protect them from the wind and the sand.

The journey was the same regardless of your reasons for making it. Ousmane had taken a route sometimes referred to by migrants from West Africa as 'the back way to Europe'. Smuggling networks would bring people to Agadez, a desert city in Niger. From there, they would board trucks and pickups that crossed the Sahara in convoy, towards Libya. This trip usually cost around 300 dollars, according to a 2015 report in the *Wall Street Journal*. Other clandestine routes to Europe existed – through Morocco to mainland Spain, or from Mauritania to the Canary Islands – but these had been largely closed off in the mid-2000s. The route to Libya had become increasingly popular. Agadez, once a medieval trading post, had become a boom town; according to one estimate, cited in the *Wall Street Journal*, more than a hundred million dollars was spent there by migrants in 2015. The route was dangerous because you could be robbed by bandits, or forced into servitude by the smuggling networks, or have an accident in the desert.

Before we parted company, Ousmane offered to take me for a walk around his new neighbourhood. Ispica is on a plateau, surrounded by farmland in the valley below, and a hot, dry wind was blowing through the town's streets. At the end of his road, there was a football pitch. 'We play here most evenings,' he said, 'with the Tunisians.' Many of Ispica's inhabitants are Tunisian. Migrant workers from Tunisia began to arrive in Sicily in large numbers in the 1980s; initially they came to work on farms as seasonal labourers, but many settled in towns on the south of the island. At first, they were able to take ferries back and forth across the Mediterranean, but when Italy imposed restrictions on their movement, in line with EU policies, the Tunisians were some of the first to take clandestine routes into the country. An amnesty in the late 1990s gave citizenship to the undocumented.

A young boy from the neighbourhood walked past us. 'We're playing at seven?' he asked Ousmane in Italian.

'*Sì, sì*, at seven,' Ousmane replied.

15 · FATIMA

In the summer of 2015, when Ousmane and Caesar had already been in Italy for almost a year, a thirty-five-year-old Nigerian woman called Fatima made a decision she'd been putting off for months. Tripoli still wasn't safe; so, in July, she too allowed herself to be herded onto a smuggler's boat at a beach outside the Libyan capital. Fatima was a pragmatic, sometimes brusque woman, but as she got on board, she found herself making a bargain with God. 'Let me live,' she said, 'and I will make it my mission to help people who come through Libya, to raise the alarm about what is happening, especially to women and children.'

At Augusta, once Fatima had disembarked and been questioned, registered, fingerprinted and screened for diseases, she was sent to the same reception centre outside Siracusa that Ousmane and his friends had passed through a few months earlier. That summer, rescued migrants continued to arrive in Italy at a rate of over 20,000 a month, according to the UNHCR, although the balance of nationalities had changed. Far fewer Syrians were making the journey from Libya now, since most who were there had already left; the proportion of migrants from sub-Saharan Africa was higher. By the end of 2015, Nigerians had become the second-largest group, after Eritreans. The EU's response to the crisis was beginning to take shape:

an increasing emphasis on tackling the smugglers, combined with a scheme to relocate refugees who had already arrived in Italy and Greece. The first part of the plan received enthusiastic support – Operations Triton and Poseidon received more funds, while a joint military operation against smugglers was agreed in June – but the second part stalled as northern European states resisted the proposed relocation scheme.

I met Fatima in August, six weeks after she had arrived. I had come back to eastern Sicily because I wanted to find out more about the women who were passing through the port. The boys whom I'd followed from Augusta had moved through almost exclusively male spaces since they arrived in Italy. This was partly due to a policy of separating single young men from women and families, but also because men were far more numerous; according to the UNHCR, between 70 and 75 per cent of the arrivals each year between 2014 and 2016 were men. (Women made up between 11 and 14 per cent of arrivals, and children between 11 and 16 per cent.) For many women who arrived at Augusta, this reception centre was their first stop before being transferred elsewhere.

The centre was in a suburb of Siracusa, on a ridge that overlooks the city. A ribbon of industrial development stretches down Sicily's east coast and this suburb had originally been built to house workers; it was called Città Giardino and had apparently been modelled on an English-style garden city – although, when I visited, the resemblance wasn't easy to discern. The centre was a three-storey concrete barracks, surrounded by a high wall and guarded by a police van at the gate. Clothes hung out to dry fluttered from the windows and the sound of children playing in the yard floated over the wall.

Fatima had been sitting in the shade of a tree by the back wall of the centre, waiting for a bus to take her into Siracusa. She was from Lagos in Nigeria, a widow, with two children whom she'd left behind. When another journalist I was with approached her, she'd apologized and said she had to run for the bus, so she could get to work, but she promised to meet us the next day. She seemed nervous about meeting in front of the reception centre and suggested we meet at a cafe around the corner.

I was waiting at the cafe with my friend when Fatima arrived. She sat down, looking flustered, and apologized for not having her hair covered with a scarf. 'We must cover in Libya. I try so hard here to be covering, but the summer is so hot.' Fatima was wearing a vest top with the word SEXY spelled out across it in plastic crystals. We were sitting outside – the weather was hot and humid – and Fatima shifted uneasily in her seat as she talked. On her way out of the centre, she said, she'd had to break up a fight between two younger women. 'I was very annoyed by it,' she said.

'This is the first time I've had to live in ghetto conditions,' Fatima continued. 'Even in Libya, I had an apartment with two bedrooms.' We asked Fatima to describe the reception centre. Looking around, as if someone might be listening, she said about 200 people lived there, several to a room, and that women and families were kept separate from the single men. It was clean, she said, but the main problem was that people were being kept there for months. When she'd arrived, she'd been told she'd only be there for two weeks before she'd get transferred to somewhere more permanent. Eritreans and Syrians left the centre of their own accord, usually after a few days, but the people from West Africa tended to stay.

Fatima didn't know where to go next. 'Some people have told me that it's not easy to stay in Italy, but if I have work here, my dream is helping children and mothers. I want to make a charity that helps women split from her accidental husbands.'

I didn't understand what she meant by 'accidental husbands'. Fatima explained that she kept meeting women in the centre who had been approached by men in Libya – or even on the boats – who told them to say they were married when they arrived in Italy, because it would get them better treatment. 'The men tell them, "If we say we are married, our documents will come quick, because of the kids."' Fatima clapped her hands together for emphasis. 'Now, when they get to Europe, they see that a woman can live without a man. I've seen a lot of women suffering in love. Not enjoying the love. One woman came to me today because she wants a separation from this unexpected husband. She has two children.'

Some of the women were 'tricked' by the men into sex work, while others did it by choice, said Fatima. 'Some women use whatever they have to get what they want.' She smiled, wryly. 'The women do feel the pressure to get out and start making money for their families.' Fatima said she'd seen the same thing happen in Libya and had tried to stop it. 'The way our girls, especially the Nigerian women, were doing prostitution, doing dirty work . . . I went to the embassy, but I couldn't find anyone to support me.'

Fatima brought our conversation to an end, as she said she was giving an Italian lesson to some of the children in the centre. We'd only been talking for about twenty minutes and I don't think she knew whether or not to trust journalists yet.

'Can we meet later in the week?' I asked.

'OK, I'll call you the day after tomorrow.'

*

We met again two days later, in the early evening, at the train station in Siracusa. The city is the provincial capital, and buses from the outlying towns stop here, which makes it a popular meeting point for people who live in the local reception centres. If they need to do shopping, or see their lawyer, or have an appointment with a branch of the Italian state – their asylum interview, for instance – then they need to come into Siracusa. It's not an easy journey, when living on sixty or seventy euros a month; from Città Giardino, it's a round trip of at least three hours by bus, or four hours on foot. Many of the inhabitants cycle, using donated or second-hand bicycles.

Fatima found me waiting outside the station. 'Come,' she said, and led me into the centre of the town. Fatima seemed less nervous today; I could see a flash of her assertiveness as she batted away my questions and told me she had errands to run. First, we passed a row of internet cafes near the station. It was here Fatima did the 'work' she'd referred to at our first encounter. The reception centre gave her a five-euro phonecard every few days, and she would sell on her unused ones here, for two or three euros each. 'The pocket money they give us doesn't last long; it runs out after one or two weeks,' she said.

Fatima said hello to a young man outside. 'You see him?' she said, after we'd moved on. 'He's from Guinea-Bissau, and five days ago, he fought with his wife. They woke us up early in the morning by screaming. She was shouting, "You're not fit to be my husband!" The police had to come in to break it up. They were sent to separate camps after that, but they couldn't divorce because they already signed the documents at the port. This is why I am trying to tell women, don't sign yourself into trouble.'

We carried on into Siracusa. In the town centre, nineteenth-century shopping streets are joined by bridges to the island of Ortigia. The island has been continuously inhabited for nearly 3,000 years. It's the place most tourists visit, to pore over Greek, Roman and baroque buildings and ruins, but it's also still the city's administrative centre. Fatima led me to the *prefettura*, where a man was waiting for us. 'This is my cousin, Ife,' Fatima said.

Ife looked like he was in his mid-thirties. He was wearing a dark blue shirt and perspiring in the heat. 'Hi, Mr Daniel,' he said, grinning, as he shook my hand.

'Where is your car?' Fatima asked me. 'We need you to drive us somewhere.'

I was interested to see where this would lead. We walked back to the car; Fatima got into the back and Ife the front passenger seat. 'Drive this way,' he said, waving a hand in one direction or another each time we got to a road junction. We made our way into the traffic-clogged sprawl of modern Siracusa. Almost every time we stopped at a major junction, a black man would approach the line of cars, polystyrene cup in hand, asking for spare change.

As I drove, with Fatima sat behind, rather than facing me, interview style, she was more forthcoming than she had been two days before. She claimed that the centre was overcrowded, and that when she'd arrived, she'd had to sleep in a room with sixteen other people. She also claimed that 'When the inspectors come, they send us out and arrange things nicely. Then, when they leave, they ask us to come back.

'We get in trouble if we talk to journalists,' Fatima said.

'Because, for the people who run the centre, it's business. They're making money off us.'

Some reception centres in Italy were well run, but there were numerous reports in Italian and international media of alleged corruption ranging from claims of petty fraud to serious organized crime: pocket money being withheld; clothes being sourced from charity donations, even though the government provided money to buy them; lack of access to health services or legal advice; no hot water or electric light at one centre in Calabria; a mafia ring said to have corruptly obtained contracts to run centres in Rome. I didn't know how the centre at Città Giardino was run and I was not able to find out what the centre's response to Fatima's allegations was or to see for myself because my requests to visit or meet the management had been ignored, and the security guards at the door stopped me from entering when I tried.

'The food is the same every day,' Fatima complained. 'Chicken and rice or couscous for dinner.' The food was made by a catering company and delivered in little sealed packets. 'Sometimes it arrives cold, sometimes it's sour, sometimes the water has particles in it. Mothers with young babies have to give their children cold food because you're not allowed to cook for yourself. If you bring gas in, they confiscate it.'

We pulled up outside a block of flats. 'Wait here,' Fatima said, and she and Ife went inside. Fifteen minutes later, she came out alone, carrying two heavy bags of shopping. 'Help me put these in the back.'

On the way back to Città Giardino, I asked Fatima about her life before she came to Italy. 'I made the journey to Libya twice,' she said. Both times she'd taken the smuggler route across the desert, through Niger. The first time was in 2010, and she hadn't left Lagos by choice. 'Where I lived, there is a crude oil pipeline. People were illegally tapping it. People high up in the establishment – they would come at night with trucks. And when they finish, they don't close the pipeline, so the oil spills out and it poisons the area, spoils the water, kills the marine life.' Fatima helped organize protests, she said, but she was visited by representatives of the oil thieves, who told her she'd be killed if she didn't shut up. Fatima had two children – her husband had died some years previously – and she sent them to her mother to be looked after.

The first time Fatima went to Libya, she opened a Nigerian restaurant near the city of Sabha, in central Libya. 'I know bakery, how to make African pastries,' she said. Sabha was the point where two migration routes converged: one from West Africa, via Agadez, and one from the east, used mainly by people from Sudan, Eritrea and Somalia. Many migrants stayed in Sabha to work in the surrounding farmland. In the late 1990s, Gaddafi had started encouraging migration from beyond the Sahara as a way to build influence in Africa. There were between 1.5 and 3 million migrant workers in the country before 2011, according to information compiled by the Global Detention Project. Black people had always faced racism in Libya – in 2000, several migrants were lynched in riots – and as the economy became less stable, Gaddafi blamed them for crime, disease and unemployment. Libya started to restrict immigration after its rapprochement with Europe in the mid-2000s, and by the end of the decade it operated at least twenty detention centres. These were notorious for overcrowding, poor sanitation and the abuse of detainees – so much so, in fact, that Italy offered to build 'model' detention centres with higher standards in Libya, which could then be copied.

The Libyan police left Fatima alone because she had applied for a work permit, but they would often come and check the papers of her customers. It ruined her business: 'They were catching people too much, so we don't open the shop again.' Shortly after Fatima had closed her restaurant, in early 2011, war broke out in Libya and the Nigerian government evacuated its citizens by plane. She went back to Lagos, but hid in a part of the city where she wouldn't be recognized.

In January 2013, Fatima took the route north across the Sahara again. This time, she said, she saw women being forced into sex work along the route, and swore she would never make the journey again. Libya seemed to have stabilized after Gaddafi's overthrow. A new government had been proclaimed, and it was trying to suppress the unauthorized militias that still controlled parts of the country. 'I came to Tripoli. Many people come to Tripoli for work. You see black men lining up by the side of the road in the morning, waiting for cars to come and take them. For their skills – carpentry, plumber, electrician. You need to be agile. Young men can do it. Young women can come and do it. I started as a cleaner.' Fatima worked in a hospital at first, she said, before moving on to clean the houses of wealthy Libyans. Because she spoke good English, she was able to pick up teaching work, too, giving lessons to the children of the people whose houses she cleaned. Eventually, she got a job at a private school, run by Americans. 'It was very hard to get work, but I cleaned, then I did my CV, got better jobs,' Fatima said. She was so matter-of-fact about it, she made it sound simple.

The situation in Libya deteriorated sharply in 2014.

Islamist militias opposed to the government had set up a rival administration in the east of the country. In May, fighting between the two factions reached Tripoli, with airstrikes, rocket fire and a fierce battle taking place for the city's main airport. 'The second time war started, it was very dangerous because there were so many bombs. The Americans were attacked, they had their schools bombed and they closed them.' Fatima lost some of the protection she had enjoyed. She explained that, for a black person in Libya, the most dangerous time was the journey to and from work. People would be robbed, or assaulted, or worse. 'One morning, on the way to work, I saw a girl being raped and her throat cut. She was thrown on the road to die. If men saw a black couple together, they would come and ask to "borrow" the woman.' The Americans who ran Fatima's school used to drive her to and from work, but they left the country in mid-2014. 'That's what made me tired and think, I need to leave this country. Even in the night, you sleep with one eye open. All night, men knocking at your door, asking for money, asking if you're a woman.'

Fatima had a dilemma: there was more work available to her now that the American teachers had left, but Tripoli was becoming more dangerous. In July 2015, she embarked on her journey to Europe. 'When I saw the boat, I said, "Oh God, it's a balloon!" They were blowing it up, like—' Fatima blew her cheeks out.

The previous year, with Italian ships patrolling international waters, smugglers in Libya had realized they could get away with sending their passengers shorter distances. Poorer migrants were crammed into inflatable boats and were often told to sail north for a few hours before making a call to the Italian coastguard on a phone the smugglers provided. Prices fell and demand rose as Libya became more dangerous, accelerating the trade throughout 2014 and 2015. 'I never pray,' said Fatima, recalling the moment she boarded the boat, 'but . . .' Her voice tailed off and she started shifting in her seat again. I didn't ask more.

There was another reason why Fatima had left Libya. Earlier in our conversation, Fatima had told me she'd become well known by West African migrants in Tripoli for intervening in other people's problems. She scolded men she thought were exploiting women, she tried to talk women out of sex work and she had protested about their living conditions to the Nigerian embassy. Eventually, she'd been ostracized, to the extent that, when she'd arrived at the beach to board a boat for Europe, some of the other migrants had recognized her and complained about her presence. When she told me, she had laughed at the memory. 'They had to take me at night so nobody else would see me.'

16 · CAESAR AND OUSMANE

I wanted to catch up with Caesar and Ousmane before I left Sicily. First, I went to see Caesar, driving up to Catania one evening in early September. He was there, waiting on the porch as usual, headphones in, illuminated by the street lamp. Caesar was listening to music; I knew the names of some Malian musicians, so I tried them out on him. 'Nah, that stuff's for tourists. I like hip hop,' he said, offering me a listen.

This time, Caesar invited me into his home. The hallway floor was tiled, and several bikes were stacked against the staircase. We went into a room on the right and sat down on the sofa. Caesar had been watching TV before I arrived. On France 24, the global French-language news channel, scenes from the Keleti train station in Budapest, of migrants clamouring to board trains for western Europe, were playing on a loop. On 24 August 2015, Germany had announced that it would give asylum to any refugees from Syria who arrived on its territory, accelerating the rush of people through the Balkans from Greece. It was the peak of what the media were calling Europe's worst refugee crisis since the Second World War.

My host gestured towards the screen. 'You see? The cameras don't come here any more because it's only blacks arriving in Sicily now.' Caesar was right that attention had shifted to the Balkans, although journalists were still coming to Italy, too. I could see he was angry again, at the apparent distinction being made between migrants. 'What they're doing now in Europe, how can you divide us like this? It's not as if one person has "refugee" printed on his forehead and another has "economic migrant", just because of their nationality. How can you tell?'

Caesar was brooding, so I let him talk.

'I'm shocked by the TV here. The only time you see Africans, it's on an advert saying, "Donate nine euros," and it's always a picture of a sick woman. But, at the same time, politicians are saying Africa is rich? It's disinformation, if you ask me.' He said he was thinking of leaving Italy again. 'I've changed my mind. Italy's a conservative country, it's like Ancient Rome. *Franchement*, it's difficult to live here. They treat us like children, like we haven't been to school, like we can't reason.'

He'd still not managed to find any work, five months after arriving in Sicily. I was surprised, I said, because Catania was a big city and you saw lots of street traders from different parts of the world in the centre, selling sunglasses, or jewellery, or plastic trinkets. Was even that kind of work off-limits? 'Yes, because you have to have the right networks,' Caesar explained. 'Ninety-five per cent of the Africans selling stuff are Senegalese and they've been here for years. You can't get work with them.' The rest of the street selling was done by men from Bangladesh and Pakistan, he said. They made deals with the Chinese wholesalers, who ran shops in Catania's suburbs. They'd take fifty selfie sticks on credit, sell them all and then pay back a cut of the money they made. But Caesar was shut out.

In any case, he'd become fixated on a new destination.

'I need you to find out some information for me,' he said. 'How does Norway treat Malian refugees? Does it do Dublin returns to Italy? And what categories are exempt? How can you get regular papers in Norway? And can you travel there if you've been given refugee status in Italy?' I noted down his questions and promised I'd try to find out.

Caesar offered to show me around the house. As he led me up the staircase in the hallway, he pointed to a row of handmade posters that bore pictures of Africa and the Mediterranean. One had the slogan *No to racism* drawn in multicoloured felt-tip pen. 'You see that? They got us to do that. They treat us like children here,' he repeated. He was sick of asking for help from managers, lawyers and public officials, who always gave him the same sympathetic but unhelpful answers. 'They're always telling me where to go, where to sleep, even though I'm older than some of them. You can't leave the centre for more than three days without permission, and if you do start working, they penalize you and take your pocket money.' It was the same story I'd heard from Ousmane's Gambian friend, Alimamo, in Ispica; accounts of this practice were widespread.

There was a kitchen upstairs, where one of Caesar's housemates was eating dinner: pasta with tomato sauce, precooked, delivered by a catering service in a sealed plastic packet. The housemate stopped eating and said hello. He introduced himself, in English, as Abdul-Majid from Kashmir. I noticed a familiar accent. 'Yeah, I lived in Bradford for two years,' Abdul-Majid said. 'I studied business management in Wakefield. But my visa ran out and I had to leave, so I came to Italy and claimed asylum.' He'd got his refugee papers and was living at the SPRAR until he could save up enough money to rent an apartment, he said. He'd been in the north of Italy, but had come down to Catania to work in one of the Chinese-run clothes shops.

We left the kitchen. Caesar opened a door that led off the corridor and showed me into his room. It was sparsely furnished: a small wardrobe and a single bed to my left, and another bed to the right, where a young man was sitting listening to music through headphones. He looked up, startled. 'That's my brother,' Caesar said. 'He's twenty-one. We were in Libya together.'

Caesar hadn't mentioned his brother before. If he was twenty-one now, in 2015, he must have still been a teenager when they fled Mali in 2012. As we went back downstairs to the TV room, I wondered what it was like for Caesar to make that journey while having to protect his little brother. Caesar broke the silence: 'Everyone who entered Libya regrets it, but once you enter, you can't leave again. The image you have of Libya from the outside is very different from the one you have inside. Outside, you know it's not stable, but you think, Maybe I can find a life. Like you see Gaza on the TV: they have lots of problems with Israel, but life goes on, all the same. But the conditions when you cross the border into Libya are like entering another world. You are no longer your own; you're at the mercy of the smugglers. They treat you like beasts. Europeans have no idea; they only see the airport.'

These short bursts of detail about the journey to Europe were like watching objects break the surface of a lake.

Before I left, he reminded me to look up the information about Norway for him. I said I thought France would be much easier, since he spoke the language, but he insisted. 'I don't want to go to France; I want to go north. I want to go far away, change my life and forget the past.'

If he went back to Mali, he said, he'd be punished for having survived. 'They'll say I must have been one of the rebels, otherwise how could I have lived?'

Not even Europe felt quite safe. I asked Caesar once how he got his name; it seemed unusual to me, but perhaps it was common in Mali. He laughed. 'Caesar's not my real name, you know – it's just some stupid joke I put on Facebook so that nobody could find me.' He told me his real name, but made me promise not to reveal it.

*

At Ispica, I found Ousmane in almost the same situation as when I'd left him four months earlier. He was still waiting to appeal his asylum decision; in the meantime, he had the temporary six-month identity documents issued by the Italian government to people whose claims were delayed. These gave Ousmane the right to work, and the manager of his centre had promised she'd try to help him find a placement in a restaurant kitchen. In previous years, this practice had functioned as an unofficial way of providing cheap labour in Italy's agricultural and service sectors. The countryside around Naples was infamous for the *caporalato* system, where undocumented migrants and asylum seekers were given exploitative work on farms, in some cases for many years. But the people crossing the Mediterranean were now arriving in numbers that outstripped demand.

We sat in the dining room, TV blaring from one corner, like the last time I visited. I didn't recognize the people who came in and out. Ousmane told me that most of the residents from a few months ago had left, with or without documents. 'Germany, France, Spain, Sweden,' he listed. His two friends from the *scuola verde* in Augusta hadn't left Italy, though. Mamadou, the younger boy, from Senegal, had been given refugee status and had moved from the centre at Siracusa to a town in the south of Sicily, not far from Ispica. He seemed to be happy there; I had seen Mamadou on Facebook, posing in fashion boutiques with Italian teenagers.

Boubacar, the footballer from Mali, was still near Naples, but he'd turned eighteen and had been moved to another centre, for adult men. I'd spoken to him and he was living in an out-of-season hotel at Palinuro, a seaside resort, with men from other francophone West African countries. The men were angry, and held protests demanding that the system move faster. In the evenings, they would talk about what an injustice it was for Europe to treat them – people from former colonies – this way. 'We remember the past, we remember slavery; they started the world wars and we fought for them,' one had said to me when I later visited Palinuro. Boubacar himself seemed more interested in finding a team to play for than discussing politics. Palinuro was named after Palinurus, the navigator in the *Aeneid*, who steers a boat of refugees from ancient Troy to their new home in Italy.

Ousmane told me he had to go soon, because it was his turn to cook dinner; it was spaghetti tonight. 'I learned to cook here,' he said. 'At home, in Guinea, my big sister cooked.' I asked him to tell me a bit more about his family, and his home. His sister was married now, and he had an older brother, who worked as a lorry driver. 'There's lots of Chinese in Guinea, working, building roads, buildings,' he said. 'Lots of raw material in Guinea.'

On my way out, Ousmane showed me a set of child-sized lockers, no doubt left over from the reception centre's original use as an infant school. They'd been told to draw pictures to identify their own locker, Ousmane said; most of the doors had a piece of A4 paper fixed to them, covered in coloured pencil. Ousmane had drawn the coast of North Africa, and then the sea, in which a wooden boat packed with people was surrounded by leaping dolphins. 'Was that the kind of boat you travelled on?' I asked.

'Yes,' Ousmane said. 'Not a good boat.' His expression warned me off asking anything else about it. He'd looked the same earlier, when I'd tried to ask about Libya; all he would say was that he'd been in a detention centre for five months.

Ousmane had turned eighteen while he was waiting here, being asked to make coloured-in drawings. He spoke at least three languages fluently and, as he picked up Italian, was adding another one to his list. He still hadn't found any work, and he knew his asylum claim was never likely to be accepted. He could either stay in Italy, and hope to earn money during the years it took for his asylum appeals to be exhausted, or he could leave for elsewhere in Europe and work on the black market. Or he could ask the Italian government to send him back to Guinea. But Ousmane wouldn't consider the latter option. 'There's nothing for me in Guinea,' he'd told me when I asked. He spoke to his family about once a month, via Facebook, and he'd told them that he had a job and was doing fine.

As I left, I was struck by how differently Ousmane seemed to be responding to his situation, compared with other people I'd met. Fatima and Caesar were telling themselves very strong stories about who they were, how they'd ended up here and why. Fatima was going to warn people of the dangers in Libya; Caesar was determined to disappear into everyday life. Fatima had made her bargain with God; Caesar was convinced of Europe's moral responsibility towards migrants from Africa. But they were older; they'd had lives of their own before they'd been displaced. Ousmane had spent the last of his childhood on the move, and he'd become an adult at Europe's border, caught between arrival and acceptance. He seemed to be taking it with equanimity. But still, I asked myself, did he feel adrift?

17 · FATIMA

I added Fatima on Facebook after we met in Siracusa, and noticed she'd set up a discussion group, to 'tell the truth' about being a migrant. Its members were mainly from West Africa, some of whose locations were displayed as towns in Italy. Throughout the autumn and winter of 2015, Fatima had posted something there every week or two. She warned about the risks of the journey, she wrote that the struggle didn't end when people were out of the sea – and above all, she implored women not to be 'tricked' by men. On her own wall, Fatima posted inspirational quotes, pictures of kittens and praise to Allah rendered in English and Arabic.

In September 2015, the European Commission held another summit. They finally agreed on a scheme to relocate 160,000 refugees living in Italy and Greece to elsewhere in the bloc; to launch a system of 'hotspots' to process new arrivals, weed out the economic migrants and deport them more quickly; and to establish a 'Trust Fund for Africa' that would provide billions of euros in aid to promote stability. A follow-up summit in November, between the EU and the leaders of various African countries, revealed that much of this money was to be spent on strengthening border security.

Over the months that followed, some of the hotspots

were opened, but the relocation scheme stalled again, under strong opposition from Hungary, the Czech Republic, Poland and Slovakia. Britain opted out of the scheme altogether. By the spring of 2016, fewer than 2,000 of the proposed 160,000 had been relocated. In Italy alone, more than 150,000 people were living in its asylum reception centres, according to the interior ministry – more than double the number who were there in 2014.

With little immediate prospect of stability in Libya, the smuggling trade continued to thrive, and the networks that moved people from sub-Saharan Africa were becoming more efficient. A journey that might have taken several years was now, in some cases, taking as little as a few weeks. Towards the end of 2015, according to the UNHCR, the number of crossings dropped because of the winter weather, but they increased again in early 2016, at a substantial rate, although slightly lower than the previous year. Over 9,000 people arrived in March, and the same number arrived in April. The vast majority now came from sub-Saharan Africa, with the largest groups from Nigeria and Eritrea.

In April 2016, I went back to Sicily for the last time. In Siracusa, walking by a palazzo in the old town of Ortigia, I noticed a sign for a conference on *innovation, integration and the migrant crisis*. In the courtyard, there were displays from social enterprises and NGOs from around Europe, promoting their projects: a mobile app for learning Swedish; a restaurant in Athens that brought cooks from different backgrounds together; a ludo-style game, where the players have to cross borders; a public-information campaign from a local council in Lisbon.

In the conference room, I saw Fatima sitting at the front of the audience. She listened patiently and took notes as the chair asked people to brainstorm ideas, pinning their suggestions to a hexagonal diagram on a whiteboard. At the end of the session, when the chair asked for comments from the floor, Fatima pushed forwards to get in line for the microphone. She introduced herself as a women's rights activist. When she said she was a refugee, and that she'd recently received her papers, the audience of white European professionals applauded politely. Fatima said it was her dream to set up a social enterprise to help migrants find work. 'It's very difficult here for refugees and migrants, especially the blacks,' she said. 'I'm seeing people begging – women, carrying their children, begging – things that aren't working. So don't just come and ask me questions and sell my story or sell my voice; we need a change.' There was more applause.

During the lunch break, I went over to say hello. Fatima told me she'd just been given two years' political asylum in Italy. 'Everyone at the centre says, "Oh, you're so lucky." I got the decision on my first hearing. The blacks usually get turned down; it's the Eritreans and the Syrians who get given asylum.' By 'blacks', she meant the West Africans. Fatima said she was still staying at Città Giardino while she waited to find somewhere else to live.

Fatima was nervous again, like when we'd first met. She beckoned me into a quiet part of the courtyard, took out her phone and played me a recording she'd made. I could hear a young woman sobbing, and then Fatima's voice saying, 'Don't worry, the white people will help you.' She stopped the recording and told me that two teenage girls from Nigeria, both aged seventeen, had been brought to her reception centre by police. They'd been placed in a secure room for their own safety, and the staff had asked

Fatima to go in and speak to them, thinking they were more likely to trust her because she was from Nigeria too.

Fatima sent the file to me via WhatsApp and I listened to some more of the recording. The girls were from villages in Edo State, in Nigeria. One did most of the talking. She said that a family friend had come to her house and asked her parents if they'd like to send their daughter to work in Europe. The friend didn't say what kind of work she would be doing, only that she would earn money she could bring home, after she had paid back a bond of 5,000 euros. They took her to the village magician and made her swear an oath that she would honour the debt, then sent her north, across the Sahara. By the time she reached Libya, she had discovered that, when she arrived in Europe, she would be forced into sex work.

On the recording, I could hear Fatima's voice asking direct, precise questions about the traffickers' contact in Italy. The girls were part of a group of five. Upon arrival, their instructions were to wait until they'd left the port and been transferred to a reception centre, then to phone a Nigerian woman, who would bring them to a brothel. The two girls had told an aid worker at the port they were being trafficked – the other three had kept quiet – and they'd been handed over to the Italian police. Now, they were worried because of the oath they'd sworn. One was telling Fatima she should phone her contact; Fatima was reassuring her she was safe now.

She told me she'd seen a lot of these cases, and usually they didn't come to the attention of the police. 'Girls are always disappearing from the centre. If ten arrive, five will be gone in a few days. They go to prostitution houses. The madam [who takes them in] says, "Let me contact your madam," and they make an arrangement to pay her back.'

Older women who arrive might have been sex workers in Niger or Libya, paying for their passage to Europe, but the girls, Fatima said, 'they bring fresh to Europe.'

The trafficking of Nigerian women to Europe is not a new phenomenon; in Italy, sex workers from Nigeria and elsewhere in West Africa started arriving in the early 1990s. They are brought by criminal networks that stretch from their home towns into various cities in Europe, and although some women might earn a degree of independence once they pay off their debts, the traffickers frequently use violent intimidation and threats to family members back home, to keep their workers obedient. Women also risk being deported if they are caught in police raids and do not have the correct documents. The Libyan route became increasingly attractive to these trafficking networks, because it was cheaper and didn't require forged ID. The IOM estimated that 80 per cent of the 5,633 Nigerian women who arrived in Italy by sea in 2015 had been trafficked.

Most of the trafficked young women she'd met came from rural towns, Fatima said. 'They work as shop assistants or on farms. Their mothers pressure them because they see other girls coming back from Europe with nice clothes and money, but they don't know how they earn it. People come and offer work in Europe, promise they will work in a bar or a hotel or a restaurant.' She made a noise of displeasure at the back of her throat. 'The girls are so little. And some of them are pregnant when they arrive in Italy.'

The area around Siracusa's train station was used by sex workers at night, some of whom were still living in Fatima's reception centre. 'The authorities in the camp see prostitution happening and turn a blind eye,' Fatima said.

'Once, I was walking past the station at night and an Italian man came up to me and said, "Are you selling?" I said, "What do you think you are saying?" and he was very sorry: "*Scusa, scusa.*"' Fatima laughed. 'This is why I am talking to girls on Facebook, telling them, "Don't come to Europe. Do you know what it's like? Do you really want to earn money this way?" Telling the girls in the centre, "Tell your friends at home what it's like and not to come."'

Our lunch break finished and Fatima went back to the conference room. 'Meet me tomorrow, and I'll tell you more about what I've found,' she said. I saw her once again that day; in the evening, the conference organizers had arranged a theatre performance, by refugee actors, in the town hall. I was watching from the back, and when it finished, I saw Fatima walk to the front and insist on taking the microphone from the compère. She said her dream was to set up a theatre group specializing in African music and dances. 'I plead with the European community not to waste our talent. Help us.'

*

The next morning, I went to meet Fatima at the city hospital. 'It's near the big church,' she'd told me. Fatima didn't know most of the street names and she was still navigating Siracusa by its landmarks. The church she meant was easy to find: a modernist concrete tower that stuck out in a city of ancient buildings and low-rise twentieth-century sprawl.

I found Fatima inside the hospital, waiting near the reception desk. She was working there two mornings a week as a cultural mediator, helping doctors communicate with West African patients. It was the end of her shift and she was in conversation with a doctor, speaking broken but working Italian, when I arrived. In the hospital, Fatima kept an eye on the patients who were brought in from reception centres around the province. 'I check on them to make sure they're not forgotten, and bring them food, because the hospital food is not enough.' Often, she said, the centres would send patients here and then forget about them for days. She played me another recording she'd made on her phone. This time, it was a young man, eighteen years old and from Gambia. He was telling her that, in his reception centre, the staff wouldn't give him his pocket money unless he sold packets of cigarettes on the town's streets.

Being a cultural mediator was the second job she'd found. 'I worked two months selling flowers, six hours a day, and all day on Tuesdays and Thursdays. It only paid fifteen euros a day. They kept saying they would have more money for me, but it never came. I kept doing it, so I could learn more Italian, but I gave up because it was so much work and it didn't give me any time for activism.'

We left the hospital. 'I need you to drive me somewhere,' Fatima said, 'but first we have to go shopping.' She took me to a Sri Lankan-run mini market, on a side street, that sold imported goods from Asia and Africa. Fatima picked out packets of smoked catfish, bitter leaf and dried peppers. 'It's the only place in Siracusa you can get this stuff, and it's expensive.'

In the car, Fatima directed me to her cousin's house. Ife had moved, and was now living in a one-storey terrace in a run-down neighbourhood. Fatima invited me in for lunch, and went into the kitchen with Ife to make soup while I waited on a sofa in the living room. There was a bed made up in one corner and another mattress propped up against the wall. Above the sofa was a Nineties-style art print of two zebras fighting. The paper had a burn mark along one side of the print. Ife and Fatima brought the food through, and we were joined by two other men. Four of them shared this apartment, which only had two rooms. They'd been living here for a few months, Ife said, but the electricity still hadn't been connected.

After lunch, Fatima asked me to take her back to Città Giardino. Ife came along with us; once we dropped Fatima off, we drove back into Siracusa together. He hadn't talked much when Fatima was around, but now he started to tell me his story. He'd come to Europe, 'in hope of a better life,' in 2011. He'd tried to cross Libya, but had been caught in one of the Gaddafi regime's immigration prisons, then released when the war started; in a gesture of defiance, Gaddafi had opened the prisons when NATO intervened against him.

'I didn't know what I would do in Europe, just come and after six months maybe find a job, in a factory or something.' He'd left Italy and gone to Switzerland, where, he told me, he'd sold drugs. Other Nigerians had told him how to do it: 'You go to a European contact and take a large amount of cocaine from them and sell it on the street, then you pay them back. Swiss people were the customers, or other Europeans. Most of the Africans I knew didn't take the drugs. I never took them.'

After six months, his temporary permission to stay in Switzerland ran out. 'My fingerprints were in the system, so they sent me back on a plane, in handcuffs, from Zurich to Milan.' In the north of Italy, he'd tried dealing drugs again, but had run away to Siracusa when the police raided his house. 'Here, the blacks can't deal drugs, only marijuana,' he said. 'The mafia deal cocaine and they don't let the blacks do it. There's no other work for us. That's why the women do prostitution and the men do begging. Or they leave and go to other countries.'

He said that the prospects for earning money had got worse since he'd first arrived. 'Even Italian citizens are finding it difficult. And there are too many refugees, so the money you earn is less. You can't earn as much helping people with their shopping at the supermarket or going to the car park to help direct the cars. I did it yesterday and an Italian woman said to me she'd already seen twenty people begging at the traffic lights.'

I dropped Ife off at his house. Earlier, Fatima had told me that all of Ife's housemates earned money by begging. 'It's not enough,' she said. 'You need to pay for all this – the apartment, the gas, the electricity – before you can send anything back home, before you can save anything for yourself.' She tried to send money back to her children and their grandmother whenever she could. 'I didn't send them money when I was in Libya because I didn't think it was good for them.'

Fatima was kicking hard against the current, trying to give her life some shape. It was as if, by declaring herself a women's rights activist, or a social entrepreneur, or a theatre producer, she was trying to will one of these roles into existence.

18 · CAESAR

I still didn't understand what it was really like to make the journey from Libya. People seemed to spend months there before they even got onto the boats. What did they do? What was daily life like? Of my three interviewees, I thought Caesar would be the most likely to tell me. Despite his frustrations at the slow pace of Italy's asylum system, he seemed to be the most rooted, the most sure of himself. I went back to Catania, to propose a longer interview. He was at home when I called on him, one Saturday afternoon in April 2016, and he invited me in. Since we'd last met, he'd had his first asylum interview and his claim had been turned down. 'They've divided everyone from Mali into "north" and "south",' he said. 'The south is safe to go back to, so if you're from there, they turn you down.' He'd had trouble explaining himself during the interview, he said, because the translator provided by the court came from a different ethnic group and didn't speak his language properly. The asylum commission hadn't believed Caesar when he said he'd been living in the north of Mali; he hadn't managed to produce a residency certificate, so he was trying to get hold of one in time for his appeal hearing. 'It's not like one person has "economic migrant" written on their forehead and another has "refugee",' he repeated.

I told Caesar why I'd come back to visit, and asked him if he'd talk to me at length. He thought carefully for a few moments.

'OK, I'll do it,' he finally said. 'But I want some time to think about *mes paramètres* first.' He wanted to think about what he was prepared to reveal and what he wasn't. 'Could you come back in a week?'

*

The following Saturday, I went back to Catania. It was mid-April, a year since the two shipwrecks that had precipitated Europe's refugee crisis, and local activists had chosen this day to commemorate the deaths. At the city port, a small crowd gathered to throw flowers in the water and listen to speeches from representatives of different left-wing groups. Afterwards, several hundred people set off on a protest march through the city centre, playing Italian political songs from a set of speakers on wheels.

I went to meet Caesar at the point where the march was supposed to finish, by the medieval Castello Ursino, on the edge of the city centre. We sat on a bench, I took out my Dictaphone and he began to speak. Caesar talked for an hour, interrupted only by my occasional questions – and, once, when a tramp came over to ask us for a cigarette.

Caesar's problems had started in 2012, when Tuareg rebels, who wanted their own independent state, took over northern Mali. It was another side effect of the war in Libya: Mali's conflict was fuelled in part by weapons – many of which originally came from European manufacturers – looted from arms dumps in Libya during the uprising against Gaddafi. The rebels had taken over Caesar's city, and then negotiated with the government so that elections could be held. 'They signed an agreement to send civil representatives to organize the elections, but the same day they decided this, a rumour started that the government was sending the army to retake the town.' Caesar and some of the other residents organized a protest. 'We didn't want the army to come, because every time the army comes to retake a town, it's war, it's civilians who take the hit and, at the end, the army flees and abandons the people to their fate.'

During the protests, spies working on behalf of the army noted down the names of the ringleaders; Caesar was well known in the town, because of his electronics shop. During the night, after the protest, militiamen and government soldiers raided the houses of Caesar and the other organizers. The soldiers killed Caesar's mother and assaulted his wife in front of him. Then they took Caesar and his younger brother away, into the desert region of northern Mali.

'They brought about sixteen of us to their base and told us we were traitors and that we supported the rebels. They discussed whether or not to kill us, but decided, if there were bodies, there would be questions, and that would cause problems. So they said they'd take us out to the desert and throw us out there, in the sand, where we'd die of thirst or of hunger. So, like that, they took us and threw us in a lorry. We drove for more than a hundred kilometres. And when they were far enough away from the town, they left us in the desert. They said it would be a waste of bullets. Because they'd beaten us so much and we were sick, it was certain we would die.'

Caesar's group lay there in the sand until they could no longer hear the sound of the soldiers' vehicles. 'In the desert, you travel by the lights of the cities,' he said, repeating what he'd told me at one of our earlier meetings, 'so we looked for where there was the most light and we walked in that direction. On the way, by God's grace, we met some shepherds who took us and gave us first aid, something to eat, something to drink.' The shepherds warned them not to walk closer to the lights. 'It was a town called Essouk and they said, "Yes, even in Essouk the army is present and, if you go there, they'll inform on you. The army will take you and kill you for sure." So the shepherds said that, since they sell their livestock in Algeria, they could put us in their livestock lorries and take us to Algeria.'

The shepherds took them to a place near the Algerian border, where Caesar's group could find someone to take them across. 'In the south of Algeria, people use several ways to travel,' he said. 'There are smugglers, but it's a closed network and they're hard to find. People also travel, as we say, *dondi, dondi* – little by little. You can find someone – for example, a shepherd, a livestock farmer, a cattle trader. You tell him, "I'll work for you, sir; you'll take me there."'

A farmer took Caesar and his brother across the border. They had no money, since they'd been abandoned in the desert with only the clothes they were wearing. The farmer brought them to his land, where he said they'd have to work to pay back their debt. 'We were kidnapped,' Caesar said. 'We spent two months with him, working on a chicken farm, then he said he was going to transfer us to Libya. So he left us with a driver.' The vehicle they travelled in was a pickup truck, smaller than the flatbed trucks Fatima and Ousmane had travelled in on the route through Niger. The pickup was about the size of a small van: four indoor seats for the driver and passengers, and an open cargo area at the back, into which the driver crammed thirty-two people. They drove across southern Algeria and crossed into Libya near the city of Ghadames.

It was mid-2013 when Caesar arrived in Libya, at which time the country was split into areas controlled by different militias. Outside Ghadames, the pickup stopped at a roadblock enforced by armed men. 'We didn't know if they were policemen, or if they were bandits. They came to the car and made some of us get out. They said that we hadn't paid for the transport, that we must pay, otherwise they'd take us to jail.' In Libya, Caesar explained, migrants would have to pay forty or fifty dinar at each roadblock. The driver usually negotiates on your behalf, because he speaks Arabic, Caesar said. And if he tells the men at the roadblock that you haven't paid, then you haven't paid.'

'What if someone refused to pay?' I asked, and Caesar laughed.

'If you refuse . . . You just can't refuse. If you saw the conditions in which . . . Your life is on the line. You're not given a choice. Either you do what they say or you go to prison, and that's a total hell. Or, by misfortune, they can kill you on the spot.'

Caesar and his brother went to prison. They were taken to a compound close to Ghadames, where several hundred other black men and women were held captive in an over-crowded room. The Global Detention Project lists a semi-official detention centre near the city, but it was impossible for Caesar to know who was in charge; Ghadames has been controlled by local militias since the fall of Gaddafi. 'Every morning at four a.m., the guards came to wake people up. They would make you go out into the court-yard. You were made to lie on your stomach. They would take your clothes off and pour water on you. Then they would start whipping you, hitting you, until sunrise.'

'Every morning?' I asked.

'Every morning.'

'Did the guards say anything while they were doing it?'

'They'd say, why did we come to Libya? Who asked us to come here? They did whatever they wanted to us in that prison. Often, they had sexual appetites. Some of them had homosexual desires. And they'd take out their desires on the people in prison there. They raped girls. They did everything. Whatever they wanted.

'In the morning, around nine a.m., they'd give you a little cup and you'd go to a tap to fill it. You could drink it then, or you could save it for later, because at midday they'd give you a piece of bread to eat. In the afternoon, at around four p.m., they'd bring us back to our rooms. Often, there would be people who'd ask us to go and work in their houses. If you stay there a long time, you'd start to learn Arabic. Then they'd tell you, "Good, you're going to work; if we pay you for the evenings, you'll earn money." And when you earned a certain sum of money, they'll say, "OK, you're free."'

The prisoners were put to work doing masonry or construction, or farming. Their captors would tell them they had to help rebuild Libya, and, according to Caesar, they reserved particular anger for people from Mali. 'They would target us because the former president of Mali, Amadou Toumani Touré, was very close to Gaddafi. They even said he sent soldiers to defend Gaddafi. So, in Libya, after the war, if they knew you were Malian, the situation was even more difficult. Because, when they see Malians, they think straight away of Gaddafi.'

It is likely that Gaddafi used at least some mercenaries recruited from sub-Saharan African countries during the 2011 war. One BBC report, for example, estimated that as many as 10,000 had been recruited, from Sudan, Chad, Mali and Niger. But 'mercenaries' or 'foreign fighters' had become a general term of abuse for the hundreds of thousands of black people living in Libya, both settled migrants and people trying to make their way through the country.

Caesar was kept prisoner for two months. Throughout that time, more people kidnapped at the roadblocks were being sent to the prison, and their living quarters were becoming even more crowded. The prisoners began trying to dig their way out. 'We tried to smuggle little pieces of stone inside the prison and we used them to chip away at the bricks, little by little. Over time, as we did it, the wall became fragile.' One night, they pushed at the prison wall and part of it gave way. 'About half of us got out. They only left two or three people to guard us during the night. They had guns and they'd shoot whenever they wanted, but they were scared because so many people had got out and they thought we were going to attack them, so they ran away. I heard of other places where people had killed their guards.'

In the distance, I could hear the music from the demonstration getting louder, as the protestors marched closer to the Castello Ursino.

After Caesar and his brother escaped from the prison, they started working their way across Libya, *dondi, dondi* again. 'We made our way north, to Tripoli. Since I'm an electrician, if I found opportunities to do that, I would, but you just wanted to find any way of surviving.'

I asked if he'd thought of going to Europe by that point.

'Us, we just wanted to save our lives,' he said. 'Because, when we arrived in Libya, it was really, really, really a catastrophe. But once you're inside Libya, it's easier to leave by sea. Even that, you don't know how it's going to happen. Your life is at stake. It's not certain you'll manage to cross the desert. The number of people who die crossing the desert, it's more than the number of people who die in the sea. But there's nobody in the desert to see. The sea is amplified because the Europeans are saving people and so the media are there, but there's no media in the desert, there's nobody to save you.'

I thought of a video Fatima had once posted to Facebook: a clip of a wrecked vehicle in the Libyan desert. The driver, lifeless, was still sitting at the wheel; all around were bodies half-covered by sand. In 2015, the IOM estimated that the death toll for migrants in the Sahara Desert was at least as high as that in the Mediterranean.

Caesar and his brother would arrive at a town, ask around for work – like the men Fatima had seen lining the streets every morning – then try and find someone who would drive them closer to Tripoli. It took him several months to reach the Libyan capital, travelling from town to town in the back of crowded pickups. 'Even with vehicles, it's very difficult to travel from one town to another,' he said. 'The desert is so big and the drivers zigzag all over the place. I once asked the driver, I said, "I don't understand; I thought we are supposed to be following the stars to head north," and he told me, "No, we're chasing after the wells." Without these wells, it's impossible to make the journey. They tell everyone to buy a twenty-litre water container, and each time you find a well, you fill it.'

The drivers, who came from different countries – Chad, Libya, Nigeria, Algeria – and were usually armed, would deflate their tyres to give them more grip on the sand, but this would increase the risk of crashes. The passengers held onto a rope strung around the back of the vehicle. 'If you fall off, you're finished. They say it's a piece of luggage that has fallen. If you tell the driver that person has fallen, he makes you get out and stay there with them.'

'Why did they have that attitude?' I asked.

'Because they're on drugs. You can't be in your normal state and say you're going to do this journey. For them, it's a job. For example, we were transported by one driver, a Chadian, who said it had been his business since he was fourteen.'

Caesar and his brother arrived in Tripoli at the start of 2014. At the time, the war had calmed down. 'There were still clashes, but you have hope that it'll settle down to let you live. Whoever aspires to life has hope, even though you see the situation deteriorate every day. It becomes worse and worse, but despite that, you hope. You try to forget, you act as if it's nothing, as if it's normal to be able to have the minimum of life. But this is not normal. Reality makes you understand every day that this is not normal.'

What did Caesar mean by 'not normal'?

'It's never normal because sub-Saharans are viewed very badly in Libya. The simple fact of being black there is a problem. Anyone could attack you. It doesn't matter at what moment, for anything. In the evenings, when you leave work, one day a Libyan will come up to you and ask for a cigarette, money; they'll search you. When you say you don't have money, they'll say, "Why?" Children do it in front of their parents and the parents say nothing. Everyone makes the law there, everyone. They can do what they like. Take you to work, not pay you. Kidnap you, imprison you. You can't say anything. Who are you going to complain to?'

In the summer of 2014, clashes between rival factions

escalated into another civil war. 'I didn't decide to leave,' Caesar said, 'circumstances decided.' The two brothers had found work on a farm outside the city that grew dates, tomatoes and potatoes. 'A few hundred migrants worked there. We told the man we worked for we wanted to leave, so he made contact with the smugglers, but he said that, because I was with my brother, we'd need to work for him for three months to earn the salary to pay for the trip.'

Caesar knew they would be leaving Libya by boat, but the farmer wouldn't tell him when or how it would be arranged. 'One night, he came to us with his car and put us in the boot. He said, "Now you're going to leave Libya." We drove for more than an hour and a half. When the car stopped, we were by the sea. Two or three other Libyans were there. We said, "You told us we were going to leave Libya, but not in these conditions." When you arrive at the sea, you don't have a choice. They all have weapons. This was our only chance. If you survive, that's it; if you die, that's it. He closed the car door and we told the Libyans we wanted to go back with him. But they beat us with the butts of their guns and told us, "Get out."'

The brothers had arrived at one of the beaches west of Tripoli – Caesar didn't know which one, exactly – that smugglers used for boat launches. Different networks ran different launch points; at Zuwara, the most frequently used point, the smuggling trade was run by ethnic Berbers. Their language, culture and economic prospects had been suppressed under Gaddafi and smuggling had provided a livelihood for many years. After 2011, they had initially waited to see if the new Libya would provide them with a better deal, before resuming the trade once again. Other networks controlled smuggling from other coastal towns, but their structures were similar: a senior coordinator would give orders to managers in charge of safe houses, boats and workers. One such kingpin was reported to have sent 45,000 people to Europe in 2015, according to a report in *Der Spiegel*. The managers would oversee the workers in charge of security, or loading the boats, or running farms where migrants like Caesar were made to work to pay for their journeys. Recruiters, often from the same countries as the migrants themselves, would gather customers in Tripoli and other big cities, and bring them to the departure points in minibuses.

'When we arrived, they blew up two of those boats on the beach,' said Caesar. 'You've seen them – they put a hundred, a hundred and fifty people inside a boat that has room for thirty or forty. On our boat, there were more than a hundred and twenty people, all sub-Saharans, but when we left, there were still others waiting.'

Before boarding, the passengers were told to undress to just T-shirts and shorts, then they were given a water can and a packet of biscuits each. 'We saw that Arabs waiting for the boats were being allowed to carry all their necessary materials. They were allowed to carry bags.' The smugglers in charge told Caesar's group that they'd only be in the water for an hour or two, before the Italian navy would come and rescue them.

Dawn had arrived by the time Caesar's boat set off. The boat was propelled by a motor at the back and the driver was a migrant who had been trained by the smugglers to operate it. 'I think they'd given him a satellite phone with GPS coordinates too, but I couldn't see easily.' Most of the passengers were men, but a dozen or so women were on board. Caesar noticed that two women – from Somalia, he thought – were pregnant.

After a few hours, the Libyan coast slipped out of sight. It was September, and the sea was calm. Nobody moved, because they were packed in so tightly that, if anybody upset the balance, the boat would have capsized. Some more hours went by. The sun dipped, and dropped below the horizon, and the passengers spent a night at sea. Eventually, the fuel ran out and the boat drifted. There was no sound, Caesar remembered, except for the noise of the waves, and the voices of people reciting verses from the Koran or the Bible under their breath. 'I was sitting at the front of the boat, next to my brother,' Caesar said. 'We just prayed. I started to ask my wife and son to forgive me for all the bad I'd done. I was leaving my wife a widow and my son an orphan.'

The boat drifted for another day and a night. On the third day, they were spotted by a helicopter, and shortly after, an Italian navy ship arrived to take them on board. They were plucked from the sea, and given foil blankets to sleep under.

*

I asked Caesar to stop his story there. The journey from being kidnapped in Mali, to being rescued at sea, had taken nearly two years. It must have been doubly hard, I thought, to have to look out for his younger brother all that time.

'I had to be big brother, dad, mum, everything,' he said. 'I told him, "You shouldn't worry; it's fate, nobody can escape their fate." Because I told him always, "Death is everywhere. If someone's day comes – their fate, the day it stops – it's over, no solution. Everyone will die one day or another. If your day has come, even if you're in the presidential palace, you're going to die. Death doesn't discriminate." My brother stopped being afraid.'

That wasn't an attitude they'd shared before being forced from Mali, he said. 'We never thought we'd live in a situation like that, with these kind of difficulties. Me, for example, it's been years since I've seen my son, since I've seen my wife. I long to take them in my arms and hold them close to me.' Caesar told me his family was safe for the moment; he often posted photos to Facebook of his son, who had grown from a baby into a little boy since Caesar left Mali.

'I've tried to make my brother understand that what he's lived through, for a kid, is very heavy,' Caesar continued. 'So, he shouldn't memorize it; he should forget it, as if it were a nightmare. Because, if he doesn't forget it, he won't be able to live his life as he wants.'

I understood better, now, what Caesar had meant whenever he'd told me that he wanted to forget about the past. 'Often, when you sleep at night, you wake up abruptly and you're afraid,' he said. 'The memories start coming back to you. When you start to think of the desert and how it was . . .'

He paused, then picked up a new thread.

'For me, the main thing is safety. After that, it's security, whether I can earn my bread, regardless of location. The key is to be able to earn my living, support myself. I do not want the Italian authorities to give me that, or the European authorities to give me that. I want to work myself to earn it. Because I value my dignity. I do not want to be a burden on Italy or on Europe, no. I want to contribute to the evolution of Europe, do my bit, even if it's as small as a grain of sand, bring at least my share of contribution.'

During our previous conversations, Caesar had been

angry at what he saw as Europe's role in his misfortune. He'd complained, at various points, about the spread of European-made weapons in Mali, and about France's role as the former colonial power. He'd felt ignored since arriving in Italy. But, as the demonstrators finally caught up with us and approached the square in front of the Castello Ursino, I asked him again how he felt about Europe.

'In the Bible – I do not know if you read the Bible – Jesus said, if your enemy strikes you on the right cheek, we must turn the left cheek. Even if somehow it is true that Europe does not contribute much, I recognize them for one thing and I thank them for that: the fact of going to save me on the sea. That makes up, in some way, for what I lost. They could have let me die at sea there. The fact of going to save me, this is important. Europe is about 500 million people. Nobody says the 500 million inhabitants are reflected by European leaders. No.'

We left the square, and Caesar walked me back to where I'd left my car, by the train station. On the way, he quizzed me about British politics. 'What happened to Gordon Brown? Was he a good prime minister?'

19 · FATIMA AND OUSMANE

I saw Fatima one last time before leaving Sicily. We met inside the church near the hospital; little groups of tourists moved in and out as we stood near one of the entrances so Fatima could use a plug socket to charge her phone. As we waited, I translated an information board for her: the church had been built in honour of a miracle that supposedly took place in Siracusa in the 1950s when a picture of the Virgin Mary above the bed of a newly married couple was said to have started shedding human tears. Fatima looked impressed. I said I didn't believe in miracles and that I thought the Church used them to earn money and gain influence. Fatima opened her mouth in shock and told me to shush. She paused, then said, 'Oh, well, people do that in Nigeria, too.'

I'd noticed Fatima had taken to wearing a crucifix around her neck, and that, on Facebook, she had begun sharing Christian, as well as Muslim, religious memes. Was she changing religion?

'No,' she said. 'I am Muslim. But I don't want to be more on the side of one religion than the other. Because I want to help people and I want them to be able to come to me.' I thought perhaps that flexibility also helped her better negotiate the Italian asylum system, where lots of the support services were provided by church groups.

We left the church and Fatima told me to drive to a small park on a hill near Siracusa's football stadium. We went into the park and trod carefully through a patch of scrub until we reached a large rock that jutted out from the hillside. Siracusa is surrounded by limestone cliffs, and its inhabitants have used the caves in them, both natural and man-made, for millennia. Ancient chroniclers claimed that 7,000 survivors of the war in 413 BC between Athens and Syracuse, the Greek forerunner of modern Siracusa, were imprisoned in an old limestone quarry outside the city. Here, in the park by the stadium, Fatima showed me evidence of more recent inhabitants. At the base of the rock, in a large alcove, were mattresses, discarded clothes and a cooking pot with a half-eaten meal still inside it. The inhabitants, men from West Africa, were out earning money, she said. Like her cousin Ife and his housemates, they were begging or directing cars to free spaces in the local supermarket car park. 'They work in the town, but they come back up here to sleep. They are ashamed to be seen.' Fatima said she was documenting these cave dwellings wherever she could find them. A cat sat on a nearby rock and watched us as we picked our way through the detritus surrounding the mattresses.

A report by the humanitarian news agency IRIN in April 2016 found that rescued migrants were being made homeless by the new 'hotspots' system. At these EU-funded processing centres, two of which are at ports in Sicily, new arrivals were being questioned by police about their reasons for coming to Europe. If they were deemed to be economic migrants, based on a limited set of responses to a questionnaire, they were issued with a piece of paper telling them to leave Italy within seven days. The rejected migrants had no means of leaving Italy, and with no access to the official asylum system – no place in a reception centre, and no lawyer who could help them appeal – they were ending up on the street.

I drove Fatima back to her reception centre. On the way, she told me she still hadn't been paid for her work at the hospital, more than a month after starting the job. 'They say they want to help you. Is that help?' she said, with a rare flash of anger. 'I signed up for thirty euros for every three hours. People here just want to drain you, to use you. Look at that conference they did. How many refugees did you see there? And they said it was for refugees.' Fatima was sick of being asked to help all the time at her reception centre. 'Because they know I help people, they ask me to help with everything, but when I ask them to help me find work, they shout at me and say everyone must help themselves.'

Her low mood didn't last long, and she was soon telling me she had a new scheme. 'I want to open an African kitchen – here, in Siracusa. Because how long can people keep begging? There are people who have been doing it for years. I tell them, "You can't keep begging. In Libya, if you beg, they would stone you to death. Because there is work to do."'

Fatima asked me to stop the car at a junction. She got out, looked through a wheelie bin for a few minutes and came back, carrying an old suitcase. 'For a pregnant girl at the centre,' she said.

*

I left Sicily without seeing Ousmane again. We'd been in contact on Facebook until the middle of March 2016, but then he'd gone silent and I hadn't managed to get a response. In the last few weeks before we lost contact, he'd been messaging me a lot, but he wouldn't say much, just *Sava pas* – 'Not OK' – when I asked how he was. When I asked why, he said, *Pour le papier* – 'because of the documents'. In one of his last messages, he'd written, *I want to leave.*

I tried asking his friends from Augusta. First, I spoke to Mamadou. He had moved on from Sicily; once his documents had come through, he'd left for Paris. I spoke to him on the phone there and he said he was living in a suburb to the west of the city, waiting to enrol in school. He hadn't heard from Ousmane, and he sounded lonely in his new surroundings. On his Facebook wall, I saw he'd posted a photo of himself with his arms around an elderly Italian couple, who I assumed had been his hosts in Sicily; he was smiling, but his eyes were full of tears.

Boubacar, still living in the seaside resort near Naples, didn't know where Ousmane was either, when I asked. His own asylum claim had been accepted, and he'd found a football team to play for. They were in Serie D, an amateur league, but just below professional level. 'I'm really happy, *mon grand*,' he messaged me.

I thought perhaps Ousmane had left for another country, but, at the end of April, I finally got a message back from him. *Hi Daniel*, it read. *I'm in a clinic. I'm a bit ill.*

What's wrong? I asked, but I didn't get a reply for another week. When I did, he claimed that the manager of his reception centre had been conspiring against him. I asked Ousmane for the name of his clinic, and, when I looked it up, I discovered it was a psychiatric hospital in central Italy. Over the summer of 2016, Ousmane kept writing to me, every few days. Again, he wouldn't say much, just *Sava un peu* – 'Not great'. In September, around two years after he'd been rescued from the Mediterranean, he wrote to me again: *I want to leave, but the doctors say I've got an illness in the head.* When he was finally let out, he told me, he wouldn't go back to Sicily.

I don't know exactly what had happened to Ousmane; there are different factors, some biological and some environmental, that might cause a person to develop a mental illness. But I knew from the stories I'd heard in Sicily that anybody who'd crossed through Libya and over the Mediterranean in the way he did would have seen and experienced things that marked them for life. A survey of migrants who'd taken this route, carried out in mid-2016 by the MEDMIG research project, found that over 75 per cent of respondents reported having been beaten, while over 25 per cent had seen someone die. Although Ousmane never told me about his experience of detention, I knew what Caesar and Fatima had told me. I had also read a Human Rights Watch report from 2014, the year Ousmane was there, that detailed numerous accounts of torture.

In Sicily, Ousmane had not had access to psychological support, except for the emergency care provided by hospitals. Médecins Sans Frontières offered therapy at a handful of reception centres, but not his one. It was difficult for charities to provide wider support; there weren't enough translators and cultural mediators, and the Italian health service wasn't set up to provide this kind of care, even to its own citizens. 'Mental health gets worse after arrival,' the coordinator of the MSF project had told me. 'Arrival is a relief, but then all the trauma comes back. The future is a big worry, too. Stress becomes a disease if it's not dealt with.'

Ever since I met Ousmane, Caesar and Fatima, a story that Caesar told me about his journey has played on my mind. It was one of those details that emerged in the middle of a conversation about something else, while we were sitting on the sofa watching TV, or standing on his porch under the street light – I can't remember which. Adrift at sea, off the coast of Libya, Caesar and his fellow passengers would see ships on the horizon and hope that one would come close enough to spot them. After two days, a ship began to approach. 'One came within two metres of us: a Portuguese ship, with a big Portuguese flag flying,' he said. 'We saw the captain looking at us through binoculars. It was so close, we could hear them talking. We were saying, "Praise God, we are saved!" And then he put the binoculars down and the ship just sailed on.

'It just sailed on, and I thought, That's it; we're dead. I will never forget that as long as I live.'

When I think about that now, I think about the people crowded into Italy's reception centres. Their bodies may have been saved from the ocean, but I wonder how many of them are still scanning the horizon, looking for help to navigate this next stage of their journey.

CONTINENT

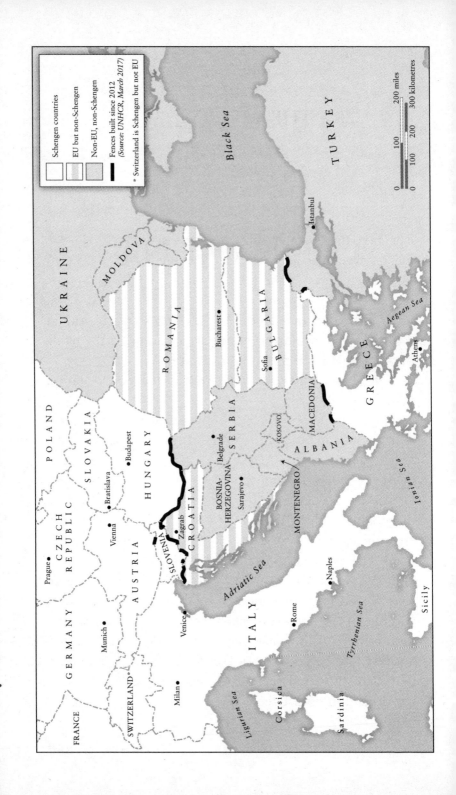

Schengen countries

EU but non-Schengen

Non-EU, non-Schengen

Fences built since 2012
(Source: UNHCR, March 2017)

* Switzerland is Schengen but not EU

200 miles

300 kilometres

UKRAINE

MOLDOVA

ROMANIA

Bucharest

Black Sea

TURKEY

Istanbul

Aegean Sea

Athens

GREECE

Sofia

BULGARIA

SERBIA

Belgrade

KOSOVO

MACEDONIA

ALBANIA

POLAND

SLOVAKIA

Bratislava

HUNGARY

Budapest

Prague

CZECH
REPUBLIC

Vienna

AUSTRIA

Zagreb

SLOVENIA

CROATIA

BOSNIA-
HERZEGOVINA

Sarajevo

MONTENEGRO

Adriatic Sea

Ionian Sea

GERMANY

Munich

SWITZERLAND*

FRANCE

Milan

Venice

ITALY

Rome

Naples

Tyrrhenian Sea

Sicily

Ligurian Sea

Corsica

Sardinia

20 · THE RIVER

The taxi driver can't find the cemetery, but he knows where the mufti lives, so he drives me there. Nobody's in; the windows of the mufti's white villa are shuttered. My driver looks at me and shrugs his shoulders. What now? He had sounded alarmed when I got into his cab at a town in the far north-east of Greece and said the name of the village I wanted to visit: 'Sidiro.'

'OK, but I'll have to take you to the police station first.'

Sidiro is on top of a hill overlooking the Evros river, which winds its way through the southern Balkans, from Bulgaria towards the Aegean Sea. For the final 200 kilometres of its journey, the Evros forms the border between Greece and Turkey. It's a natural frontier, but it also marks the point at which the two states, fighting for territory after the collapse of the Ottoman Empire, reached stalemate. The 'population exchange' of the 1920s, when two million Greeks from Anatolia and Muslims from Greece were forced from their homes and made to swap places, was one of the first great refugee movements of the twentieth century. The arduous journeys they made, and the hostility and contempt they faced on arrival in countries that were supposed to be their homelands, have passed into legend in both Greece and Turkey.

Sidiro, a mainly Muslim village on the Greek side of the border, is an inconvenient reminder to some that nations are never pure. Its inhabitants are Pomaks: speakers of a Slavic dialect, who converted to Islam under the Ottomans, but stayed put during the population exchange. Not Turkish enough for Turkey, yet not Greek enough for Greece; for many decades they were regarded with suspicion by the Greek state, as a potential Turkish fifth column. In the 1960s, the government tried to dilute the Muslim population by settling ethnic Greeks there, and, until the 1990s, Sidiro was encircled by checkpoints on the roads connecting it to its neighbours.

We stopped at a police station near Sidiro, where they made me sit on a bench as six officers crowded round a desktop computer and leafed through my passport. It wasn't only my destination that had made them suspicious; the day before, I'd crossed into Greece from Turkey. Until 2012, crossing the Evros was the most popular route for undocumented migrants who wanted to enter the European Union. Smugglers in Turkey would bring their charges up from Istanbul, only a three-hour drive from the Evros border. At night, they would send the people in inflatable boats across the kilometre-wide river, pulling them across with a rope strung between the two banks. In summer, when the water level dropped to one or two metres deep in places, people would try to wade across, their clothes stuffed into a plastic bag. The local UNHCR office estimated in 2011 that as many as 350 people were making the crossing every day.

Once across, the often bedraggled migrants would build shelters and fires to keep warm until the morning, when, if they had paid the smugglers enough, someone would be waiting to take them to Thessaloniki or Athens.

If they had not paid enough, they would have to try and make their own way there without being caught by the police and sent to one of the region's detention centres.

'Sorry,' the taxi driver had said as we left the police station. 'If they catch me with an illegal immigrant . . .' He knocked his wrists together to signal handcuffs.

*

It's just after noon when we turn away from the mufti's house in Sidiro. We can hear dogs barking and the call to prayer from the village mosque. Driving around, we ask villagers if they know the way to the cemetery. I have its name in Greek, written phonetically, on a piece of paper: *NEKROTAFIO METANASTON* – 'the migrants' graveyard'. I had read about this place, where they buried the bodies of people who drowned in the Evros and couldn't be identified; it was one of the few physical markers that hinted at the many thousands who had made secret journeys through this region.

An elderly lady, walking chickens along one of Sidiro's mud tracks, points us towards the village cafe. There, they tell us which road to take, to a nearby hilltop. As we pass by fields, we see a man in beekeeping gear, bending over a hive. He tells us we're on the right path and points to the top of the hill.

We reach the graveyard – a clearing on the hill, where the long grass has been cut back – around one p.m. There's little to announce its presence, except for a chain-link fence that surrounds it. I get out of the taxi and walk around the edge. Inside, large unmarked mounds of earth are set in rows, the older ones grassed over, the newer ones covered in gravelly soil and the tips of weeds. I find a sign, pockmarked by air-gun pellets, lying face-down in the long grass. The sun is out and it's almost silent, except for crickets and a breeze that comes across the tops of the graves and makes the grass rustle. Turning around, I can see back down the hill to the Evros; beyond that is another set of hills, which must be in Turkey. Hundreds of people, perhaps as many as a thousand, from various parts of Asia and Africa, are buried under the mounds at Sidiro; the cemetery has been in use since the early 2000s. They were given funerals by the mufti, on the assumption that they were probably Muslim.

Later, I visited the pathologist at the hospital in Alexandroupolis, near the mouth of the Evros, whose job it is to try and identify the bodies when they are brought in. The Evros is fast flowing and muddy, so people who drown in it are sucked downstream and often not discovered until the water level falls in summer. He showed me a set of photos on his computer, of greyed, bloated and skeletal corpses, still wearing jeans or patterned floral dresses, to underline how difficult the task was. In winter, people were more likely to freeze to death once they had crossed the river. They carried few possessions, and no identity documents. Each body is photographed and a DNA sample is taken, in case any relatives eventually come looking, before it is sent up to the mufti at Sidiro.

The doctor showed me a list of the number of bodies found each year. The figures climb steadily throughout the late 2000s, reaching fifty-four bodies in 2010 and fifty in 2011, before they drop sharply and tail off from 2012 onwards. It's an index of the political shifts happening around this border, which not only marks Greece's boundaries, but also the south-eastern frontier of the European Union. Geographical barriers like the Evros last for thousands of years; national borders may last for centuries.

Around them, we are constantly engaged in drawing and redrawing lines of threat and safety: ally and enemy, who belongs and who doesn't.

'Every death is one history,' the doctor at Alexandroupolis told me. The living, those who tried to cross the Evros and survived, have their own histories too.

21 · HAKIMA

My directions were to get out at the Victoria Square metro station, on the north-west edge of central Athens, and walk. It was dark, mid-evening, after rush hour had died down, when I left the station. Outside the Pakistani-run grocery stores that dotted the streets in this neighbourhood, men kept watch. The roads they surveyed were quiet, save for the occasional whine of a moped. The mood felt tense, which wasn't unusual for Athens at this time: the late autumn of 2012. It was the tail end of a year in which tens of thousands of Greeks had come out into the streets to protest the harsh austerity policies imposed by the EU after the financial crisis. In the city centre, riot police in protective gear lounged at street corners. There had been a large left-wing demonstration a few days earlier and reinforcements were drafted in, tear gas at the ready.

But there was a different source of unease in this neighbourhood. I crossed another square, dominated by a large Orthodox church dedicated to the fourth-century martyr, Saint Panteleimon. The cafes around the square were open, but the square itself was largely deserted. On the ground, in front of the church steps, was a slogan spray-painted in blue and white, the same colours as the Greek flags which hung limply from surrounding apartment balconies. It translated as 'Foreigners Out, Greece for the Greeks'. On a nearby street, angry scrawls of graffiti chased one another along a wall. Blue squiggles that looked like part of a meander design on Ancient Greek pottery had been crossed out in black paint, or supplanted by circle-A anarchy symbols.

I arrived at an apartment doorway, where a woman called Kaniz was waiting to meet me. She was Afghan, as were the people I had arranged to meet, and she had agreed to translate for us. A man with a nervous demeanour answered the door, introduced himself as Sakhi and motioned for us to take off our shoes. We walked through the front room, where a sheet, hung from the ceiling, divided the kitchen area from the rest. Four men lived here, Sakhi said. His family had the back room. We went through a door into their living area, where mattresses had been cleared away to make a space where we could sit on cushions and a carpet.

Sakhi's wife, a woman in her late twenties with a thin, serious face, was sitting there holding a baby. Two other young children – a boy and a girl, both under ten – drew pictures on a piece of paper next to her. She said her name was Hakima.

I tried to make conversation, by asking about the baby. 'Was she born here?' I asked, meaning in Greece.

'Yes, here,' Hakima said, and pointed to the carpet.

Hakima handed the baby to Sakhi. She went into another room and came back with a bowl of boiled sweets and cups of tea, and we began our interview. I was in Greece to report on the country's political crisis, and I had wanted to know how refugees were being affected. Hakima did most of the talking. They were virtually prisoners in their own home, she said. Sakhi had worked on a building site, but he had been beaten up by racists and lost his job while he was in hospital. Since then, the police had beaten him, too, in front of his children. Without work, the family had to rely on help from friends who still had jobs, and donations provided by a local church group.

Did that affect their social life? I asked.

'How can we invite our friends round to socialize?' Hakima said impatiently. 'We have no money, they have no money, they eat food from the garbage, they take things out of the garbage to sell them.' She described how, with other Afghan women in the neighbourhood, she would look through rubbish bins to find useful items. They were so worried about being attacked, she said, that they only went out at night to do it, in groups. 'We thought we would come here, we would be safe, we would be comfortable,' Hakima said, shifting her baby from one arm to another as she talked. 'The people here don't treat us like human beings.' She said there was little difference between the racists who attacked them, the police and the rest of Greek society. 'They all hate us.'

It was difficult to find the common ground needed for a real conversation. The details of their story seemed so bleak, and Hakima was describing them so starkly, that it didn't leave me much room to respond. After twenty minutes or so of conversation, Hakima lost her patience. She let out a stream of invective in Dari, which my translator relayed to me in English. 'We keep having journalists visit, and they want to hear our stories, but, tell me, what can you do? Nothing changes.'

I mumbled something that I thought would sound encouraging, about how other refugees had been here before them, that members of my own family had been refugees once, and they had got through it – but my words fell on stony ground. There didn't seem much more I could usefully do there, so once I'd got the details I needed for my story, I thanked the family politely and left.

I've thought about this incident a lot since, as I've encountered more people in situations like Hakima's. I've also been asked the same sort of question – what can you do for us? – by other people I've met. Often, journalists like to think that what they're doing is going to provoke a change. It's rarely the case, at least not in any direct way. The myth we believe is that exposing something we consider unjust is enough to fix it. But it's usually not. Most writers do not, and will not, get the chance to uncover a shocking new piece of information that makes a government or a society change its course. Instead, if there's anything useful in our work, it's more like fitting the pieces of a shattered mirror back together, to explain how a person, or a community, has come to find itself at an impasse. As writers, we have the luxury of distance. We can step back from a situation, try to untangle the web of cause and effect that surrounds it, and retell it in a way that makes sense.

That's what I want to do with Hakima's story here.

*

Hakima arrived in Greece in 2008. I don't know the exact date she arrived, but I know the route she took. She left her village in the eastern Afghan province of Ghazni, and crossed to Iran. From Iran, she paid smugglers to take her across the country, led on foot through mountain paths near the border with Turkey. At Van, in eastern Turkey, a city that serves as a transit hub for people-smuggling routes from central and south Asia, she was transferred to the first of several lorries that took her across Turkey, past Istanbul, into continental Europe. Somewhere near Edirne, a Turkish city close to the Greek and Bulgarian borders, she was brought to the banks of the Evros. A smuggler contact was waiting on the other side, to take her to Athens.

Hakima made this journey with her eldest child, the boy, who was a young child at the time. Her husband had left Afghanistan four years previously and was waiting for her in Athens. Ghazni province had escaped the worst of the violence that followed the US-led invasion, but it wasn't totally safe. The couple are Hazara, a Dari-speaking ethnic group made up largely of Shia Muslims and which faces persecution by the Taliban. Fighters for the deposed regime attacked rural areas, which made it difficult to move around. Sakhi had taken a job as a police officer, after the new Afghan government created tens of thousands of new posts, but corruption and violence were rife and he started to receive death threats, so he fled across the border to Iran.

Sakhi was now part of one of the world's largest and most enduring refugee diasporas. Afghans have been fleeing their country in waves since the civil war and Soviet invasion of the late 1970s. There were as many as six million refugees at one point, most of whom settled in Iran and Pakistan, according to the UNHCR. Until the war in Syria broke out, Afghans were the world's largest group of refugees by nationality, and their fate points to what happens when states are unwilling to fully accept the presence of newcomers. Afghans in Iran and Pakistan, even the ones who have been there for decades, are denied full civil rights; their right to stay is precarious and they are frequently mistreated by officials. Sakhi, who had crossed the Iranian border without permission, was arrested and put in prison for several months. Once released, he left for Europe. He sent for Hakima and their son when he'd earned enough money to pay for the trip.

By the time Hakima arrived in Athens, an Afghan community had grown up around the square of Saint Panteleimon. They were not the first migrants to arrive in this neighbourhood, which expanded during the decades after the Second World War. In the 1970s and 1980s, the original inhabitants of the apartment blocks – urban professionals and military officers – left for less polluted suburbs, and were replaced by poorer Greeks from the countryside, who set up small businesses in the streets around the square. In the 1990s, after the fall of the Iron Curtain, they were joined by new arrivals from the communist bloc: Albanians, Bulgarians and others. Like the generation before them, the Greeks who had arrived in the 1970s prospered, and began to move out to the suburbs too. They sold or rented out their old apartments in the inner city, often to the new immigrants. In a typical Athens apartment block, the cheaper, smaller flats are at the bottom, and the roomier ones are at the top. Today, if you look at a front-door buzzer, you're more likely to see Greek names on the upper floors, and a mix of nationalities on the lower ones.

In the 2000s, migrants began to arrive from Asia and Africa, making use of Greece as an entry point into the European Union. Afghans were one of the largest groups, and while they may have had other countries in mind as their final destination, many of them stayed in Athens for long periods while they looked for a route out of Greece. Arriving in the city with little or no money, they would head for Saint Panteleimon, which they knew as 'Hadji

Yasin', the name of an Afghan businessman who owned a block of apartments that overlooked the square. For a few euros a night, you could rent space in a shared room. Hadji Yasin was just one of several landlords – others of whom were Greek, local residents told me – who put these new migrants into apartments built for single families. Others would illegally let space in the basement, or even allow people to live on the roof in the summer months. The more settled residents of the neighbourhood started to complain about the signs of this overcrowding: washing lines strung from windows, or rubbish thrown from the tops of buildings.

This was how Sakhi lived as he waited for Hakima and their son to arrive. The EU's asylum rules made his situation more difficult. Under the Dublin system, he was expected to claim asylum in Greece, as it was the first EU country he entered. But Greece's asylum system didn't work properly; there was such a backlog of cases, it could take many years to reach a decision. In the meantime, Sakhi had to live on temporary identity documents, which needed to be renewed every six months at one particular police station in the city. Sakhi found a job on a building site; it was hard, low-paid work, and his boss didn't always pay him.

In 2008, the year Hakima joined Sakhi, there were 5,000 Afghans intending to stay in Greece, according to one community activist's estimate, but a consistent turnover of between 12,000 and 15,000 coming and going. As well as those who wanted to stay and the ones who had recently arrived, there were the ones who had left for elsewhere in Europe but were being sent back to Greece under the Dublin system. Most of the Afghans were in Athens, and many gathered around Saint Panteleimon. A more stable kind of community emerged. An Afghan restaurant and an internet cafe opened around Saint Panteleimon square. Hakima and the other parents took their children to play on the swings at a playground in front of the church. Those families with some sort of income, like Hakima and Sakhi, were able to rent more space. Around Athens, new migrant communities – not just Afghans, but Pakistanis, Bangladeshis and people from West Africa – were becoming more visible.

But the overcrowding and slum conditions caused tensions. Those people who didn't have any money at all lived in squatted buildings or slept rough in the city squares and parks. Some turned to drug use, or sold sex in the parks at night to make money. Greek residents began to feel uneasy about the effect this was having on their neighbourhood. Some were worried about crime, and reports and rumours of muggings spread quickly among the customers of the little shops that still lined the streets around Saint Panteleimon. Others complained to the city council, which they felt wasn't doing anything to crack down on slum landlords, nor was it providing public toilets for the rough sleepers.

At the end of 2008, a petition from a group calling itself the 'citizens' committee' circulated among residents. It called on the city council to do something about the migrant 'problem'. Hadji Yasin's building was evicted, but the group kept going. In January 2009, the 'citizens' held a protest on the square of Saint Panteleimon, in which they brandished Greek flags, and speakers denounced the immigrants. One morning, a few weeks later, residents woke up to find a padlock on the gates of the playground, placed there during the night. On the ground in front, sprayed in the blue and white of the national flag, was the word *ΕΛΛΑΣ*: 'Greece'.

*

Shortly after the citizens' committee emerged at Saint Panteleimon, worrying stories started to circulate among the Afghan community. People were being attacked, at night, as they crossed the square. The Afghans had experienced hostility before, including harassment from the police, but a new pattern started to emerge. At night, when crossing the square in small groups or alone, Afghans would be approached by a child. The child would ask them where they were from. If they said, 'Afghanistan,' a group of adults standing nearby would come over and assault them. Sometimes it would be kicks and punches, other times it would be a plank of wood or a broken bottle. Worse still, the police would look on and do nothing, or they would come over and start pushing the assaulted people around themselves.

Although it wasn't obvious at first, the citizens' committee had been infiltrated by Golden Dawn, a neo-Nazi party hitherto confined to the fringes of Greek politics. Founded in the 1980s, it took direct inspiration from the German Nazi party in its profound biological racism, its mysticism – Golden Dawn's meander symbol looks like a Greek take on the swastika – and its militaristic structure. For the first few decades of its existence, it operated as an underground network, occasionally providing security for other right-wing movements, or sending its members to act as strike-breakers in industrial disputes. But it had larger ambitions. A map, seized by police from the home of a Golden Dawn MP in 2013, appeared to contain plans to take the left-wing Exarchia neighbourhood of Athens by force.

Golden Dawn had been forced out of other city neighbourhoods by anti-fascist activists before it arrived in Saint Panteleimon, but the new citizens' committee gave it an opportunity to target migrants instead. Leading members of the group had been active in the committee from its inception, as had a few local supporters. They worked to draw in other local residents, spreading rumours of crime committed by migrants and smearing the reputation of Greeks who criticized them. In August 2009, a few months after the playground outside the church had been locked shut, a Golden Dawn official – a businessman who had been charged and acquitted of murder in a case linked to a protection racket – and his brother opened a cafe-bar on the square. This became a base for Golden Dawn's activities in the neighbourhood.

Throughout 2009 and 2010, the attacks continued, and they seemed to be targeting Afghans, Pakistanis and people of African origin in particular. The citizens' committee became more vocal, too, holding more demonstrations in the square, and demanding a halt to the 'Islamization' of the neighbourhood. Locals were asked to hang Greek flags from their balconies – often the upper floors of the apartments, where elderly residents still lived – to show their support. But, for Hakima, as for many other Afghans, this growing hostility was just one of several worries. Greece's economy had slowed sharply, work became scarcer and Sakhi's employer paid him less often. In 2009, Hakima gave birth to a second child, a girl; her son started at the local primary school the same year. Soon, he was switching between Greek and Dari with ease; the family was putting down roots, despite the circumstances.

*

As the attacks and intimidation continued, Golden Dawn campaigned for elected office in Athens, presenting itself as the only party that could clean up the city's streets. The financial crisis had led to rioting and protests; shops were closing down at an alarming rate; narcotics users were seen more frequently on the streets of Athens; and opinion polls showed that public fear of crime had risen sharply. For Golden Dawn, the presence of migrants was just another indicator of disaster. *GET OUT OF GREECE YOU ARE NOT WANTED HERE*, read an unsigned poster that appeared on lamp posts around Saint Panteleimon, accusing the migrants of rape, child abuse, dirt, drug dealing, disease, prostitution and robbery. 'We are angry with this government and all politicians that brought you here and support you and defend you AND WE ARE DETERMINED TO PUNISH THEM AND YOU.' At the end of 2010, the party's leader, Nikos Michaloliakos, was elected to the Athens city council.

In the summer of 2011, a Greek man was stabbed to death near Saint Panteleimon square, in a robbery by two men of Afghan origin. He had been getting ready to take his pregnant wife to hospital. Word of the attack quickly spread, and a member of the citizens' committee was interviewed on television, pointing out the ethnicity of the assailants. Within hours of the murder, protesters had converged on the scene of the crime, chanting, 'Foreigners out!' and, 'Greece is for Greeks!' Over the next few days, groups of young men, often dressed in black and wielding knives and baseball bats, attacked migrants in central

Athens. They were chased around city squares and dragged off buses and beaten up. The violence appeared to be coordinated, and senior members of Golden Dawn were filmed leading the crowd's chants at the protest.

After the attacks, which are referred to by many people in Athens as the 'pogrom' of 2011, life became markedly worse for the Afghans and other migrant communities. Assaults in the street became even more common, taking place in daylight and carried out by black-clad squads of men. Afghans were chased into hiding. They stopped congregating in Saint Panteleimon square, and Afghan-owned shops were repeatedly attacked until they closed down. Yonous Muhammadi, the head of Greece's Afghan community association, started showing newer arrivals a map of the city with a red line drawn around areas they should avoid. 'This is exactly what I used to do in Afghanistan with the Red Cross about places people shouldn't go because of fighting,' he told Human Rights Watch. Sakhi was attacked and hospitalized during the summer after the pogrom; he became nervous and suffered fainting fits.

This is what forced Hakima to become the family breadwinner, going out at night to search through bins with the other Afghan women. But her family was caught on a political fault line that stretched far beyond their neighbourhood.

According to the best available statistics, the number of immigrants in Greece actually fell slightly in the years after the financial crash, as people went elsewhere to look for work. But many politicians and media outlets treated 'illegal' immigration as a symbol of all that was wrong with the country. Other European states, themselves seeking to crack down on migration, started to pressure Greece to seal its borders. In 2012, Austria's foreign minister accused the Evros of being 'open like a barn door', just as Greece was gearing up for a general election. The governing centre-left party, PASOK, perhaps seeking to deflect public anger at its acceptance of EU austerity measures, proposed a set of law-and-order policies. It promised to close the border and expand detention camps for undocumented migrants. One minister talked about the 'public health time bomb' threat which irregular migration posed. PASOK's main election rivals, the centre-right New Democracy, vowed to 'take back' Greek cities from the immigrants.

Against this background of xenophobia, Golden Dawn received an unprecedented 450,000 votes in the May 2012 general election, gaining their first seats in the national parliament. It was enough to provoke an international scandal, but the winners of the election were New Democracy, who presented themselves as a middle way between two extremes: Golden Dawn on the right, and the anti-austerity Syriza on the left. The new government's first moves included the construction of a fence at the Evros border, and the launch of a police operation in Athens to round up and detain undocumented migrants. Human Rights Watch recorded allegations that police taking part in the operation mistreated people in their custody; one black American tourist who was accused of being an illegal immigrant alleged he had been handcuffed and then punched in the face.

Hakima had left Afghanistan because her home wasn't safe. She had crossed several countries where she was unwelcome. She arrived in Europe where, in theory, a system existed to protect her, but in practice it made her an outcast. Here, she became the target of resentment from a population wrapped up in its own anxieties and a government whose response was to aggressively police the borders. It must have seemed as if, on every level, solidarity had broken down.

That wasn't quite true. Throughout the whole period, there were Greek residents of Saint Panteleimon who did what they could to oppose the fascist voices in their midst. I spoke to residents who had formed their own, rival neighbourhood committee to challenge the Golden Dawn gatherings and hold anti-racist cultural events. Anarchists living in a nearby squat tried to organize a community defence of the neighbourhood. But, in 2012, they were too weak to push back effectively, and residents who spoke out found themselves on the receiving end of malicious rumours and intimidation. One Greek woman I spoke to left the country for several years because she received threatening phone calls. She came to London, using her right as an EU citizen to move freely.

*

I didn't visit Athens again until the end of 2014, two years after I'd met Hakima. In the meantime, Golden Dawn had all but disappeared from the streets of Athens. In September 2013, a Greek rapper, Pavlos Fyssas, had been stabbed to death in a confrontation with supporters of the group. The murder shocked Greece in a way the violence against migrants hadn't; Golden Dawn's leaders were arrested and charged with membership of a criminal organization. The trial is set to conclude in 2018. Almost immediately, the black-clad gangs that terrorized migrants vanished from the city.

My contacts in the Afghan community said they didn't know where Hakima and her family were, but they would try to find out. While I waited, I asked a young community activist called Mohammad if he'd show me where the Afghans were living now. We met one evening by the metro station at Victoria Square. People hadn't gone back to Saint Panteleimon after Golden Dawn departed; instead, this was their new centre. Victoria was busy, surrounded by bars and cafes popular with students. On the side streets, the Pakistani-run grocery stores I'd seen two years previously were still there. Groups of young people and families with children sat around on benches or on the ground in the middle of the square. Some of them had suitcases and bags, as if they were waiting to catch a bus.

These were new arrivals, Mohammad said. Around 50,000 people had crossed the Aegean that year, according to the UNHCR – at the time, a record number for this route. They were arriving in Athens and looking for a way to continue their journeys to other European destinations. Outside the Greek parliament, the week I visited, a group of refugees from Syria were staging a hunger strike. They asked that either the Greek government give them housing and let their children go to school, or that it open its borders and let them continue their journeys across the Balkans, towards northern Europe.

I asked Mohammad if Athens was safer for Afghan migrants, now that Golden Dawn was less visible. Not really, he explained. It was one less worry, but they were still harassed by the police. People were especially scared of being arrested and detained; thousands of migrants were arrested in Athens during the police operation and the number of inmates in Greece's detention centres had soared. According to international standards, detention for 'administrative convenience' – holding someone while their status is assessed, rather than as punishment for a crime – is meant to last for short periods only. An EU directive sets the maximum length of detention at eighteen months, but hundreds in Greece had been locked up for even longer, according to several human-rights organizations.

Mohammad introduced me to a young Afghan man, just out of adolescence and wearing a white shalwar kameez, who he said could tell me what it was like to be detained.

'I was arrested while I was asleep in my house in Athens,' the young man said, 'and, because I didn't want to apply for asylum, they sent me to a detention centre. I was there for eighteen months.' He described scarce food, no hot water and no clean clothes. 'People tried to kill themselves,' he said. 'People cut themselves with glass, or they ate shampoo or chemical materials. The police kept telling us to go back to our own country, but if we didn't have a problem, we wouldn't have come to Greece. They told us we were dirty and that we brought illness to Greece. I spoke with a lot of policemen there and I told them, "Once, we had a country, and once, we were clean in our country, but we lost that."'

We talked to some of the families sitting in the square.

'The Iranian government are making it very difficult for Afghan refugees now,' said a man with an Elvis-style quiff and sideburns, who had recently arrived in Greece with his wife and children. 'We were living in different cities, but recently they decided to collect us in one place by force and put us in camps.'

A couple with four daughters sitting in a row on a bench, in pink, white, black and silver headscarves, told us a similar story. The parents had left Afghanistan in the 1990s, and had lived in Iran as refugees for eighteen years. The Iranian government made it difficult for refugees to take up work, they said, and refugees' children were only allowed to go to school up to primary level. 'Most of the younger generation haven't even seen Afghanistan,' said the father. 'They have a very bad image of the country – bomb blasts against different ethnic groups – so they want to come to Europe.'

These stories, of being displaced for so many years and still not settling, reminded me of something another community activist had told me. 'Afghan joke,' he had said. 'Americans land on the moon and they're surprised to see people already there, moving around. It's Afghan refugees – we get everywhere.' The long-term displaced were being joined outside Afghanistan by a growing number of people who had recently left the country. Emigration had risen, from 2014 onwards, as the US began to withdraw its occupying troops, leaving behind a precarious economic and security situation.

*

I still hadn't heard news of Hakima. Had her family left Greece? Or had they, too, ended up in a detention centre like the one described to me by the young man in Victoria Square? I wanted to see for myself what detention looked like, so one afternoon I took the bus with a Greek friend to the outskirts of Athens. We passed through run-down suburbs with Golden Dawn graffiti scrawled on the side of buildings, into the foothills of the Parnitha mountain range to the north of the city. Central Athens can be warm in December, but up there it was chilly.

We were heading for Amygdaleza, which was then one of Greece's largest detention centres, although 'detention centre' is a euphemism. It was a prison camp, in the middle of a police training school, surrounded by perimeter fences topped with barbed wire, and overlooked by guard towers.

More than a thousand people were detained there at the time of my visit. Most were men, most came from Pakistan, Afghanistan and Bangladesh. All of them were migrants who had been caught without the correct papers.

When we arrived at the visitors' gate, a dozen men were waiting in line, carrying shopping bags full of biscuits, bread and toiletries. They were allowed in, three at a time, to visit friends and relatives inside. One of the men in the queue, a Kurdish refugee from Syria, who was there to see his brother, told us that detainees were given one meal a day, and any food brought in from outside had to be in sealed packets. We joined the queue, but were picked out by police at the gate, who wanted to know what we were doing there. My friend had got hold of an inmate's name and his section number, and we were told to say we had an urgent message from his parents. We were ushered through and driven by patrol car to the section where he was being held.

The section consisted of a series of high-fenced pens, separated by a central path. Inside the pens, each of which was no more than twenty metres across, were two or three converted shipping containers, in which the inmates – all men – lived. According to the newspaper *To Vima*, an internal police investigation found that a group of six or seven officers formed a 'hit squad' to torture detainees; they were accused of switching off the air conditioning during the summer, leading to temperatures approaching fifty degrees Celsius inside the containers. Inmates had recently rioted, and some of the containers had been burned. Their walls were buckled and blackened, but people still appeared to be living in them. As we passed, the inmates walked up to the fence and tried to catch our attention: 'Deutsch? Deutsch? Where are you from?'

When we reached our contact's pen, the police officer escorting us shouted his name – Farhan – and beckoned him towards the fence. Two men approached. Farhan had a bushy moustache and was dressed in a green tracksuit; his companion had a blanket over his head, to protect him from the cold. Farhan spoke enough Greek to communicate a few details to my friend: he was twenty-eight, from Pakistan, and had arrived in Greece in 2011 by sneaking across the Evros. He had been selling fruit and veg at a market when he was arrested. That was in 2012. He told us he'd been in detention for eighteen months and twelve days – a breach of the EU's time limit.

'Do something for him,' said his friend with the blanket, who spoke a little English. 'He is walking around all the time, very sad. The toilets are dirty, it's freezing inside and the food is awful.' As he spoke, he became more agitated, and the police officer, who had been hovering behind us, stepped in to cut off the conversation.

'OK, you need to leave, now.'

I had just enough time to give Farhan my phone number before we were rushed back to the visitors' gate.

That evening, I went back to the square of Saint Panteleimon. It was empty, except for a group of children playing football outside the church. Golden Dawn's graffiti had been painted over by anti-fascists. The playground had been demolished and all that remained was a patch of gravel with a scrap of someone's patterned scarf trampled into the dust. I remember thinking the pattern looked like the ones on the dresses I had seen in the photos of bodies found in the River Evros.

Everyone had a reason to move on from what had happened here: anti-fascists wanted to claim victory; the residents who had supported Golden Dawn wanted to disassociate themselves from the violence; the government wanted to put the unwanted migrants out of sight and out of mind; and the Afghans who had lived through it wanted either to rebuild their community down the road, or slip out of the country unnoticed. But the memories of what had happened would persist. Perhaps, one day, parents like Hakima and Sakhi would try to explain to their children what those early years of their lives meant.

But that would be their decision. I received an email from one of my contacts, saying the family had moved to Germany: *I'm sorry, Hakima isn't here anymore.* I never did manage to find her.

22 · THE AHMEDS

Nisrin Ahmed, born in Syria's Hasakah province in the 1960s, never learned to read and write, but she was determined to make sure her children got an education. Hasakah, a cosmopolitan province on the border with Iraq and Turkey, is home to a large Kurdish population, who have historically been discriminated against by Syria's rulers – denied full citizenship, or forced to travel elsewhere for work or study. The aim was to weaken the demands of Kurdish nationalists for an independent state, but what it did instead was contribute to a diaspora with networks of support, trade, travel and language.

Nisrin didn't leave Hasakah; she married a railway engineer and together they had three children: two boys and a girl. When her husband died, shortly after the birth of their younger son, Nisrin became the only protector of the family. Her children had the need to work hard at school impressed upon them. By early 2011, on the eve of Syria's civil war, she could survey the results of her endeavours with pride: all three children had graduated from high school and gone to university.

Nisrin's younger son, Azad, was studying petroleum engineering at Homs university, in the west of Syria, when people first started to demonstrate against the government of Bashar al-Assad, in March 2011. Homs was a centre of opposition to the regime and played host to some of the largest anti-Assad protests in the early days. Azad watched developments with unease; he agreed with the protesters, who wanted democratic reforms, but when peaceful demonstrations were met with a brutal military crackdown, and then opposition groups took up arms against the state, he grew wary. Mainly, Azad wanted to finish his degree and get on with his life.

As the Syrian government laid siege to Homs, the university dorm rooms where Azad lived during term time were caught in the middle of the fighting. On one side was the neighbourhood of Baba Amr, a rebel stronghold; on the other were regime troops, who would launch rocket strikes and fly jets low over the roofs of the university buildings. Sometimes the troops would enter the university and use it as a base for attacks on the rebels. Once, Azad came back to his room and found that, while he was out, a bullet had passed clean through the window and lodged itself in the opposite wall. Dust was everywhere. He touched it, and his hand came away bleeding, cut by pulverized glass. A few days later, an oil pipeline near Baba Amr was blown up. Soon after, Azad took a bus home to Hasakah. But he went back to Homs to continue his studies, leaving during the vacations on a coach that made its way back to Hasakah via a string of regime and rebel military checkpoints.

At home, at first, the fighting was more distant, but the effects of the civil war were felt all the same. Transport connections out of the province were being cut off. People began to lose their jobs. Food prices rose sharply and the value of the currency fell. Early on in the war, the Kurds, who had their own defence forces, had made an uneasy peace with the regime. Assad forces occupied the airport in

Qamishli, the largest city in the region, but ceded control of the province to the Kurdish armed 'people's protection units', the YPG.

At the edges of their territory, however, the Kurdish forces were vying for control with a range of Islamist rebel groups. Fighting between the government and the al-Nusra Front, the Syrian affiliate of al-Qaeda, got closer to Hasakah; some villages on the edge of the province were bombed by helicopter. People displaced by fighting in other parts of Syria had been streaming into Hasakah for safety, and they brought with them stories of the horrors that would follow. A cousin who had been working at a state-run hotel in Damascus came back to Hasakah, saying his employers had tried to force him to join a gang of irregulars, to beat up demonstrators. Another ran away to avoid conscription into Assad's army. In 2013, the fighting intensified, killing 22,000 civilians and creating the first great surge of refugees. A million people fled the country that year, most of whom were hosted in Lebanon, Turkey and Jordan. Millions more were internally displaced.

In the towns and villages along the border, where Nisrin and her family lived, people were weighing up whether to leave or stay. Those who wanted to leave began selling their possessions. It was a buyer's market and a few opportunists were buying up property. If you had the money and weren't tied down by sick or elderly relatives, and you weren't fighting with the YPG, then your destination was Turkey. The Turkish government had thrown open its borders to Syrian refugees early on in the conflict – a declaration of solidarity with opponents of the Assad regime. The only catch was that, if you presented yourself at the official crossing points and told the Turkish officials you were a refugee, you'd be put into one of the tent camps in the south of the country, where you were supposed to stay until it was safe to return to Syria. If you wanted to reach one of the big Turkish cities, to find work or continue your journey, you had to pay smugglers to take you across.

In the summer of 2013, Azad finished his penultimate year of university. That August, he took the bus home. On the motorway, as it reached the edge of Hasakah, Azad's bus was ambushed by Islamists. Kurdish men were separated from the other passengers and taken off the bus at gunpoint. Azad and the other men were held hostage for five days in a darkened room; they were taken outside at random and subjected to mock executions, a sword held against their neck. After a few days, the hostages were released when Kurdish and Islamist forces negotiated a settlement.

By the time Azad arrived home, his family had already given him up for dead. 'It's like you've been born again,' said his mother. She took it as a sign: the family had to leave Syria now; Azad's studies would have to wait. They started to sell everything they owned: the television, the kitchen set, the living-room furniture, the beds, the family home. Everything went at knock-down prices. All they kept were their clothes, their Syrian ID cards, their phones and a couple of laptops. One night, at the end of August, a family friend showed the Ahmeds to a quiet stretch of border where they could cross without being spotted by Turkish soldiers. They hid in a drainage ditch for several hours before they crossed. The family stayed for a few nights with relatives in Mardin, a city in southern Turkey, before heading to Istanbul.

Istanbul was fast becoming a hub for Syrians who wanted to reach Europe. But, since 2012, the smuggling routes had shifted. The land border into Greece, at the

River Evros, was now closed. You could either go to Izmir and pay to travel on a boat, or you could travel by land into Bulgaria. Azad's cousins had already crossed into Bulgaria, and they gave him the contact of a smuggler in Istanbul who could take the Ahmeds there for 400 euros per person. There were thieves in the forest that separates Bulgaria from Turkey, warned the smuggler, so it's best if you get rid of your valuables here. The Ahmeds sold their laptops.

At the end of October, the smuggler drove the Ahmeds, in a minibus, north from Istanbul. At Edirne, they changed vehicles and were driven out to the forest. It was three in the morning when they joined a group of seventy people, mainly Syrian and Afghan, who were all making the same journey. 'Walk that way,' the smuggler said, and pointed towards an old lumberjack route that made a path through the trees. The refugees had few possessions with them; they'd all been told to travel light. By the time they'd made the six-hour walk through the damp autumn forest into Bulgaria, some people would have even lost their shoes.

For the Ahmeds, something else had changed. Since leaving Syria, Nisrin was no longer in control. Her elder son, who had worked in Turkey before the war, had negotiated much of their passage towards Bulgaria. Now, on the threshold of the European Union, the only one who could speak English was Azad, the baby of the family.

*

Just before lunchtime on 5 December 2013, Azad resumed the routine he'd been following for a month. He went back to his container, picked up a notebook that held a list of names, ages, dietary requirements and shoe sizes, and walked over to the camp gates, where two lorries with *Aladin Foods* written on their sides had just pulled up. A dozen other men, each with his own notebook, had also gathered around the back of the lorries. Each one shouted out his order in Arabic, to a man unloading the cargo; each one was handed a stack of polystyrene boxes that steamed gently in the winter air.

I followed Azad, with his stack of boxes, back across the camp. We were in a derelict military base at Harmanli in southern Bulgaria, cordoned off from the outside world by a concrete perimeter wall, low enough to see the tops of trees in the street beyond, but too high to see passers-by. The main square, overlooked by windowless barrack buildings, had been given over to rows of green military tents, which were gradually being replaced by recondi-tioned shipping containers. Police officers guarded the gate, asking visitors for ID and preventing their guests from leaving. 'This isn't supposed to be here,' one of the aid workers who had helped me sneak into the camp said.

The derelict camp at Harmanli was a remnant of the Cold War, when Bulgaria's border with Turkey was also the border of the Eastern bloc; Soviet troops were once stationed there, facing off against NATO members Greece and Turkey. In 2007, that border took on a new geopoliti-cal meaning, when Bulgaria joined the European Union. As Bulgaria was cautiously welcomed in by the EU – the country is still not part of the Schengen zone – it was given a new role in keeping people out.

In the second half of 2013, Harmanli was hurriedly pressed back into service as the number of refugees cross-ing Bulgaria's border with Turkey rose dramatically. The previous year, only a few hundred people in total had claimed asylum in Bulgaria, according to figures given to me by the country's migration ministry; between August and December 2013, over 12,000 refugees arrived, via similar routes to the one the Ahmeds had taken. Most of them were from Syria, with a smaller number from Afghanistan and a smattering of other nationalities. The Bulgarian authorities had run out of places to put them and had opened a series of 'overflow' camps, where the rough conditions – no hot water, no fixed shelter, no medical services – caused a ripple of surprise in the international media. In 2013, these were unusual scenes in Europe. Bulgaria, one of the EU's poorest countries, was being left to meet the refugees' needs largely by itself. In October, the aid agency Médecins Sans Frontières opened clinics at Harmanli and elsewhere.

Before the Ahmeds reached Harmanli, Azad told me, they were found wandering, lost in the forest, by Bulgarian border guards. The Turkish smuggler had said there would be someone on the other side of the border, waiting to meet them – he'd even given them a description – but the contact was nowhere to be found. First, the police took their group to a detention centre at the town of Elhovo. It had been built to accommodate 240 people, but the police had run out of space, so they were housing migrants in a basketball court, divided into sections by ethnic origin: Syrian, Afghan, sub-Saharan African. 'They caged us like animals,' Azad said. At the time, I thought this was an exaggeration, but I found photos of the basketball court online that showed the inmates were literally locked up in metal cages. Their doors were unlocked from eight a.m. to eight p.m., and they were allowed to walk around a small exercise yard. Refugees whose clothes had got soaked in the rain at the forest on the border had to stay in them until they dried.

We reached Azad's row of containers in Harmanli and he distributed the boxes: meals of fried chicken and rice, supplied by a Bulgarian chain of kebab shops. The notebook told him how many to deliver to each home. He'd either knock at the container door and hand them over to the occupant or leave them waiting on the doorstep. 'See?' he said. 'In ten minutes, we can feed the whole camp.' They used the same system for clothes and children's toys, which were donated by Bulgarians and arrived every few days. When his family had arrived at Harmanli, over a month before, Azad told me, there had been no such system. The inhabitants would crowd around the vans and grab whatever they could. Fights often broke out.

Now, the residents ran their own distribution network. Each row of tents or containers – around a dozen homes, in total – would nominate one person to collect the deliveries. It was partly based on trust, and it helped that many of the refugees had known each other before they arrived in Bulgaria. Most of the Syrians in this camp were Kurds from Hasakah province. Azad told me his neighbour in the camp had been a neighbour back at home. Some of his cousins were there, too. Around twenty-five people from his town alone were in the camp.

After the food had been delivered, we went for another walk. People were scouring the ground for firewood; most of the trees had already been stripped back to bare stumps. Between two containers, a man had strung up a sheet and put a chair behind it; a queue of people were waiting for haircuts at this makeshift barber's shop. In the first month the camp was opened, Azad explained, conditions had been harsher. First, they were given sheets and mattresses infested with bedbugs. They weren't allowed to leave the camp to receive money transfers from relatives, or to go shopping. The police opened a shop in the camp that sold goods at twice the price they were available for in the village. Then the Syrians protested, burning their bedding in a pile outside. Media started to arrive at the camp, and the police relaxed the rules. The Syrians, who were in the majority here, seemed particularly well organized and assertive. The smaller group of Afghan refugees, who mainly lived in a disused shower block, were quieter. And there was an even smaller group of black African residents, who were made to live in a concrete guard house with bars on its windows. They walked the camp despondently, alone or in pairs.

We poked our heads into a tent. A family – parents, four children and a grandmother – were cooking dinner on a gas stove and invited us to sit with them. They were also Syrian, but from the Yezidi ethnic and religious minority, and had fled when ISIS fighters destroyed their village and massacred many of the inhabitants. Their path into Europe had been diverted by the new border defences at the River Evros. 'The police pushed us back from Greece to Turkey,' said the father, Ayman, as a pan of tomato and onions steamed over the stove. 'Into the river, then into the forest.' The group his family was travelling with had managed to cross the Evros by night, but they were found by police the next morning, shivering, in one of the Greek border villages. Ayman said that the police had detained them and taken away their money, documents and mobile phones, before making them cross the river, back to Turkey. His account seemed to fit with a report that appeared in the *Guardian* in December 2013, in which residents of the village of Praggi said they had seen a group of 150 Syrians forced into police vans and driven to an unknown destination. By the time we left Ayman's tent, it was getting dark and people had lit fires in old oil drums, or on the ground, to keep warm.

Before I left the camp that evening, I went back to the Ahmeds' container: two small rooms, lined with cushions and mattresses, plus a little bathroom and kitchen area by the door. Nisrin bustled around anxiously, making sure I was comfortable. Neighbours dropped in, curious about the new visitor. 'This is my neighbour from our village,' Azad said, introducing one man. 'And now he lives in the container next to us here.' Some of the Ahmeds' cousins came in, bringing their two young girls. Azad entertained them by throwing a balloon back and forwards, while his brother looked at a map of Europe on the back page of an exercise book and pointed to different countries, asking me which ones were in Schengen. The Ahmeds wanted to go to Germany, Azad said. 'My brother has a degree in economic management, my sister is a qualified psychologist – but people here think we're animals.'

His brother asked to look at my passport. 'We heard the best three are UK, US and Finlandia,' he said. 'They have the most countries where you don't need visas to visit.'

One of the girls asked if she could keep the passport; I held my photo page up to her face and the others laughed.

The container's electric heaters were on full blast. Outside, it had dropped below zero.

At the end of 2013, the European Union responded to Bulgaria's request for help, with 5.6 million euros of emergency funds to improve reception conditions. By contrast, according to Amnesty International, fifteen million euros from the EU's External Borders Fund was being spent on a networked surveillance system, which used cameras and motion sensors along the border with Turkey.

In December, Bulgaria started building a fence along part of the border, too.

*

The Ahmeds spent the winter at Harmanli; at Christmas, they sent me a Facebook message to show me that the Kurdish residents were marking the festival: they had set up a stage and were performing traditional songs. An accomplished folk musician was among the refugees there and he had been posting videos to YouTube of his performances in one of the containers. When I'd visited Harmanli, nobody had internet access, but a few weeks later people had pooled their money and bought Wi-Fi routers and internet subscriptions, which were shared among residents of each 'street' of containers.

In April 2014, I visited Sofia, the Bulgarian capital; the police restrictions at Harmanli had softened, so Azad was able to take a bus and meet me there. It was a 200-mile journey, but he insisted; he had friends in Sofia and he wanted to see how they were, too. That month, according to Bulgarian government statistics, there were 3,500 refugees accommodated in camps around the country. The majority of these were Syrian, and there were another 3,000 living at private addresses, at their own expense.

Both Azad and I were new to Sofia, but when we met outside the bus station, he already had a set of directions to follow. We navigated by landmark, rather than street name. Azad's instructions were to walk first to the 'Arab' market near the bus station, surrounded by shops run by Middle Eastern immigrants. He pointed out which shops were run by Syrians – immigrants who had come here for work before the war. Azad knew English and a few words of Bulgarian, but if he wanted to read a shop sign written in Cyrillic script, he took a picture with his phone and an app would translate the text.

From the market, we walked down to a grand nineteenth-century bridge at the northern edge of the city centre, flanked by stone lions. This, Azad explained, was the landmark the Syrians in Sofia used most often to navigate by. On the other side of the bridge, we walked past a shop selling plastic jewellery and mobile-phone covers. A man, who had been watching the street from the doorway, stepped out and greeted Azad. They spoke in Arabic for a few minutes. 'He's my neighbour, from home,' Azad said. 'I haven't seen him for a year and he was telling me that he heard I had been kidnapped. He wanted to know how I got out.' The friend, Sherwan, was thirty years old, and had been a tailor before leaving Syria. He had ended up in Sofia after a man posing as a lawyer visited his camp in southern Bulgaria and sold him a fake contract that claimed to guarantee him accommodation in the capital. The scam was widespread in the autumn of 2013; an aid worker at Harmanli had shown me a copy of one of the fake contracts, which he said had been issued with the connivance of local police officers. Sherwan was renting an apartment in Sofia, paid for with money he'd borrowed from relatives still in Syria and the ten lev (five pounds) a day he made from working at the jewellery shop. Others, though, had been left homeless by the scam. 'They were sleeping at night in the park, down there,' Sherwan said, pointing in the direction of a sixteenth-century mosque, built when Sofia was under Ottoman rule. 'But then, in the winter, it started to snow. Sometimes we saw people hungry and we took them into our house. Other people took Syrian passports from the embassy and went back to Turkey.'

After we parted company with Sherwan, Azad and I

took a bus east from the Lions' Bridge, into the city suburbs. We drove past billboards advertising the TV channel of a far-right political party, Ataka ('Attack'). One of its MPs had recently condemned 'Islamists described as refugees'. Hostility to the new arrivals had ebbed and flowed in Bulgaria since the summer of 2013. In the first few months, politicians from parties like Ataka tried to stoke public fears; there were local protests outside some of the newly opened camps and, in Sofia, fascist street gangs carried out 'ID patrols' around the Ottoman mosque, beating up foreigners. But public opinion had swung in the opposite direction by the following spring; the media coverage of conditions in the camps had provoked widespread public sympathy and a flood of donations. One group of volunteers had set up a website where individuals from across the country could send second-hand goods to wherever they were needed most.

Our bus reached a neighbourhood of poorly maintained communist-era housing blocks and garish new shopping malls. The neighbourhood was called Nadezhda – 'hope'. A thin, middle-aged man with a bushy moustache was waiting for us there, at one of the bus stops, with a teenage boy. The older man introduced himself as Siwan, and the boy, his son, as Khalid. They led us into one of the blocks and up to a third-floor apartment.

Inside, Siwan's wife, Aveen, greeted us and the family beckoned us to sit down on the living-room sofa. Their baby son stood and stared at us from a corner of the room. The apartment was decorated with china ornaments and old prints; it looked like the previous inhabitants had only recently departed. Aveen and Siwan were from the same province in Syria as Azad, although they had only met him for the first time in the camp at Harmanli. They had been caught out by the fake contract scam, too. The 'lawyer' they paid told them they were going to be taken to accommodation in Sofia, but they were dropped off outside a random hotel they had to pay for with their own money. Now, they were using their savings to rent this two-bedroom apartment.

Because they were not living in a camp, Siwan explained, they didn't receive the monthly sixty-five lev stipend paid by the government to asylum seekers. The only money the family had was from selling their house in Syria, plus Siwan's savings from working as a taxi driver. 'We've spent 12,000 euros in five and a half months,' he said. 'We don't have anything in Syria now; what I built in twenty-five years has been destroyed.' As more Syrians arrived in Sofia, rent and hotel prices were starting to shoot up. 'Before, an apartment cost only 150 euros a month. Now it's 400,' Siwan said.

Aveen went into the kitchen and brought beer, served in little cut-glass thimbles presumably left by the previous occupants. She sat down with us again and explained the family's options. They could stay here and wait for their asylum claim to be processed, then try to find work before the money ran out. But they only knew of a few other Syrians who had found jobs here, and these people were all earning a pittance, making sweets or serving kebabs, or working at the market. If they ran out of money, they could beg the state refugee agency to allow them back into one of the camps. There were three camps around Sofia, and they were all overcrowded and dirty; hepatitis and tuberculosis had been detected there. The inhabitants were supposed to leave once they'd been given refugee status, but many stayed because they had nowhere else to go.

If they didn't want to stay in Bulgaria at all, they could

leave for western Europe, where they might find a better deal. That was by far the most popular option among the Syrians here. 'All the refugees want to go to Germany,' Aveen said. 'Maybe Germany doesn't have the ability to take all of us, but then why don't other European countries divide us between themselves?' The most direct route to Germany was to travel north, through Romania, then west through Hungary and Austria. Once they reached Hungary, they would be in the Schengen zone of free movement, and could travel more easily – but there were two sets of border checks to pass first, because Bulgaria and Romania were not Schengen members. Until early 2014, these borders had been relatively easy for refugees to cross, as long as they'd received their documents from the Bulgarian government. But by the spring of 2014, the route had become more restricted.

It all depended on what document you received, Aveen explained. Syrians were either being issued with full refugee status, which came with a five-year ID, or they were being given 'humanitarian protection', a more temporary status, designed for people fleeing war zones, who, in theory, could go back once the war had died down. Forms of subsidiary protection like this, which stop short of full refugee status, have been used increasingly in Europe since the 1990s, allowing states to avoid giving permanent citizenship to large numbers of refugees. In Bulgaria, this lower status came with a three-year ID. Romanian border guards had recently started to turn away holders of these documents when they tried to leave Bulgaria, in an effort to slow the passage of people west. If they couldn't get out of Bulgaria by legal means, Siwan said, the only other way was to pay smugglers; you could find a contact at the market near the bus station in Sofia.

It was late afternoon by the time we'd finished talking, and Aveen insisted on cooking dinner before we left. As we waited, the men got out their phones and started scrolling through images. Khalid showed me a picture of him and a young woman, both dressed in the fatigues of the YPG, the Kurdish defence forces that controlled northern Syria. They had volunteered for the security police in their hometown. The woman was now dead. 'I found out three days ago. Jihadists cut her neck,' he said. Siwan showed me some video clips he'd downloaded. One was of YPG fighters inspecting the body of a jihadist they'd just killed in battle. They laid out his bloodstained identity documents and bank cards to show he wasn't from Syria. Then Siwan played another clip, showing captured soldiers from the rebel Free Syrian Army being beaten by Assad regime soldiers. The men were kneeling and lined up against a wall, which was dripping with their blood. A soldier kicked one of them in the head, while a voice off-camera shouted obscenities. Before the clip ended, one of the prisoners leaned around to look at his assailant, an expression of total fear on his face.

Azad and I made one more stop that day, at an apartment on the fourteenth floor of a tower block near the bus station. Two young men who Azad knew from Harmanli were living there; one had a job, working in a kebab shop near the market. When we arrived, they were hunched over the kitchen table, peering into a smartphone. They were playing with Azar, a clone of the web service Chatroulette, which randomly connects you for video chats with other users; when you're bored of one, you swipe the screen leftwards and it connects you to another.

The young men were flirting and joking in broken English with people from all over the world: Ecuador, South

Korea, Kentucky. Three teenage girls from Ukraine appeared, and they teased the young men about their English. 'I love you, bye-bye!' shouted Azad. His friend swiped the screen. They heard a familiar language. 'Sy-ri-a!' the three shouted in unison. The two men at the other end of the line were indeed Syrian, but the location details in one corner of the screen said they were in Germany. 'Are they letting you stay?' One of the men in Germany said yes, and that he knew of a smuggler in Sofia who could get them there, via Belgrade, for 1,300 euros. The mood in the room became more serious as they pressed him for details. Then Azad swiped left again and the Ukranian girls were back. There was laughter, and the two groups blew kisses at one another.

*

I stayed in touch with the Ahmeds throughout the summer of 2014 and, in August, I went to see them again – this time in Germany. They told me they were staying at a town called Eisenhüttenstadt, in the east of the country, a forty-minute train journey from Berlin. Azad came to meet me at the station. As we walked back to the family's new home, he told me they'd arrived in Germany a few months earlier. He didn't want to say exactly how they'd done it, although I could guess.

Eisenhüttenstadt – 'ironworks city', originally 'Stalinstadt' – was once the showpiece of East German communism. Most of it was built in the 1950s to house industrial workers. Each new layer of the city, built in successive decades, reflected the GDR's declining fortunes. Ornate Stalinist buildings at the centre were ringed by housing developments built with increasingly cheap materials. After reunification, the state-owned steelworks was privatized, almost completely closed down, and the population of Eisenhüttenstadt plummeted. The town is on the west bank of the River Oder, which forms the border between Poland and Germany. During the communist period, that had given it symbolic power: it was a sign of Soviet influence in central Europe. Now, it felt pushed to the margins. There wasn't even a bridge connecting it to the Polish side.

As we made our way through the town, I was struck by the number of posters urging people to vote for the NPD, Germany's largest neo-Nazi party. Azad didn't know what the posters said; I translated them for him and he was shocked. He had thought that his family might have left that kind of hostility behind them, in Bulgaria. But Eisenhüttenstadt has an uncomfortable history in this respect. In the early 1990s, after reunification, it was one of several towns in the former GDR to see outbreaks of violence against refugees. The newly unified Germany practised a system of dispersal, sending asylum seekers to live in all parts of the country while their claims were being heard. Many were sent to towns in the east, where it was cheaper to accommodate them. But the sudden arrival of people in communities that had little previous experience of hosting refugees, and which were going through their own crisis as the east's economy struggled, was seized on by neo-Nazi extremists. In the port of Rostock, during the summer of 1992, a block of flats housing asylum seekers was attacked by gangs throwing stones and petrol bombs. A wave of copycat attacks followed, including in Eisenhüttenstadt. Two decades later, the NPD, a fringe party whose voter base was strongest in this part of the country, were hoping to capitalize on similar feelings.

We arrived at a block of flats, a concrete and pebbledash affair, built at some point in the 1980s. It had been a youth hostel, now given over to housing families like the Ahmeds; it was an improvement on the container at Harmanli, at least. They had two rooms and a small kitchen to themselves, plus a bathroom they shared with other people on their corridor. It was more like a dormitory than an apartment, and the only furniture they had was the beds. Azad and I sat down on one, in the main room. On the tiles above a sink in the corner were stickers of teams from the 1998 football World Cup.

The family had applied for asylum in Germany, Azad said. But they were stuck in limbo, waiting to see if Germany would accept them, or send them back to Bulgaria under the Dublin system. Several thousand others were in the same situation; it seemed as if Germany was quietly allowing them to stay, but they couldn't be sure. Slowly, over the course of a year, most of the Syrians who had arrived in Bulgaria in 2013 had made their way west. Of the seventy-two people with whom his family had walked across the forest between Turkey and Bulgaria in October, Azad said, only one he knew of was still in the camp at Harmanli, and that was because he didn't have the money to leave. His cousins were all in Germany, too; some of them were being housed in Kiel, in the north, others near Dortmund, in the west. Siwan and Aveen, the couple we had visited at home in Sofia a few months earlier, were now in France with their children. 'We get 330 euros a month from the German government,' Azad said, 'but a lot of it goes to pay back people we borrowed money from when we were in Bulgaria.'

By now, the summer of 2014, the Bulgarian route had become much more difficult for refugees travelling via Turkey. As with Greece, a year earlier, the extra defences at Bulgaria's southern border had reduced the number of crossings, at a price. A report by Human Rights Watch, published that September, showed evidence that the police had been pushing Syrian refugees back to Turkey, against international law, and had beaten some of them. 'Three of my friends from university tried for three weeks to cross the Bulgarian border,' Azad said. 'But it was too tight. They went back to Istanbul and paid 9,500 euros each to a smuggler. They're in Brussels now.'

The flight from Syria was gathering pace. Practically everybody in the country had been touched by violence in one way or another. Since the Ahmeds had left, an uncle had been killed by a jihadist car bomb in Qamishli and one of Azad's university teachers had been killed fighting for the rebel Free Syrian Army. After the first surge of refugees in 2013, another, greater movement had begun. Increased bombing, largely by the Assad regime, as well as a destroyed economy, the rise of ISIS and the threat of forced conscription into the government forces were all reasons given for leaving, by people fleeing the country. Most of the refugees were still living in Lebanon, Turkey and Jordan, but it was hard to build new lives there. In Turkey, which denied work permits to most Syrians, many people had to take black-market jobs with low pay and little protection. Child labour was rife; Syrian children even worked in sweatshops, making clothes for European high-street brands. Those who had the means were trying to find ways out.

If you made it to Turkey, there was a range of options for how to reach Europe. For around 12,000 euros, you could buy a false passport and go by plane. Because of all the identity checks involved in air travel, this route was difficult and sometimes involved flying to a southern African country with lax security, like Zambia, then taking a plane towards Europe. For 8,000 euros, you could pay to be hidden inside a lorry. 'Two of my friends went by lorry from Turkey to Italy,' Azad said. 'It took four days. They brought bottles to piss in and they only ate biscuits, so they didn't need to go to the toilet.' You could fly to Libya or Egypt and pay 1,000 dollars for a place in a smuggler boat, if you were willing to risk it. Or you could go to Algeria, cross into Morocco, and then enter Spain via its heavily fortified North African enclaves of Ceuta and Melilla. But the cheapest way was to go to Izmir and be smuggled across the Aegean; as the land routes into Europe were closing off, this was emerging as the most popular option.

Nisrin came into the room to say hello, and see if I was comfortable, but Azad ushered her out again. It had been a year since the family had left Syria, and ten months since they had crossed into Bulgaria. The dynamic between mother and son had changed again since my last visit. When they'd left Syria, his mother had been in charge of the family, but since they reached Europe, her lack of English had meant she'd retreated into the home. Azad, on the other hand, had been made to take care of everything outside of the home: arranging travel, getting documents sorted, negotiating with officials. In Bulgaria, this had given him a degree of independence. He'd made friends with the aid workers, volunteers and journalists who'd passed through Harmanli. Now, in Eisenhüttenstadt, it seemed as if his world had shrunk.

I stayed the night at the former youth hostel, but Azad wasn't talkative; he spent most of the evening hunched over his phone, looking at football clips. I asked him to show me a map of his home town. 'That's the road where I was kidnapped,' he said, pointing to a highway that cut through the countryside. He switched to Google Earth and zoomed in until you could see the tops of the houses. 'There's mine. There's my grandfather's house. There's my school.' I asked if he knew anyone who had stayed. 'The town is almost empty,' he said. 'But my grandmothers are both there. We asked them to leave with us and they said, "We were born in this land and we'll die in this land."'

*

I didn't visit the Ahmeds again for over a year. In that time, the refugee crisis of 2015 had peaked. In August, the movement of people through the Balkans had intensified when Germany announced it was suspending returns under the Dublin system for Syrians, which effectively meant that any who reached its territory would be given the opportunity to claim asylum. But this was a decision made largely after the event; throughout the summer, Syrians, Iraqis, Afghans and others had been moving through the Balkans in unprecedented numbers. Their movement was chaotic, with unpredictable border closures and little coordinated response from the EU or from national governments. Local citizens and international volunteers flocked to places along the route to offer the migrants practical support.

In October, two years after the Ahmed family first set foot in Europe, I went to see them. They had moved again; the German government had decided they could stay and had given the family full refugee status. After a few months of trying and failing to find a place to rent in Berlin, they had moved to Dortmund, where an uncle who had emigrated ten years previously lived. Eurostat, the EU's statistical authority, would later show that Germany received nearly half a million asylum applications in 2015, and almost 750,000 the following year: a record number, and the highest in the EU. At train stations in major cities, it was now common to see groups of migrants huddled around bulging rucksacks and suitcases. There were Afghan families who looked like the ones I'd seen waiting in Victoria Square, in Athens, a year earlier, as well as young Arab and Kurdish men and women. They often had a distant look in their eyes: tired, perhaps, or apprehensive.

Azad was friendly when we met, but much warier than on previous occasions. Something around us had shifted. For most of the last two years, his family had tried to slip by unnoticed. Now, refugees – in particular, those from Syria who reached Germany – were subject to even more intense scrutiny. Their movement had been accompanied by hostile rhetoric from politicians in many European countries, including Hungary's prime minister, who claimed Muslim refugees posed a threat to Europe's Christian identity. Among the taunts thrown at refugees was the accusation that the men were cowards and should have stayed at home to defend their own country. 'In Eisenhüttenstadt, when you walked past people, they would speak and you knew they were insulting you. They didn't want us here,' Azad said. Things had improved when the family was transferred to a small village in rural Brandenburg. 'There, they told us this was the first time in 600 years people had come here. The neighbours spoke English and helped us with things.'

I told him I wanted to write about his family's journey in my book, and Azad looked suspicious. 'What are you going to write?' he asked.

Before visiting his house, Azad wanted to go for a walk, so I suggested he showed me the Borussia Dortmund stadium. It was the afternoon, and a match was starting in a few hours, so we walked alongside crowds of football fans in black and yellow. Azad told me about a friend, who had been studying medicine at his university in Homs: 'All 165 doctors from his training course are in Germany now.' Azad told me stories of couples who had split up during the journey, but reunited in Germany; or would-be lovers who had arrived and found that their partner had settled down with someone else. He was more bothered about his studies, he said; he needed to find a place on a German language course so he could reach university standard and restart his degree. Azad had already managed to retrieve his university certificates from Homs; the university had sent the documents to Damascus to be stamped, then they were sent by plane to Qamishli, where the government still controlled the airport. A friend who had gone back to visit the Kurdish provinces took the certificates with him to the Netherlands, then gave them to Azad's uncle. Now, Azad just needed to collect them.

He told me he wanted to work on a deep-sea oil platform, somewhere far away, when he graduated. 'In Kurdish society, the mother stays with the sons, and the daughters get married,' he said, 'but I want to escape.' I asked if he'd ever consider going back to Syria – at the time we were speaking, the Kurdish provinces in the north had carved out a degree of autonomy, and it seemed as if there was at least a chance of stability returning. He was sceptical. 'Everyone respects the sacrifice of the YPG, but the political parties are just interested in themselves, all fighting for their own interest.'

This surprised me. I'd always seen Azad as being very proud of his Kurdish identity. He posted pictures of the Kurdish national flag and videos of Kurdish songs to Facebook; he'd tell me at length about Kurdish history or contemporary Kurdish politics. But perhaps one could be proud of this, yet still not want to fight. I asked him if that was true.

'I don't want to kill people,' he replied. 'Even if it was ISIS and I had a gun in my hand, I wouldn't do it.'

We arrived at his family's home, an apartment in a modern suburban housing block. Nisrin greeted me as usual; Azad's brother was there, too. They were polite, but, again, more guarded than they'd ever been before. Nisrin brought out some food – rice, soup, salad and a chicken stew – and laid it on a mat on the floor of their sitting room. Everything in the room was new: a large television, leather sofas, clean Ikea-style furniture. The uncle who lived in Dortmund had helped them set up home, and each month they kept some of their support payments aside to buy a new item of furniture.

I'd wanted to interview the whole family in detail about their two-year journey, but the answer was no. That chapter of their life was now closed. Before I left, Nisrin served us tea, from a brand-new metal pot, warmed underneath by a candle in a glass tray. I thought about the various times they'd offered me tea at different stages of their journey, in plastic cups or chipped mugs – or, on one occasion, from a kettle with the tea bags hung directly over the side. Now, they had an opportunity to arrange their lives the way they wanted. I wondered what the home they left behind in Syria had looked like.

23 · FARHAN

It took a dropped pin in Google Maps and a thumbs-up emoji to work out that I'd gone to the wrong place. Farhan had said to meet him at the 'station', but now I realized he'd meant 'bus stop'. These sorts of misunderstandings had been common in our exchanges since I'd first spoken to him through the detention-centre fence in Amygdaleza, in the autumn of 2014. A few days after my visit, I'd started getting calls on my mobile, usually at night, just as I was falling asleep. If I answered, we wouldn't be able to make ourselves understood, since he didn't speak much of my language and I didn't speak any of his. If I let the phone ring out, when I woke up the next morning there would be a message waiting: a pause, then a Punjabi-accented voice saying 'Hello?' two or three times before the line went dead.

I left the station and crossed the village, which was in the northern German countryside. Farhan's phone calls had carried on throughout the final months of 2014 and into the first months of the new year. Eventually, I gave him the name of my Facebook account, which worked better. Every now and then, he'd send me a message in phonetic English, which I'd try to decipher:

- 5 day no food
- why greece police not give stay pepar
- i am lafing
- i want out her from camp

In February, he sent me another message: *I'm reeliz now*. The left-wing party, Syriza, had won elections the month before and formed a new government. They had pledged to close the detention centres and replace them with more humane accommodation. 'I'm here to express my shame,' the newly appointed minister for public order said on a visit to Amygdaleza, 'not as a minister but as a human being.' Their first move was to release inmates who had been locked up for longer than the EU's eighteen-month limit. Farhan, who had been detained for around twenty months by February, was released.

We didn't speak for several months, and then, in July 2015, he wrote to me again: *I'm in Hungary*. Next, a grid of photo thumbnails dropped into my inbox. I clicked on them. The first picture was of a long queue at a Greek train station. The next was of Farhan – looking leaner than when I'd met him a year before, and with his moustache shaved off – standing in a clearing surrounded by trees, wearing a heavy backpack. It was summer, and he had a pair of sunglasses propped up on his head. The rest showed Farhan and a group of South Asian men waiting at small train stations, or eating by the side of the road – until, finally, they were posing outside a row of reconditioned shipping containers, like the ones I'd seen in Harmanli, or the ones in Amygdaleza that had escaped the fire. A few weeks later, Farhan messaged me again, to say he was in Germany.

Now, it was November 2016, and I had come to meet

him. I reached the village bus stop, at a deserted cross-roads near an industrial estate. I waited for a few minutes, wondering if I'd got the right place, then I saw Farhan approaching me on a bike a few sizes too small for him. In the months since our first encounter, he'd been a ghostly presence: a disembodied voice, or one end of a Facebook conversation in which we could never quite make ourselves understood. My image of him was of a figure in distress, behind a prison fence; now, he was cycling with his knees stuck out at angles. He was wearing a blue tracksuit and his hair was slicked back and shaved at the sides, in a vaguely hipster style.

*

Farhan led me through the industrial estate, to a patch of recently cleared ground which lay behind it. This was his new home: a two-storey set of Portakabin blocks, which were being used to house male asylum seekers. Most were Syrian or Afghan, he said. There were about a hundred residents in total. Farhan brought me to his room, which was narrow, but big enough to fit a bed, a fridge, a small dining table and an armchair. He motioned for me to sit at the table, offered me a bottle of Coca-Cola and went off to find some glasses. When he came back, seven other men filed into the room behind him, each shaking my hand and nodding as they passed me. Four went to sit down on the bed; the other three sat on the armchair, one in the middle and two perched on the arms. Farhan sat down on the other chair at the table, took out a pouch of tobacco and began rolling a cigarette.

The man sitting in the middle of the armchair introduced himself as Nawaz. He spoke good English and translated for the others as they introduced themselves. All were from Pakistan; most of them were in their late twenties or early thirties, and had lived in Greece for several years before coming to Germany. Two younger men, sitting at the far end of the bed, were both eighteen and had made the journey to Europe, via Turkey and the Aegean, this year.

First, I said, I wanted to know more about how Farhan had ended up in Germany. As Nawaz translated for us, Farhan spoke in long sentences, staring at the table or tapping his cigarette into the ashtray. After he'd been released from Amygdaleza in February, he said, the police had given him an order to leave Greece within thirty days. He'd gone to stay with friends in Athens, and had looked for work, but he couldn't find any. Farhan didn't know what to do; the only ways out of Greece were to go back to Pakistan, or to pay a smuggler to take him elsewhere in Europe, but he didn't have the money for either. And he was scared that, if he stayed, the police would arrest him and put him back in detention. 'He had no other choice but to come here,' said Nawaz, summarizing Farhan's words for me and adding his own explanations.

In the spring of 2015, the number of people crossing the Aegean by smugglers' boats leaving from Turkey climbed to record levels, according to the UNHCR. So, too, had deaths by drowning. On Lesvos and other Greek islands, new graves like the ones near the River Evros were dug to bury the people who couldn't be identified. By the summer, over 30,000 people a month were arriving on the Greek islands. Most were travelling to Athens and then making their way north. To slow their progress, the EU had relied on the Balkans as a kind of buffer zone; in previous years, migrants had to pay smugglers to take them through Macedonia and Serbia before they could rejoin EU territory in

Hungary and make their way through the Schengen zone. Now, under weight of numbers, that route was being forced open and it was easy to tag along and follow others who had gone before. In July, Farhan and two of his friends decided to try it.

They met in the morning, at the Larissa train station in Athens – close to the neighbourhood where Golden Dawn had terrorized immigrants a few years previously – and bought tickets to Thessaloniki, in northern Greece. Thessaloniki, a five-hour train journey from Athens, is about fifty miles south of the border with Macedonia. They didn't know the exact route, but it was obvious when they arrived in Thessaloniki – the station was crowded with people, all wanting to cross the border. 'We walked. Thousands of people were going in the same direction, so we just followed them.' It was high summer, and along the route, groups of volunteers were handing out bottles of water and supplies. In his bag, Farhan had two spare jackets, so he wouldn't get cold at night; a spare pair of trainers; packets of biscuits and bottles of water; and 400 euros he had borrowed from a friend in Athens.

It took sixteen hours to walk from Thessaloniki to the Macedonian border. On the road, they met a dozen other Pakistani men and decided to travel together. More men, from Iran and Syria, joined them, so that they were less likely to be robbed on the journey, and their group expanded to around fifty people. Each time somebody needed to rest, they would sit by the side of the road, wait for the others to pass, and rejoin at the end. A long column of thousands of people walking in the same direction stretched along the road between Thessaloniki and Macedonia: families, children, single men and women.

Close to the border, their path diverted from the main

road and turned west, towards farmland outside the Greek village of Idomeni. Here, several kilometres from the official border crossing, migrants had been trying to walk into Macedonia. 'The police said nothing, but they wouldn't let you in and just pushed you away. They were in riot gear, with sticks and guns.' When Farhan's group had set off from Thessaloniki, they'd heard the border there was open, but by the time they arrived, it had been closed. Farhan's group waited until it got dark, then walked along the border for a few miles, until they found a spot that was less heavily guarded. Many others were doing the same thing. 'The police were there, but it was dark and they couldn't see us, so we ran away.'

From the Macedonian border, they walked until morning, when they arrived at a provincial train station. Hundreds of people were waiting for a train to arrive, on a line that ran a two-carriage service. Each time one arrived at the station, people pushed and fought one another as they tried to board. Police watched on, hugely outnumbered by the migrants. Farhan's group sheltered in the woods by the station for two days, sleeping on the ground, before they were able to board. A ticket had cost fifteen euros, but once they set off, the conductor pushed his way through the packed carriages, asking for more money. 'People were scared they'd be taken off the train, so they gave him whatever money they had: fifty euros, a hundred euros.'

After eight hours, the train stopped at a station close to the Serbian border and the driver told the passengers which direction to walk in. Overnight, they walked through a forest until they reached Serbia and repeated the same sequence they had gone through at the previous border: being turned away by police, then walking along until they found a place to run across. Moving by night was preferable, because it kept them warm as the temperature dropped, as well as making it harder for the police to spot them. The technique favoured young, able-bodied single men and women. Those with families or elderly relatives, or in wheelchairs, had to wait at the larger crossing points and hope the police would eventually let them pass.

A few hours after crossing into Serbia, Farhan's group was found by police officers and taken to a detention centre. They were fingerprinted and released after three days, and given a document telling them to leave the country within twenty-four hours. They crossed Serbia by train, and crossed into Hungary by waiting for the border police to catch another group of migrants and then running across while they were distracted. Once they were safely inside Hungary, they encountered a group of journalists outside a village who told them to wait by the side of the main road so that police could spot them and take them to a camp. By July, 72,000 other migrants had entered Hungary in similar fashion, according to the government, which had opened centres to accommodate them. As soon as they could, they left the camp and made their way to Budapest, from where they could board trains to Austria, and then Germany. Farhan and his two friends had originally wanted to go to Italy, where they'd heard it was easier to get documents, but other migrants in the Hungarian camp told them the border was being heavily policed and that Germany would be better.

From Athens, the journey had taken twelve days. In Macedonia, Farhan's phone had run out of battery, and he wasn't able to charge it again, or buy a new SIM card, until Hungary. He posted the same photos he'd sent me to Facebook, to let people know he'd arrived. 'We didn't talk much during the journey,' he said. 'Everybody was tense, everybody was tired, we had no proper rest, no shower. So we were quiet.' Farhan went through two pairs of shoes – trainers made by the Pakistani brand, Servis – while he was walking. 'They're very popular in Pakistan; police use them,' said Nawaz. 'They sell them in the Pakistani shops in Athens.'

*

I asked if others in the room had made the same journey. All of them, except Nawaz, said yes. The two eighteen-year-olds had tried to go through Bulgaria at first, but they'd been robbed and beaten by a vigilante gang at the border; these gangs were now common. The older men had all lived in Greece for several years before leaving. Lack of work and the threat of detention had made them leave. One of the men on the armchair, whose name was Tahir, had met Farhan in Hungary and travelled the last leg of the trip to Germany with him. 'I was in Greece for eight years. I used to have temporary documents, but then they took them away and put me in detention for six months.' He had worked in a water-bottling plant. Another man, heavyset and perching on the edge of the bed, told a similar story. 'I paid taxes there, everything. I did farming, driving a tractor.' But life had got much harder after the crackdown of 2012. 'Whenever police see you, they're racist. They ask, "Why are you here?" Say, "Go back to your own country." They swear at you, they say bad things to you.'

'And *Xrysi Avgi*?' I asked, using the Greek name for Golden Dawn. They nodded.

Before his arrest, Farhan was earning a hundred euros a week working at the fruit and vegetable market in

Athens. He wasn't happy there, he said, not only because he could feel the hostility towards immigrants, but because the money he earned was so low it would take him years of living without papers, in semi-hiding, to save anything. In the end, the police solved that problem. One evening, on his way home from work, at the end of 2012, they stopped him to check his documents, and when he said he didn't have any, they sent him to jail.

For the first few months of his imprisonment, he was kept in a windowless cell at the police station with thirty other men from different countries: Pakistan, Afghanistan, Nigeria, Morocco, Albania. The bathroom smelled foul and three of the inmates ganged up on everyone else and intimidated them. A friend visited Farhan about once a month to bring clothes and cigarettes, and he was offered access to a lawyer and a translator. 'They couldn't do anything,' he said. 'If you have money, you can go out within a night, but without money, nothing.'

One problem with Greece's attempt to round up and deport undocumented migrants was that the government could often only carry out the first part. If someone has claimed asylum, you can't deport them until the process has concluded; if your system can't process the applications, then you never reach that point. Even when someone has lost the right to stay, you need to have an agreement with the country you want to send them back to. In December 2015, Pakistan made a plane full of deported migrants turn back from Islamabad and return to Greece with its passengers still on board, because it said the EU had not provided the right paperwork.

After Farhan had been kept in the cell for several months, he said, the inmates developed skin diseases and they were moved to Amygdaleza, which was opened in

2013. Conditions there were a little better, since you could go outside and walk for a hundred metres or so, but they were behind fences the whole time. Farhan shared his container with five other men, all from Pakistan. Fights, usually over food – it was never enough, just starchy pasta and bread – broke out often. People would rip metal bars from the bed frames and hit one another; the police would come in and beat them or withhold food for days at a time as punishment. Farhan estimated that, in the eight to nine months he was kept in Amygdaleza, he saw four people die in fights and several others kill themselves.

The riot that had taken place just before I visited, Farhan said, was over the death of a young Pakistani man. He had been ill for some time, but hadn't received any medical attention. 'When he died, we told police, but they didn't listen and they left his body there for twelve hours before anyone came to get him.' The inmates, including Farhan, were so angry that they smashed up and burned some of the containers. Some went on hunger strike; the story was even reported in Pakistani media.

The main link with the world outside was via a smuggled phone, which was shared between the men living in Farhan's section. In Farhan's container, when it was their turn to use the phone, they would go on Facebook, or watch Bollywood movie clips, or listen to Attaullah Khan Esakhelvi, a Pakistani singer. 'His songs are sad songs; like, if you listen to them, you start crying,' Nawaz explained. 'They're all about how he used to have a lover and he failed in his love. Or he loves someone, but he couldn't get her.'

'I liked listening to the sad songs in detention because I already was sad,' Farhan interjected. If they didn't have the phone, in the evenings the men would talk, usually about what would happen to them in the future. Some inmates, who'd been detained for two years by the end of 2014, had been asking to be deported back to Pakistan. Others were still saying they'd stay, and hoped to find work, maybe even get papers.

Later, I went on YouTube and listened to a few Attaullah clips. The songs were indeed sad: mournful ballads, accompanied by harmonium and other classical instruments. They reminded me, in tone and spirit, of rembetiko, the Greek popular music brought to the mainland by refugees from Asia Minor in the early twentieth century.

*

We had been talking for over an hour, and Farhan's narrow room had filled with cigarette smoke. Did he miss Pakistan? I wanted to know.

'Yes, of course, but I can't go back,' he said. 'I borrowed money to come to Europe from my uncle, from friends.' Farhan hadn't told his parents he was leaving for Europe; he'd just said he was leaving their home in Pakistan's Punjab region to look for work in Karachi. It wasn't until he'd crossed into Iran that he phoned them and told them his plans. They'd been very worried after he was arrested in Greece, and had begged him to come back to Pakistan, but he'd told them it was fine, he was being treated well in detention, he would be out soon.

The other men in the room were also Punjabi. They came from towns and villages around Faisalabad, a planned city built under the British Empire, the central roads of which are laid out in the shape of the lines on a Union Jack. All of them came from working-class families, the children of farmers and factory workers, and all except Nawaz had left school as teenagers. The only one who'd had a job before he left Pakistan was the heavyset man on the end of the bed; he had been a professional kabaddi wrestler when he was younger.

Although Pakistan is a source of refugees – a Taliban insurgency in the north-west of the country, human-rights abuses in Balochistan, gender-based violence, corruption and police torture are all things that cause people to flee – none of these men had left his home because of persecution or war. 'We leave because it's not a very good situation there; if you are not educated, you can't get any job,' Nawaz explained. 'Even the people who are educated, they don't have enough work.' The area around Faisalabad was relatively prosperous; it wasn't just the lack of work, but the knowledge that other things were possible, that motivated people to move. 'If you stay at home, your parents say, "You do nothing; you are young, you have to earn something." So people get crazy and they just want to leave. These guys –' Nawaz gestured towards the two teenagers – 'they were fighting in school and got into trouble, so their parents told them, "Go away and live your lives, stop causing problems."' Migration to Europe was harder than it had been for an earlier generation, who were able to come to Britain as Commonwealth citizens. 'If you don't have family connections and you're not educated, it's difficult.'

Ten years ago, one major route into Europe had been across the Evros. Most of the men I was talking to had been smuggled in that way. The journey from Pakistan had cost 4,000 or 5,000 euros, back then. Now, as the Balkan migration route had opened up, it looked like perhaps there was a quicker way out of Greece; the two teenagers had arrived in Germany only a month or two after leaving Pakistan. All of these men were precisely the kind of 'economic migrants' Europe's border defences were supposed to filter out. But, even after years in Greece, including some extreme hardship in the country's immigration prisons, they were still determined to stay.

'If someone comes here, they destroy their life,' said Tahir, sitting next to Nawaz on the armchair, 'but they destroy their life in Pakistan, too. You stay here five years, ten years, and you still don't have a good life; you don't have papers, you are like nothing here – but people sold their houses to come here, they borrowed money. And when they go back to Pakistan, they don't have anywhere to live and they have no work. If master's degree holders can't get work, then how can we?'

Farhan carried on smoking and stared at the table; Nawaz nodded in agreement. 'We keep moving,' he said, 'because, even though we're scared of detention, we're scared to go home with nothing. Everybody will laugh at you: "He's been to Europe and he came back with nothing." In Pakistan, it's like family, you know; everybody knows each other. If you live in one place, the whole area knows you.' The Pakistani government was already running media campaigns warning people not to come to Europe, saying that it wasn't going to be like it was for their parents' generation, he said.

'We just want to tell the guys who are still in Pakistan not to come here. Don't do it,' said Tahir.

Farhan asked if I wanted something to eat. He got up, went into the kitchen for a few minutes and came back with a dish of biryani, which he served out onto plates and shared around. As we ate, I asked Nawaz where he'd learned English. His accent suggested he'd lived in Britain for some time. 'I lived in Manchester, and then Birmingham,' he said. 'I was in Britain for four years; I had a student visa to learn English for three and a half years, then I paid 5,000 pounds applying for a new one and it was turned down.' In recent years, Britain has been making it harder for non-EU migrants to settle in the country: student visas are harder to come by; UK citizens with a foreign spouse must be earning a minimum amount, or have minimum savings before their partner is allowed to join them; landlords are required to check the immigration status of prospective tenants. 'So I paid 700 pounds to be smuggled out.'

Nawaz had taken a lorry, via a contact in Birmingham, in the opposite direction to the migrants at Calais. 'I slept in a park in France for a week, but people there told me it was shit and that, if you claim asylum, they say you have to live by your own means for seven or eight months, so I came to Germany.' He knew his asylum application wouldn't be accepted. 'We all know that, but maybe we'll be able to stay for a year or two. Maybe a lawyer will even help us stay for five years.'

Once we'd finished dinner, I thanked the men for their time and asked if there was anything I could send them from the UK. 'A cricket bat,' said Nawaz. 'We've looked everywhere and we can't find one here.'

Farhan walked me back to the bus stop. It was late evening and there was a hint of winter in the air. Without Nawaz as our intermediary, Farhan had returned to silence. We shook hands and smiled and made gestures to say thank you, and maybe I even gave him a thumbs up. As the bus pulled away, I could see the tip of his cigarette glowing in the dark.

CENTURY

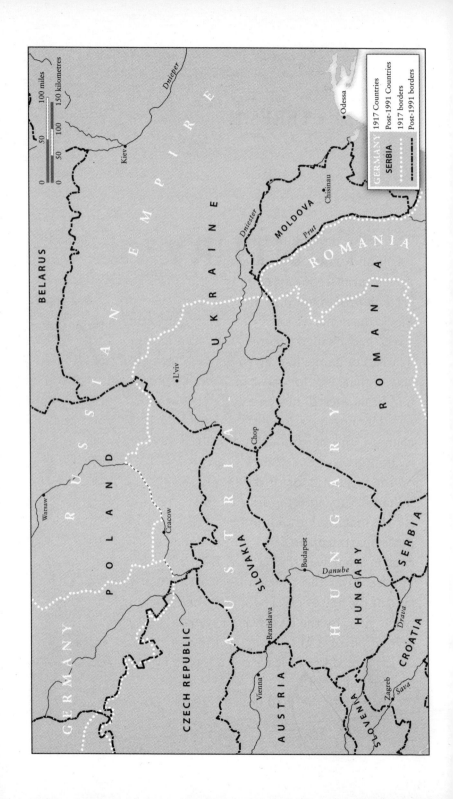

24 · TERESA

The house on Annunciation Street had changed. Painted green and white, with balconies jutting out and a Soviet agricultural scene carved in relief on the top, it was a concrete approximation of the nineteenth-century apartment block that once stood in this corner of central Kiev. The street had changed names, too. Annunciation Street, the Tsarist-era name, had given way to Gorky Street, and had stayed that way for most of the last century. But that too had been altered, more recently, to Antonovych, the name of a Ukrainian nationalist historian. Despite a century of changes, the neighbourhood appeared to have clung to its bourgeois roots when I visited in the summer of 2014; on the ground floor of the block was a showroom for an Italian luxury interior-design firm.

My maternal grandmother, Teresa, was born in one of those apartments in 1911, to Russian-speaking Jewish parents, in what was then a provincial capital of the Russian Empire. Over the course of her life, which ended in England at the age of ninety-four, she had been made a refugee twice: first, by the civil war that engulfed Russia after the revolution of 1917; then, by the rise of Nazi Germany, which forced her to leave her adopted home of Berlin, for London, in 1939.

My grandfather had been a refugee, too, although a far

luckier one; his family were Russian Jewish merchants who had left Bialystok for London after the revolution, with their money and their business intact. He had died when I was a baby, so I never heard his story directly, but for most of my childhood I either lived on the same street or in the same house as Teresa. In the later years of her life, she was partially sighted, and whenever she had to look after me and my brother, she would keep us amused by telling us stories. Teresa had three main subjects. One was the kings and queens of England, a lineage she'd learned after coming to Britain. Another was descriptions of paintings by the old masters; she had studied at the Berlin art school, but most of her paintings were destroyed en route to Britain by a German U-boat. The only book she'd brought with her was Vasari's *Lives of the Artists*. And the third, the one we liked to hear about the most, was the events of her youth. Some cheerful, others traumatic, they were retold and repackaged as stories with neat little plots, or vivid images.

In this way, they were passed on to me. I came to know a vanished world, of decrepit ancestors who had to be carried in basket chairs, or religious forebears who went through the ritual of sweeping breadcrumbs from the house with a chicken wing before Passover. I know that, in Teresa's Kiev apartment, when winter arrived and a second set of frames were attached to the windows for insulation, she would line up her toys in the gap between the two panes, on a bed of cotton wool, and watch them there, as cold air outside frosted up the glass. I also know that, in a corner of the park at the end of the street, tucked behind some trees, there was a worn wooden statue of a bear, some relic of a pagan belief system that had survived into the twentieth century.

I heard how her childhood world had begun to crumble as the Russian Civil War reached Kiev. Her father's office – he was a merchant, who traded in medical supplies across Europe – was smashed up by Ukrainian nationalists, because the sign on the door was in Russian. An uncle, only just discharged from the Tsar's army, was shot dead on his balcony, because he'd heard a commotion in the street and had gone out to look, without first removing his uniform. A militia requisitioned the apartment on Annunciation Street and moved other families into the rooms.

But it was the stories of escape that made the strongest impression on me. The first took place in around 1920, when Teresa was eight years old. Her father, thanks to his trading connections, had been able to leave Russia. He got hold of false documents and sent them back to his wife and daughter in Kiev. At a train station near the Polish border, the pair were stopped by soldiers, who wanted to see their identity documents. They were carrying two sets – one false, one real – and if their deceit was uncovered, they would probably have been shot. Teresa's mother asked her to go to the toilet and flush away the genuine papers, which were hidden in her shoe, but a soldier came into the cubicle with her and she couldn't do it. They were kept there for hours, during which time Teresa charmed their guard by drawing pictures of horses.

Eventually let go, mother and daughter crossed the Polish borderlands on foot, walking after dark and sheltering in peasants' houses during the day. They paid guides to show them the way, although they were warned that some might try to rob them. Teresa's mother had sold the family's possessions and bought a platinum cigarette case with the money, which she had sewn into the lining of her coat.

Teresa remembered hearing gunshots in the distance as they crossed the border.

In 1921, the government of what was by then the Soviet Union issued a decree that stripped Russians beyond its borders of their citizenship. The decision rendered millions of people stateless, an unprecedented situation. In Europe, the First World War had led to the collapse of several multi-ethnic empires, the spread of the nation state and a wave of mass displacement across the continent. There was no international system for dealing with the displaced civilians. Instead, it was generally left to individual states to accommodate or protect ethnic groups they considered their own people. Two groups in particular lost their old citizenship but could not find a new one: Russians outside the Soviet Union, and those Armenians displaced by the Ottoman genocide who did not go and live in the new Soviet Republic of Armenia. This affected millions of people; 800,000 Russians were stripped of their citizenship by the decree of 1921 alone.

Teresa and her parents moved to Warsaw, then Berlin a year later. More than a quarter of all Russian refugees, many of them Jewish, settled in Germany at this time. In 1922, the League of Nations, at the initiative of Fridtjof Nansen, a Norwegian polar explorer who became the League's first high commissioner for refugees, issued international passports for stateless Russians. These 'Nansen passports', as they became known, allowed the bearer to travel among countries that had signed up to the scheme. In 1933, they were also issued to Armenian, Turkish and Assyrian refugees, and by the end of their lifespan, the passports were recognized by fifty-two governments. It was the first serious attempt to create an international system of refugee protection, an effort to resolve a paradox of the modern world: if certain rights are supposed to be universal, why can they only be guaranteed through membership of a nation state?

When we were children, my grandmother spoke of her Nansen passport in reverential tones. She would describe it in detail: a white card with the bearer's photo attached, which, in her telling, allowed the holder to travel wherever they wanted, and didn't tie them down to any one nation. She would bemoan ever having to give it up. Teresa had eloped with a man from Berlin in her twenties and had taken his German citizenship at the start of their brief marriage. I grew up thinking of the Nansen passport as an almost magical document, a get-out-of-jail-free card that offered the bearer a unique freedom – and an escape route, if necessary.

After visiting the house on Annunciation Street, I found a park nearby; perhaps this was the one that Teresa had visited as a child. It was hard to tell. The ground had been landscaped recently, and there was definitely no sign of a wooden bear. It was peaceful, despite being only a few blocks from Kreschatik, the city's main boulevard. At the other end of Kreschatik were the remnants of the Maidan protest camp, by now looking like a stage set. Most of the players – the people who had come out onto the streets in protest the previous winter, an uneasy mix of pro-EU liberals, far-right nationalists and libertarian leftists – had departed. A Ukrainian friend had shown me around the sites, and I was struck by how the events she described seemed to be unfolding on the same ground as the stories I'd been told, about Kiev a century earlier. The uncle who'd been shot had even lived in an apartment that overlooked

Kreschatik. I said this, and told her some of Teresa's story. 'The usual, then,' my friend replied.

*

A few days later, I took the motorway west from Kiev and drove to Vinnytsia. The city was founded in the Middle Ages, but its modern history is marred by two massacres: in the 1930s, it was the site of mass killings by Soviet officials during the Great Terror; a decade later, under German occupation, Jews from the city and the surrounding region were murdered by Nazi death squads. A photograph of a man kneeling before a mass grave as an *Einsatzgruppen* soldier points a gun to his head – a grim souvenir that its owner, a German soldier, titled *The Last Jew of Vinnitsa* – has become a symbolic document of the Holocaust.

My grandmother would often tell us that we had no idea what it was like to leave our entire life behind and start again. She, after all, had done it twice. I used to think of this in terms of possessions: leaving my house, my books, my toys. But now I think it meant something more. Teresa never talked about people she knew who had died in the Holocaust, although, having lived in both Kiev and Berlin, she must have known many. Once, I looked up the names of people who had died at Babi Yar, the ravine outside Kiev where, in 1941, one of the worst massacres of Jews during the whole war had taken place. Her family name appeared several times on the list, although the people weren't relatives I'd ever heard Teresa speak about. At the very least, Teresa would have known that the communities of her childhood and her youth had largely been extinguished.

Told with hindsight, a refugee's escape takes on the quality of an adventure story. The right decisions, the right risks, taken at just the right moments. But this obscures just how contingent survival can be. If Teresa had settled at any point before London on her twenty-year journey from Kiev, she would most likely have been killed. The system of refugee protection established in the 1920s was not fit to meet the increasing challenges of the 1930s, as more groups of people were displaced by the rise of fascism in Europe. In France, internment camps were set up for refugees from the Spanish Civil War; many of these refugees were republicans who had fought Franco, so they were viewed as potential political subversives, as well as a burden on the state. As persecution in Nazi Germany intensified, other states were unwilling to offer shelter to Jews who escaped. At the 1938 Evian Conference, representatives from two dozen countries met to discuss the plight of German and Austrian Jews, who had been stripped of their citizenship by the Nuremberg Laws. Half a million were already on the move in Europe, looking for sanctuary. But, although many countries expressed their sympathy, they were unwilling to resettle refugees in any great number. 'The United Kingdom is not a country of immigration,' said the British representative. 'We have no real racial problem ... we are not desirous of importing one,' said Australia. Brazil said it would only accept Christians, while the US, fearful of refugees' impact on the economy, would not raise its immigration quotas.

Teresa left Germany in 1939. Her father had died in 1935 and was buried in Berlin's Jewish cemetery, his death certificate – which we still have – stamped with an official swastika. He had missed the acceleration of Nazi persecution, but Teresa and her mother were there for it. Teresa was in Berlin when the law forcing Jews to wear yellow stars was passed; she had been spat at in the street, had hidden male friends in her apartment on Kristallnacht. After the Nuremberg Laws of 1938, she'd been stripped of her citizenship for a second time in her life. From then on, she had to take her German passport to a police station once a week, to receive an official stamp.

Early in 1939, Teresa sent her mother, who had never given up her Nansen passport, ahead to London. But Teresa had to wait until a friend there could procure her a visa that would allow her to find work. The British government had largely kept its doors closed to Jewish refugees in the late 1930s, under pressure from much of the press, who cast the displaced as an alien threat. Teresa arrived in London at the end of August, a few days before war was declared and the borders closed fully.

*

At Vinnytsia, I had an appointment at a house on a quiet, leafy residential street. A Ukrainian woman called Svitlana was there to greet me; she ran a local human-rights NGO, which in recent years has concentrated its work on refugees. Organizations like this now have an international system of laws to refer to, and, in theory, they can use these laws to hold their own governments and institutions to account. The foundations for this system were laid in the decade after the end of the Second World War, a conflict that displaced more people in Europe than ever before: forced labourers in Germany, former concentration-camp inmates, Germans expelled from eastern and central Europe, people unwilling to return to countries now under Soviet control. Millions of people needed accommodation, or a way home, or a new place to settle.

At that time, there was political will to tackle the crisis, and the 1951 Refugee Convention is an important part of the system that emerged. Its language is bold, and sounds universal. But defining who is a refugee, and who qualifies for legal protection, means excluding those who don't meet the criteria. The 1951 Convention, for instance, at first only applied to Europeans – and, initially, only those Europeans displaced before it was drawn up. The displacement of European Jews, many of whom couldn't or wouldn't return to countries in which the local populations remained hostile, was supposedly resolved by the creation of the state of Israel, which in turn displaced 700,000 Palestinians. These Palestinians weren't – and still generally aren't – covered by the standard system of refugee protection. The millions of people displaced by partition in India and revolution in China weren't considered refugees under this new definition. Nor did the Refugee Convention provide for people who fled generalized war; this kind of protection was only created after pressure from newly independent African states in the 1960s and Latin American states in the 1980s. People forced from their homes by economic disaster or catastrophic climate change have never been included. Even today, the Convention leaves power mainly in the hands of nation states. It does not oblige its signatories to give anybody asylum, merely to hear their case and not push them back to a country where they might be in danger. The definition of 'refugee' is political, and its meaning is subject to a constant struggle over who's in and who's out.

We sat down in the front room of the house, which had been converted into an office, and Svitlana handed me a sheaf of printed-out digital photographs. They were of children and young men and women of East African origin – receiving food, trying on clothes, taking an art class. Svitlana explained that, in 2009, Somalis had started to appear in Vinnytsia, often destitute. Her NGO started to investigate and discovered cases where people had been locked up in apartments and kept there for days without being given food.

Since the outbreak of civil war in Somalia during the late 1980s, perhaps as many as several million people have left the country, while over a million are internally displaced. Their situation is a striking example of how both safety and economic concerns can affect a person's decision to move. Violence is still common in many parts of the country, but Somalia has also suffered from a drought-induced famine in recent years, and the state is weak. Families often rely on money sent by relatives working abroad; the World Bank estimates that around one in five households in Somalia receive remittances. Most Somali refugees, nearly a million, live in countries that neighbour Somalia. If they do what they're told, then they are likely to end up living somewhere like Dadaab, in eastern Kenya. This is the world's largest refugee camp – in fact, a cluster of five camps that date back twenty years and are home to over 300,000 people. The official way out is through a slow-moving UN resettlement programme.

Under such circumstances, paying smugglers to take you to Europe is a popular option. The Somalis in Vinnytsia were taking a circuitous route that went via the Gulf states and Russia, Svitlana explained. They would fly to the United Arab Emirates, which has an established Somali immigrant population, and, from there, take a plane to Moscow with fake documents or a short-term student visa. In Moscow, said Svitlana, a smuggler network would keep them in safe houses and force many of the Somalis to work in menial jobs or the sex industry to pay off their debts. Then they would be taken west by minibus, from Russia into Ukraine, and then on into the European Union. Vinnytsia was a stopover point, and a place that Somalis who were caught at the border would return to, because they knew its name and they knew they would find compatriots there. People from other countries used these smuggler routes, too, but Somalis were the most visible, because, if they were caught by the authorities in Ukraine and didn't want to claim asylum there, the government could not deport them, given the ongoing conflict in Somalia.

Svitlana's NGO had started to make a fuss about the mistreatment they had observed. They collected accounts from the migrants of alleged beatings, torture and extortion. When the NGO started to post videos of these testimonies on YouTube, its offices were raided by police. Soon after, the smuggler routes shifted, and Vinnytsia's Somalis disappeared: they were being sent via other towns.

This account was close enough to Teresa's story – clandestine journeys across similar territory; the threat of capture and punishment by hostile state officials – to make me think about them in comparison. But, today, I'm more struck by the differences. The European population upheavals of the twentieth century are now largely resolved. They may have been painful, they may have led to disasters, but they're generally seen as having provided a moral lesson for Europe today – one of several ways in which Europe declared, 'Never again.' That's one reason why comparisons of the 2015 crisis with the plight of earlier refugees hits a raw nerve. But, for much of the world, displacement is persistent, its causes apparently more complicated, the people at the centre of it afforded less significance. Often, they're given no story at all, reduced to a shadow that occasionally flits across European consciences. Perhaps, for instance, if we had paid more attention to the stories of Somalis in the 1990s, we might have a better handle on what is happening today.

The NGO was still busy, Svitlana told me. Vinnytsia was now a destination for Ukrainian citizens displaced by the war in Donbass. Her organization was helping them find accommodation, register with health services, or get their children enrolled at school. When I visited Vinnytsia, in the summer of 2014, the war in eastern Ukraine had been going on for several months and the number of displaced was approaching 100,000. Ukraine's ministry of social policy now estimates that 1.6 million people have been displaced. There is a vast refugee crisis in Ukraine, but it's generally regarded as a domestic problem – that's the difference a national border makes. Several hundred thousand Ukrainian citizens have moved into the EU since the war began, either for safety or because the Ukrainian economy has crashed, but they've mostly done so on temporary work visas. For the most part, there has been no trafficking, no detention, no deaths at the border.

*

After Vinnytsia, I headed south-west, a day's drive along potholed roads through flat countryside, punctuated every now and then by a farmstead hidden behind metal gates. Military convoys, their cargo hidden by green canvas, passed in the other direction, heading east. As I neared my destination, the landscape changed and the road crossed a mountain range, the top of which was covered in cloud. On the other side, the towns and villages looked different from the ones before: here, their narrow streets were still cobbled in some places, and the larger buildings were gabled nineteenth-century affairs, with little turrets.

This was Ukraine's westernmost region, Transcarpathia. Covering a section of the Carpathian Mountains, which stretch across central and eastern Europe, it has passed through many hands over the course of the last century. Once part of the Austro-Hungarian Empire, it was claimed by Hungary's short-lived Soviet republic, then an equally short-lived West Ukrainian republic, then Romania, then Czechoslovakia during the interwar years. After the Second World War, it was made part of the Soviet Union. A glance at a map shows why Stalin coveted it: across a span of just a few hundred kilometres, Transcarpathia borders Romania, Hungary, Slovakia and Poland – convenient for an empire looking to keep its satellite states in check.

Today, this border is part of the European Union's eastern frontier, a ragged line that runs for around 2,000 miles south from Estonia's Baltic coast, past Russia, Belarus, Ukraine and Moldova, and on to the Black Sea. The EU's political objective has been to build closer relationships with many of the countries to its immediate east, so it has tried to patrol the border while keeping it open for certain people. 'There are different levels,' a Ukrainian friend explained to me. 'If you go by plane, it's fine. If you go by train, it's usually fine, but you have to wait while they change the wheels. If you go by bus, you have to wait eight hours sometimes while they do security checks. And if you go by foot, they really go through everything and make you wait. It's hard not to feel that they're treating you like a piece of shit.'

Because the border divides ethnic groups – there are Poles, Slovaks, Romanians, Hungarians and Ukrainians in this region – anyone who lives within thirty kilometres of the frontier is allowed easier travel. Smuggling is a staple of life in the border villages of Transcarpathia. Cheap, Slovak-registered cars travel in one direction, cigarettes and contraband in the other. There is also a cargo that villagers sometimes refer to as 'the blacks': refugees and other migrants, not just from Somalia, but Sri Lanka, Afghanistan, the Middle East and beyond. For some, it's big business. In 2012, an underground tunnel, equipped with electric light and a miniature railway on which to carry goods, was discovered underneath a house in the Ukrainian town of Uzhgorod, running 700 metres under the border into Slovakia. Police on the Slovakian side believed people were being smuggled through the tunnel as well.

At Chop, a town close to the Hungarian and Slovak borders, I arrived at a Ukrainian border-police base. I was greeted at the entrance by three uniformed officers, and a staff photographer. 'It's not often we get an international journalist here,' the photographer explained, and proceeded to take pictures of me as his colleagues showed me around the base. In recent years, these border guards have been asked to take on an increasing amount of work policing Ukraine's western frontier on behalf of the European Union. A treaty signed in 2007 – part of a wider set of agreements on trade and movement – obliges Ukraine to readmit any 'third country nationals or stateless person' who has crossed into the EU from Ukrainian territory. Migrants sent back to Ukraine are tried by a court for attempting to cross a border illegally and, if convicted, are given a prison sentence of up to a year, before being deported.

Unless, of course, they can't be deported. In theory, those migrants who say they want to claim asylum should be exempt from this treatment. In practice, as at other borders of the EU, this is often ignored. A lawyer in Uzhgorod, whose organization provides legal and medical assistance to migrants, told me that they had collected numerous accounts of people being stopped by guards on the Slovakian side of the border, saying they wanted to claim asylum, but then being driven back across and handed over to Ukrainian guards. Those migrants who couldn't be deported after completing their prison sentence were faced with an unpalatable choice: claim asylum in Ukraine, where the system gave them very little means of support, or try once again to cross the border. There were cases, she said, of people who had gone through a three- or four-year cycle of border crossing, capture, imprisonment and release. She introduced me to a Somali man who had experienced this. Before he was sent off to detention, he said he had been chained to a radiator and beaten at the Ukrainian border station. 'We don't come to Somalia, so don't come to Ukraine,' he'd been told. A Human Rights Watch report, published in 2010, found that over half of the migrants they interviewed said they'd been mistreated in Ukraine, or asked to pay bribes, with a few making allegations of torture.

The Ukrainian officer showing me around the base at Chop, a lieutenant colonel, said it wasn't true that Slovak officials had been pushing migrants back to Ukraine. They were just sending back those who didn't want to stay and ask for asylum in Slovakia, but who wanted to head further west instead. That wasn't the Slovaks' responsibility. Ukraine's border guards had to be 'polite and smiling and comfortable' at all times, even while they were checking for security threats, he said. The lieutenant colonel offered to show me the detention block. We walked across a courtyard to a single-storey building with bars on the windows. In the entrance hall was a plaque bearing the

EU flag and a logo for the Catholic relief agency Caritas, which said the block had been renovated with their financial support. One obstacle to the 2007 treaty was that Ukraine's border detention facilities hadn't met the EU's minimum human-rights standards, so the EU had given them money to improve them. The regular prison system was regarded as too abusive to hold migrants, so two special immigration prisons had been built elsewhere in the country, partly funded by the EU.

Two short corridors led away from the entrance hall of the detention block, in opposite directions. One was the block for women, the other for men. The centre could hold up to twenty-four people, although, at the moment, only three were detained here. Two were from Guinea and one was from Somalia. I asked if I could meet any of them, but the lieutenant colonel apologized and said they were unavailable. Two more apprehended migrants would be arriving from the border station later, but, sadly, it would be too late for me to visit. My host showed me into one of the men's cells, a small room furnished with three camp beds. It was warm and clammy with the breath of people who must have only been removed from there a few minutes earlier. This was Europe's border system working as intended: inconvenient people kept out of sight and out of mind, with their inconvenient stories unheard.

Our last stop on the tour was the exercise yard. Here, in a concrete-lined courtyard a few metres wide, topped by a steel mesh roof, the inmates had tried to leave traces of themselves. There were slogans scratched into the walls in Arabic, Cyrillic and Georgian scripts – and, in large Roman letters across one end of the courtyard, *USA AFGHAN*.

In 1887, geographers from the Austro-Hungarian

Empire decided that Transcarpathia was the dead centre of the continent; they set up a monument to mark the exact spot, a few hours' drive from the border-guard base at Chop. We were somewhere near the heart of Europe, but a border ran through it.

AFTERWORD

The refugee crisis of 2015 might usefully be described as the period between the two shipwrecks off the coast of Libya, in April, and the Paris terrorist attacks that November. This period was one of shock and uncertainty, with mass public displays of sympathy for and solidarity with the refugees – from the volunteer lifeguards on the beaches of Greek islands, to the tens of thousands of people demonstrating in European cities under the banner 'Refugees Welcome' that September. Politicians vacillated between bold humanitarian pronouncements and reassurances that they would soon, once again, have migration under control.

After Paris, the political mood became reactionary. The attacks supplied an excuse to start closing borders again, since it appeared that one or more of the perpetrators had slipped into Europe along the refugee trail from Turkey. The Balkan migration route, from Greece to Hungary and beyond, was the first to be sealed off. In the days immediately following the Paris attacks, Slovenia, Croatia, Macedonia and Serbia began to stop irregular migrants from crossing: first, anyone who wasn't Syrian, Iraqi or Afghan; later, everyone.

On New Year's Eve 2015, a series of sexual assaults and robberies among crowds in Cologne and several other

German cities seemed to confirm the predictions of right-wing ideologues that Germany had courted disaster by allowing in so many foreigners. The perpetrators, most of whom were never caught, were said by the police to be 'of Arab or North African appearance'. A chief prosecutor initially claimed that the 'overwhelming majority' of suspects were asylum seekers; it later emerged that around half of the suspects had arrived recently in Germany, and most came from Morocco or Algeria, countries not generally associated with the refugee crisis.

Yet, for many, this was justification enough for a flood of paranoid racist fantasy about the threat posed by migrants of Muslim background, elevating the crimes of a few to a civilizational threat. One widely read political magazine in Poland proclaimed 'The Islamic rape of Europe' on its cover, casting Europe as a blonde woman being groped by swarthy hands. The sentiment was echoed, albeit in quieter tones, by a wide range of European media.

For the most hard-line of anti-immigration politicians, the backlash against refugees merely proved them right. Hungary's government announced a referendum on the EU's migrant relocation scheme, strongly urging voters to reject it. The UK Independence Party, as well as the right-wing press, used images of refugees in Europe in its campaign for Britain to leave the EU. Donald Trump has used the crisis in Europe as rhetorical justification for his own xenophobic domestic policies.

The responses of individual European states have been mixed. Some, like Germany or Sweden, are trying to keep their asylum systems relatively open, even under pressure from the far right. Others are trying to make their countries less attractive. Denmark, for example, has cut its support payments to asylum seekers and even passed a law that allows it to seize refugees' jewellery and other assets when they arrive in the country, a largely symbolic policy that has drawn criticism for its uncomfortable echoes of Nazi Germany. Britain offered to take in 20,000 Syrians from camps outside Europe, but has only taken in vulnerable migrants from Calais after sustained pressure from campaigners and a court challenge. In fact, during the last few years, Britain's share of the asylum claims made in Europe has actually fallen. Despite doomy predictions that the refugee crisis would spell the end of Schengen, what it's meant in practice is passport checks at the borders within the zone for black people, but not for whites.

Overall, while the rhetoric may vary, the actions taken by European governments have been broadly consistent: a shoring up of the old border regime, the toughening of conditions for migrants inside Europe to deter others, and the effective outsourcing of European border control to governments in Asia, the Middle East and Africa. The scheme to relocate refugees from Italy and Greece never really got off the ground. In April 2017, the EU revised the target for relocation down, from 160,000 to 33,000, after fewer than 15,000 refugees were actually moved under the scheme.

Greece and Italy have effectively become holding pens for tens of thousands of asylum seekers. At the end of 2016, around 60,000 migrants were living in Greek camps, with more outside, and well over 100,000 were in Italy, waiting for their asylum claims to be processed, according to each country's migration ministry. The migrants are the ones who lose out; neither country has an incentive to invest in their broken domestic systems and encourage people to stay, and other European countries have no interest in speeding up relocations. Mass detention has returned to Greece, despite the promises of the Syriza-led government, and enclosed, crowded and unsanitary tent camps on the islands are becoming a European version of Australia's offshore detention system. Current state policies are a stark contrast to the solidarity shown in Greece by locals and international volunteers during the summer of 2015. The money from international donors that flooded into Greece in 2015 has been described as the most expensive humanitarian response per beneficiary in history, and has diverted funds from much poorer parts of the world, yet Greece, the EU and the UNHCR were unable even to ensure between them that camps were made ready for winter conditions in 2016 and 2017. To discourage European citizens from intervening, various governments have become more rigorous in applying an EU directive that criminalizes the 'facilitation' of unauthorized migration. Among those arrested or charged with people trafficking have been a group of Spanish volunteer lifeguards on Lesvos, a French farmer near the Italian border who let migrants sleep in caravans in his fields, and a Danish campaigner for children's rights who gave a Syrian family a lift in her car. A 2017 report by the UK-based Institute for Race Relations counted forty-five people who have been prosecuted under anti-trafficking laws for carrying out humanitarian work in Europe since 2015.

The EU is also trying to extend the reach of its border control. In March 2016, a deal with Turkey came into force, which states that, for each migrant Europe sends back to Turkey from the Greek islands, the EU will resettle one Syrian directly from Turkey. The deal, which has been condemned by human-rights organizations such as Amnesty International, because Turkey denies full refugee status to non-Europeans and has forced people back to Syria, Iraq and Afghanistan, resulted in a sharp drop in people crossing the Aegean. But this is mainly down to Turkey doing what it had always been able to do: policing its Aegean coastline. It can just as easily allow the boats to sail freely once more, which is a powerful political bargaining chip. Turkey asked for six billion euros in aid, visa-free travel in Europe for its citizens and new talks on EU membership. Refugees are the currency in this exchange.

Further afield, the EU has offered up to sixty-two billion euros in investment and aid to countries in the Middle East and Africa who agree to help it reduce the number of migrants entering Europe. The EU is using coercion, too. In September 2016, the EU told Afghanistan that it would reduce aid unless the country accepted 80,000 Afghans deported from Europe. Similar deals have been considered with Sudan and Eritrea, despite those countries' widely documented human-rights abuses. And, if the EU can't deport migrants to their countries of origin, it wants to send them back to one further down the migration route: Niger, Lebanon, Ethiopia and Nigeria are all being considered. The aim is to extend a militarized border system deep into neighbouring continents. In July 2016, it was revealed that the European Commission would divert money from its budget for 'peace building' and development, to military equipment and training for armed forces in Africa and the Middle East. Border defence, not the protection of life, remains Europe's priority.

The danger of treating people in this way has become apparent as Europe tries to recreate the EU–Turkey deal in Libya. As media attention has drifted elsewhere, the central Mediterranean route has only got deadlier. In 2016, according to the UNHCR, over 5,000 people drowned in the Mediterranean; since the end of Mare Nostrum, there has been a proliferation of private search-and-rescue initiatives. In 2017, Europe stepped up its efforts to close down the route. A leaked Frontex report accused rescuers of encouraging people smugglers, while Italy has tried to introduce a restrictive code of practice for NGOs whose boats use its ports. European leaders have also been trying to make deals to control migration in Libya, which still lacks a unified government. In mid-2017, there was a sudden drop in boat crossings from Libya; it later emerged that Italy had paid a militia in the city of Sabratha to halt people-smuggling. This money then fuelled a weeks-long battle between rival militias for control of the city. In August, three NGOs – MSF, Save the Children and the German charity Sea Eye – suspended search-and-rescue operations after they were threatened at sea by the Libyan coastguard, which has received training and funds from the EU. Migrants are not much safer if they are prevented from going to sea; abuse, torture and appalling conditions in detention are still rife.

The EU's response to the crisis of 2015 is undermining two key principles of the Refugee Convention: that you treat people as individuals and that you don't force them back to danger. The outsourcing of border control to states who might want to prevent their own inhabitants fleeing contradicts the Universal Declaration of Human Rights, which, in addition to the right to move freely within a country, states that 'everyone has the right to leave any country, including his own'. Europe is already proving an inspiration to governments elsewhere who would like to wriggle out of their commitments. In May 2016, when Kenya announced plans to close the Dadaab refugee camp, a government official cited the EU's recent deal to return refugees to Turkey as a precedent: 'We will not be the first to do so, this is standard practice worldwide. For example, in Europe, rich, prosperous and democratic countries are turning away refugees from Syria, one of the worst war zones since World War Two.'

This isn't simply a humanitarian problem, it's a political one. After the Second World War, the theorist Hannah Arendt turned her attention to the new forms of state oppression that had emerged in the twentieth century: Nazism and Stalinism. *The Origins of Totalitarianism* (1951) traces the roots of these regimes and warns that they were not pathologies unique to Germany or the Soviet Union, but an outgrowth of conditions far more widespread in European society. The treatment of refugees, people who had effectively been rendered stateless, was a crucial part of Arendt's study. She had direct experience of this: Arendt was the daughter of secular Jews and fled Germany – the country of her birth – in 1940, for France, where she was interned as an 'enemy alien'.

In *The Origins of Totalitarianism*, Arendt argued that statelessness reduced people to the condition of outlaws: they had to break laws in order to live and they were subject to jail sentences without ever committing a crime. 'The best criterion by which to decide whether someone has been forced outside the pale of the law,' Arendt wrote, 'is to ask if he would benefit by committing a crime.' When I read this, it immediately resonated with the stories I'd heard from my interviewees, and the ones my grandmother had told me as a child. Being a refugee means not doing what you're told – if you did, you'd probably have stayed at home to be killed. And you continue bending the rules, telling untruths, concealing yourself, even after you've left immediate danger, because that's the way you negotiate a hostile system.

The inability of states to guarantee rights to these displaced people, Arendt argued, was a powerful tool for regimes that wanted to undermine the idea of universal human rights. Look, they were able to argue, there's no such thing; you only get rights by being part of the nation. Instead of resolving this problem, European states between the wars cracked down on unwanted migrants, giving police forces extensive powers that were eventually also wielded over their own citizens. This happened in the western European democracies, and not just in the 'totalitarian' states, Arendt warned. Far from being the barbarians they are often portrayed as – a mass of 'illegals' threatening European security and identity – rightless people appear 'as the first signs of a possible regression from civilization'.

*

But Arendt points out a threat, not something inevitable. Importantly, governments respond to pressure from below. By the time my grandmother had arrived in Britain, the government had already been forced to soften its position on Jewish refugees. Under public pressure, it had approved the Kindertransport initiative: a private scheme to resettle Jewish children from Nazi-occupied Europe. After war was declared, the authorities interned German and Italian nationals, many of them Jews, as 'enemy aliens'. Yet even as the Luftwaffe's bombardment of Britain gathered pace, there were British citizens who spoke out about the dire conditions in the camps, and, in 1941, the government closed them down.

In the autumn of 2015, public outcry over the photograph of the drowned toddler, Alan Kurdi, that circulated in international media pressured the British government into expanding a scheme to resettle Syrian refugees. Announcing the change, Cameron talked of the country's moral responsibility, and many politicians have invoked Britain's 'proud history' of welcoming refugees. In fact, Britain's history in the twentieth century might be better described as one of mainly trying to keep refugees out. The first modern border controls were introduced by the 1905 Aliens Act, aimed specifically at preventing Jews, fleeing pogroms in the Russian Empire, from settling in the UK. And Cameron was using the idea of a 'proud history' to justify excluding people – the British government had held fast to its refusal to take in any refugees already in Europe, except under compulsion, as was the case with children in Calais – as much as to welcome them. But the government was forced to listen to its critics.

In 2015, the UN's special rapporteur on migration proposed two responses that would have done much to alleviate the crisis: mass international resettlement of refugees from Syria, and a temporary work-visa scheme between African countries and the EU, so that economic migrants could come and go, without getting trapped in the deadly clandestine routes. The reason this hasn't happened is because European governments simply don't want to do it. There are domestic political pressures within Europe, and a wider crisis of the international system through which conflicts and disagreements between states are supposed to be resolved. The undermining of refugee protection is one symptom of this.

In such a context, it is easy to feel powerless, but there are two ways in which we can usefully respond. One is to be alert to the ways in which some politicians and their cheerleaders try to convince people to give up rights and protections that exist for the benefit of everyone. Any authority figure who says, 'We should look after our own before we look after refugees,' for instance, probably isn't interested in doing either. The other is to recognize the importance of collective action. There won't be 'solutions' to a crisis, in the sense of one or more policy decisions that will make refugees vanish. Wars produce refugees. People will continue to move to improve their quality of life – not only because of extreme poverty, but because they, like the rest of us, are connected to global culture and global networks of communication. Climate change has the potential to create far greater displacement than we have seen in recent years; as with refugees from war, it's likely to be poorer countries who feel the greatest impact. The question is not so much whether these things will happen, as how we respond.

What I would say for now is that you do not have to let your thinking be limited by the categories that currently exist. It is possible to defend the protections that the current system of refugee law offers, while recognizing their limits. Politicians may try to draw a distinction between 'genuine' refugees and other irregular migrants, and our economy may assign relative values to people's lives based on their use as workers, but that doesn't mean you accept that one of those people is any less a person, or that their experiences are any less real. Refugee law provides an essential protection for some kinds of displaced people, but not all of them. Drawn up in a world where power and wealth are unequally distributed, it has always to some extent reflected the concerns of the powerful and wealthy. But the universal language of human rights is a promise, even if it is a partly unfulfilled one – and the more rigidly we enforce distinctions between the deserving and undeserving, the more likely we are to accept the violence done in our name.

Europe's border system works by isolating people; one of the things we saw in 2015 was thousands of European citizens unwilling to accept that isolation. This is part of a wider pattern we have come to know in recent years, where the state is unwilling or unable to prevent a crisis, leaves volunteers to fill the gap, then cracks down when it doesn't like the result. The people who give up their time to volunteer in camps or at entry points, the money that is donated to rescuers in the Mediterranean, the activists who defy policies they see as unjust – all of this is a political challenge to the system as it currently exists.

I'd also suggest that, rather than seeing European racism as a thing of the past, the recognition of its persistence is essential for understanding the refugee crisis and some of the responses to it. Thousands of people from former European colonies, whose grandparents were treated as less than human by their European rulers, have drowned in the Mediterranean in the past two decades, yet this only became a 'crisis' when the scale of the disaster was impossible for Europeans to ignore. Even now, a hierarchy of suffering pervades much of the debate, in which people's struggles are ignored or dismissed depending on their background, with little discussion of how Europe might have contributed to the situation of the countries the migrants leave behind – either historically, or through the military and economic policies of current governments. And when local conflicts involving newly arrived refugees break out in European countries, many commentators jump seamlessly from an incident that needs a considered response, to declaration of an existential threat to Europe from its Muslim minority. At its extreme end, this is geno-cidal logic, of a kind Europe has known in its past. You do not have to accept this.

*

But the starting point should be the migrants themselves. Their experiences are often treated as secondary to the question of what to do with them. On the one hand, you have the weight of anti-immigration propaganda. On the other, you have the messages of humanitarian organiza-tions that want to stress people's vulnerability, or their good nature, or their exceptional achievements. Most, though, are neither innocents nor villains, but people trying to retain control over their lives and making com-plex decisions about what risks to take, what rules to flout, what lies to tell. Like the rest of us, they are con-stantly making and remaking stories that explain their place in the world.

Throughout 2015, as the crisis commanded the atten-tion of the world's media, I kept hearing and reading about refugees having a 'dream' of Europe. Perhaps that's the case; we are all moved at times by an ideal. But it implies a certain naivety on the part of the beholder, that someone is being pulled by an illusion that the rest of us do not share. It belittles them, while at the same time aggrandizing us. To the European audience, and by exten-sion audiences in other rich parts of the world, it is reassuring: they're dreaming of us, perhaps they need to have their illusions dispelled – but who can blame them for idolizing our existence?

Yet it is striking how often the word 'dream' seems to crop up in place of the words 'want' and 'need'. Those are less comforting words. This person has arrived in Europe and they want to go to Britain, where their uncle lives. Wouldn't you? This person needs to get to Europe to earn a living. Why can't they earn a living at home? Why is Europe a place where one can earn a living? How does the place they come from relate to the place they are headed to? Why should anyone have to put up with these conditions? What set of interests does it serve to regulate their movement? And how likely is it that states which treat migrants with such callousness will behave similarly towards their own citizens? These, I think, are the sorts of questions we should be asking.

Note on Sources

This book had two false starts. The first was an attempt to write a book about the far right in Europe; my trip to Athens in 2012 convinced me that it was more important at that moment to pay attention to the people on the receiving end of the violence, and to ask why many of them seemed also to be threatened by the actions of states governed by parties with a commitment to liberal democracy. The second was an attempt to map out the way asylum seekers were treated at the external borders of the EU; after embarking on this, I soon realized that people's troubles did not end at the geographical frontier, and that it was more interesting to keep following them and see where they ended up.

I chose a series of places around Europe – Calais, Sicily, Athens, the Evros, Ukraine's far west – which seemed to me to be 'border' areas, in one way or another: places where the fault lines in Europe's asylum system were most evident. I kept visiting them, to meet and interview migrants, residents, activists and officials, and my subjects for this book arose from contacts I made during those visits. The people who feature do so for two principal reasons: the first is to give a fairly representative – although not comprehensive – picture of the people who have come to Europe in search of asylum in the last decade; the second is because they are those with whom I felt I was able to make a connection. I followed my subjects' progress for a long time – in many cases, for several years – and we needed to trust one another to make it work.

Clearly, the book relies on individual testimony. I wanted to present that in as open and honest a way as possible, which is why I have narrated our encounters in the first person. I also did it because I want you to see these people as I did, and not to let their harshest experiences overshadow the other aspects of their personalities. For the parts of my subjects' accounts that take place outside Europe, I have cross-referenced details wherever possible – the 2008 rebel incursion into Khartoum, or the progress of the war in Libya, for instance – with contemporary media reports. In Europe, I have visited most of the places my subjects stayed in and passed through, often on multiple occasions. For example, I visited Calais repeatedly throughout 2014, and I have been to almost every location described by Zainab and Jamal. I interviewed scores of people – migrants and others – in each place I visited. I asked them about living conditions, local history, routes taken and experiences with people smugglers, to get a sense of what was typical and what wasn't. And I kept in touch with these contacts, even when I wasn't there, to see how situations developed over time.

Some of my interviewees' names have been changed, at their request.

To supplement this and provide wider context, I drew on various documentary sources. The UNHCR figures on migrant arrivals come from data provided at http://data2.unhcr. org/en/situations/mediterranean. Migration statistics are incomplete at the best of times; this is even more the case when dealing with irregular migration. But these figures give us a sense of scale, and of movement. Public statements by politicians and officials are sourced from contemporary news reports.

Specific books, reports, newspaper and blog articles I drew on are listed below. More generally, Primo Levi, Frantz Fanon, Hannah Arendt and Mourid Barghouti were on my mind while I was writing this book.

Introduction

— Bridget Anderson's *Us and Them? The Dangerous Politics of Immigration Control* (Oxford University Press, Oxford, 2013) makes a connection between today's border policies and historic attempts to control the movement of the poor.
— The research on globalization and migration patterns by Mathias Czialka and Hein de Haas is, 'The Globalisation of Migration: Has the World Become More Migratory?', *International Migration Review* 48 (2), 20 May 2014; figures on the global proportions of international migrants and of refugees come from two articles by Hein de Haas: http://heindehaas. blogspot.co.uk/2017/03/myths-of-migration-much-of-what-we.html and http://heindehaas.blogspot. co.uk/2016/08/refugees-small-and-relatively-stable.html
— Reece Jones's research on border walls is cited in his book, *Violent Borders: Refugees and the Right to Move* (Verso Books, London, 2016).
— Agreements on migration between the EU and various neighbouring governments in the years before the refugee crisis are discussed in Matthew Carr's *Fortress Europe: Dispatches from a Gated Continent* (Hurst, London, 2014).
— The comparison of EU spending on border defences and asylum conditions comes from Amnesty International's report, 'The Human Cost of Fortress Europe' (London,

2014): https://www.amnesty.org/en/documents/
EUR05/001/2014/en/
— The estimate of deaths at Europe's borders between
2004 and 2014 comes from the IOM's report, 'Fatal
Journeys: Tracking Lives Lost During Migration'
(Geneva, 2014): https://publications.iom.int/books/
fatal-journeys-tracking-lives-lost-during-migration
— Figures on refugees from Syria are available at: www.
unhcr.org.uk/uk/syria-emergency.html
— Eurostat's data on asylum claims in Europe is available
at: http://appsso.eurostat.ec.europa.eu/nui/show.
do?dataset=migr_asyappctza&lang=en

City

— The UN rapporteur's criticism of sanctions on Sudan
was reported by Al Jazeera, 'US sanctions on Sudan
under the spotlight', 2 December 2015: http://www.
aljazeera.com/news/2015/12/sanctions-sudan-spotlight-
151201120012775.html
— Figures on displacement from Darfur are available at:
http://news.trust.org//spotlight/Darfur-conflict
— Figures on the Sudanese diaspora in the UK are from the
IOM report, 'Mapping exercise – Sudan' (London,
2006): https://www.iom.int/mapping-exercise-sudan
— Figures on unauthorized entry into the EU in 2008
come from Frontex's 2009 annual report: http://www.
europarl.europa.eu/document/activities/cont/201008/
20100805ATT79751/20100805ATT79751EN.pdf
— Figures on ferry traffic between Dover and Calais come
from: https://www.gov.uk/government/statistics/
provisional-sea-passenger-statistics-2014

— Figures on Channel Tunnel traffic come from: http://
www.eurotunnelgroup.com/uk/eurotunnel-group/
operations/traffic-figures/
— The trial of the Calais smuggling gang was reported in
the *Daily Telegraph*, 'Trafficking gang offered "a la carte"
routes to UK', 29 October 2014: http://www.telegraph.
co.uk/news/worldnews/europe/france/11197058/
Trafficking-gang-offered-a-la-carte-routes-to-UK.html
— Figures on refugees from Iraq are available at: www.
unhcr.org/uk/iraq-emergency.html
— The rise in the number of migrants arriving in Calais
and trying to cross to the UK in 2014 and 2015 is
reported in the *Guardian*, 'Migrant arrests at Calais
double', 19 July 2014: https://www.theguardian.com/
world/2014/jul/18/migrant-arrests-calais, *The Times*,
'More stowaways found in refrigerated lorry', 20
August 2014: https://www.thetimes.co.uk/article/more-
stowaways-found-in-refrigerated-lorry-fkzkgg86dtj and
'Street battles in Calais as fury at illegal camps rises',
24 September 2014: https://www.thetimes.co.uk/article/
street-battles-in-calais-as-fury-at-illegal-camps-rises-
7kpgvfhpcwk, and the *Daily Telegraph*, 'Tractors,
police cars and lorries block Calais roads in migrant
protest', 13 October 2014: http://www.telegraph.
co.uk/news/worldnews/europe/france/11158322/Calais-
police-block-roads-in-protest-against-insufficient-
resources-to-handle-migrant-numbers.html and
'Welcome to the Calais jungle', 19 June 2015 (print
edition only).
— Statements made at migrant protests in Calais were
either heard directly by me or supplied by participants;
I heard directly the statements made at the far-right
rally.

— Migrants' accounts of police violence, and information on shortages in the French asylum system come from Human Rights Watch's report, 'France: Migrants, Asylum Seekers Abused and Destitute', 20 January 2015: https://www.hrw.org/news/2015/01/20/france-migrants-asylum-seekers-abused-and-destitute
— The Road Haulage Association's submission to the UK parliament is available at: https://www.parliament.uk/business/committees/committees-a-z/commons-select/home-affairs-committee/inquiries/parliament-2015/mediterranean-migration/
— The February 2016 survey of migrants in Calais is from Refugee Rights Data Project's report, 'The Long Wait' (London, 2016): http://refugeerights.org.uk/reports/the-long-wait/

Country

— The account in chapters 10, 15, 17 and 18 of the people-smuggling trade in Libya and how it developed over time is drawn from Peter Tinti and Tuesday Reitano's *Migrant, Refugee, Smuggler, Saviour* (Hurst, London, 2016).
— Further detail on smuggler communities in Libya comes from Patrick Kingsley's *The New Odyssey: The Story of Europe's Refugee Crisis* (Guardian Faber, London, 2016).
— Historical background on exploited migrant labour in Sicily is drawn from Jeffrey E. Cole and Sally S. Booth's *Dirty Work: Immigrants in Domestic Service, Agriculture and Prostitution in Italy* (Lexington Books, Lanham, 2007).
— The Global Detention Project has information on immigration detention in Libya, and immigration policy

under Muammar Gaddafi, at: https://www.
globaldetentionproject.org/countries/africa/libya
— The IOM's estimate of deaths in the Mediterranean is
taken from their press release, 'IOM Counts 3,771
Migrant Fatalities in Mediterranean in 2015', published
on 1 May 2015, at: https://www.iom.int/news/iom-counts-
3771-migrant-fatalities-mediterranean-2015
— The *Wall Street Journal* story on Augusta is, 'In Italy,
Migrant Children Languish in Squalor', 12 September
2014: https://www.wsj.com/articles/
in-italy-migrant-children-1410547308
— The claim that most West African migration takes place
within the region comes from the International Centre
for Migration Policy Development's report, 'A Survey
on Migration Policies in West Africa' (Vienna, 2015):
https://www.icmpd.org/fileadmin/ICMPD-Website/
ICMPD_General/Publications/2015/A_Survey_on_
Migration_Policies_in_West_Africa_EN_SOFT.pdf
— The IOM has a country profile of Guinea-Conakry at:
https://www.iom.int/countries/guinea
— Statistics from Italy's interior ministry on the number of
people living in reception centres are available at: http://
www.libertaciviliimmigrazione.dlci.interno.gov.it/sites/
default/files/allegati/cruscotto_statistico_giornaliero_23_
settembre_2016_0.pdf
— The figure of two billion euros spent by the Italian
government on accommodating asylum seekers between
2011 and 2015 comes from 'Mediterranean migrants
meet the Mafia at Sicily's Kafkaesque Mineo camp',
International Business Times, 5 May 2015: http://www.
ibtimes.co.uk/sicily-mediterranean-migrants-exploited-
lucrative-business-huge-mineo-camp-1498737

— The claim by academics at Goldsmiths, University of London that EU policy contributed to deaths in the Mediterranean is in the report, 'Death By Rescue: The Lethal Effects of the EU's Policy of Non-Assistance' (London, 2016): https://deathbyrescue.org/

— The *Wall Street Journal*'s report on smuggling routes through Niger is, 'Agadez Traffickers Profit From Movement Through Niger to Libya', 19 July 2015: https://www.wsj.com/articles/agadez-traffickers-profit-from-movement-through-niger-to-libya-1437002559

— The BBC story on claims that mercenaries fought for Gaddafi is, 'Gaddafi's African "mercenaries" leaving Libya', 27 August 2011: http://www.bbc.co.uk/news/world-africa-14693343

— Accounts of black African migrants being targeted for allegedly having supported Gaddafi were reported by the *New York Times* as, 'Libyans turn wrath on dark-skinned migrants', 4 September 2011: http://www.nytimes.com/2011/09/05/world/africa/05migrants.html?scp=1&sq=racism

— The IRIN story on the effect of EU 'hotspots' in Sicily is, 'How Italy's flawed hotspots are creating thousands of "clandestini"', 13 April 2016: http://www.irinnews.org/news/2016/04/13/how-italy%E2%80%99s-flawed-hotspots-are-creating-thousands-%E2%80%9Cclandestini%E2%80%9D

— The MEDMIG survey of migrants who travelled through Libya is available at http://www.medmig.info and is included in the book, *Unravelling Europe's Migration Crisis: Journeys Over Land and Sea* (Policy Press, London, 2017).

— The Human Rights Watch report on torture in Libyan detention centres is, 'Libya: Whipped, Beaten, and Hung from Trees', 22 June 2014: https://www.hrw.org/news/2014/06/22/libya-whipped-beaten-and-hung-trees

Continent

— Information on the number and location of Afghan refugees is available at: http://reporting.unhcr.org/node/4505
— A detailed history of Golden Dawn, including its activities at Saint Panteleimon, is provided, in Greek, by Dmitris Psarras in, *Η μαύρη βίβλος της Χρυσής Αυγής* (*The Black Book of the Golden Dawn*) (Polis, Athens, 2012); an abridged version is published, in English, by the Rosa Luxemburg Stiftung, at: http://www.rosalux.eu/fileadmin/user_upload/psarrasen.pdf
— The murder that triggered the Athens 'pogrom' of 2011 is reported, in Greek, by *To Vima*, '*Δολοφονία Καντάρη: «Τον μαχαίρωσα γιατί φώναζε 'κλέφτης'»*' ('Kantari Murder: "I stabbed him because he was crying 'thief' "'), 21 May 2011: http://www.tovima.gr/society/article/?aid=401942
— The recent history of Eisenhüttenstadt is told in Sabine Rennefanz's *Eisenkinder: Die Stille Wut Der Wendegeneration* (*Iron Children: The Silent Fury of the Turnaround Generation*) (Luchterhand Literaturverlag, Munich, 2011).
— Further information about racist violence in Greece, and the targeting of migrants in Athens, comes from the Human Rights Watch report, 'Hate on the Streets: Xenophobic Violence in Greece' (New York, 2012), available at: https://www.hrw.org/report/2012/07/10/hate-streets/xenophobic-violence-greece; information

also comes from reports compiled by the Athens-based Racist Violence Recording Network, available at: http://rvrn.org/

— Information on migrants detained for more than eighteen months in Greece is available at: http://www.asylumineurope.org/news/25-05-2017/indefinite-detention-migrants-greece-unlawful-rules-athens-administrative-court

— The *To Vima* story of abuse at Amygdaleza is, 'Police officers formed "hit squad" and abused migrants at Amygdaleza', 17 February 2015: http://www.tovima.gr/en/article/?aid=677906

— The *Guardian* story on refugees being forced back across the Evros is, 'Fears over disappearance of 150 Syrian refugees from Greek village', 24 December 2013: https://www.theguardian.com/world/2013/dec/24/greeks-protest-refugees-disappear-praggi

— The figures for EU investment in Bulgarian border defences come from Amnesty's report, 'The Human Cost of Fortress Europe' (see above).

— The Human Rights Watch report on refugees forced back from Bulgaria to Turkey is, 'Bulgaria: new evidence Syrians forced back to Turkey', 18 September 2014: https://www.hrw.org/news/2014/09/18/bulgaria-new-evidence-syrians-forced-back-turkey

— A case of Syrian children working in Turkish sweatshops, making clothes for European high-street brands, is reported by the BBC, 'Child refugees in Turkey making clothes for UK shops', 24 October 2016: http://www.bbc.co.uk/news/business-37716463

— The Hungarian government's figure of 72,000 migrants entering the country by July 2015 is reported by the BBC as, 'Hungary MPs approve border fence and anti-migrant law', 7 July 2015: http://www.bbc.co.uk/news/world-europe-33421093

— The *Guardian* story on Pakistan turning a plane around at Islamabad is, 'Pakistan sends deported migrants back to Greece', 3 December 2015: https://www.theguardian.com/world/2015/dec/03/pakistan-sends-deported-migrants-back-to-greece-eu

Century

— The account of twentieth-century refugee history draws on Peter Gatrell's *The Making of the Modern Refugee* (Oxford University Press, Oxford, 2013); Simon Behrman's 'Legal Subjectivity and the Refugee', *International Journal of Refugee Law* 26(1), 2014; and presentations given by Tony Kushner and Jessica Reinisch at Birkbeck, University of London's conference, 'Placeless People: What Can History Tell Us About Today's Refugee Crises?', 20 June 2016.

— Quotes from the Evian Conference come from IRIN's story, 'Look back and learn: the Evian Conference, 1938', 18 November 2015: http://www.irinnews.org/analysis/2015/11/18

— A 2017 World Bank study on remittances in Somalia is available at: http://www.worldbank.org/en/news/press-release/2017/10/05/world-bank-launched-somali-poverty-profile-first-comprehensive-snapshot-of-welfare-conditions

— Information on people displaced by the war in Ukraine is available at: http://reporting.unhcr.org/node/12004

— The Human Rights Watch report on migrants in Ukraine is, 'Buffeted in the Borderland: The Treatment of Asylum Seekers and Migrants in Ukraine' (New York, 2010): https://www.hrw.org/report/2010/12/16/

buffeted-borderland/treatment-asylum-seekers-
and-migrants-ukraine

Afterword

— Denmark's law to seize assets from refugees is reported
  in the *Guardian*, 'Danish parliament approves plan
  to seize assets from refugees', 26 January 2016:
  https://www.theguardian.com/world/2016/jan/26/
  danish-parliament-approves-plan-to-seize-assets-from-
  refugees
— The claim that the UK's share of refugees actually fell
  during the crisis comes from research by Nando Sigona
  of Birmingham University, available at: https://
  nandosigona.info/2016/04/12/there-is-no-refugee-
  crisis-in-the-uk/
— The EU's revised relocation target of 33,000 is reported
  by *EU Observer*, 'Fewer refugees to be relocated as EU
  revises targets', 12 April 2017: https://euobserver.com/
  migration/137582
— For an example of racial profiling and the
  criminalization of solidarity at Europe's internal borders,
  see my *New Statesman* story, 'The French farmer
  smuggling migrants in the Alps', 30 September 2017:
  https://www.newstatesman.com/world/europe/2017/09/
  french-farmer-smuggling-migrants-alps; the Institute for
  Race Relations's report, 'Humanitarianism: the
  unacceptable face of solidarity', is available at: http://
  s3-eu-west-2.amazonaws.com/wpmedia.outlandish.com/
  irr/2017/11/10092853/Humanitarianism_the_
  unacceptable_face_of_solidarity.pdf
— Daniel Howden and Apostolis Fotiadis have given a
  comprehensive account of how Greece became a holding
  pen for refugees in their investigation for *NewsDeeply*,

'The Refugee Archipelago', 6 March 2017: https://www.newsdeeply.com/refugees/articles/2017/03/06/the-refugee-archipelago-the-inside-story-of-what-went-wrong-in-greece

— Daniel Howden does the same for EU policy in Libya and the clampdown on NGO rescues in, 'European Priorities, Libyan Realities', October 2017: http://issues.newsdeeply.com/central-mediterranean-european-priorities-libyan-realities

— Information on the EU–Turkey deal is available in this *Guardian* Q&A, 8 March 2016: https://www.theguardian.com/world/2016/mar/08/eu-turkey-refugee-deal-qa; Amnesty International's assessment of the deal's threat to human rights, 'The EU–Turkey deal: Europe's year of shame', 20 March 2017, is available at: https://www.amnesty.org/en/latest/news/2017/03/the-eu-turkey-deal-europes-year-of-shame/

— The EU's plan to invest sixty-two billion euros in the Middle East and Africa is reported by *Politico*, 'EU plans Africa cash-for-cooperation migration deal', 7 June 2016: https://www.politico.eu/article/eu-plans-africa-cash-for-cooperation-migration-deal-europe/

— The plan to divert peace-building funds to armed forces is reported by the *Financial Times*, 'Brussels set to give "peace-building" funds to armed forces', 4 July 2016: https://www.ft.com/content/856d855c-411b-11e6-b22f-79eb4891c97d

— Pressure on Afghanistan to accept 80,000 deportees from Europe, and plans to make deals with Sudan, Eritrea, Nigeria and other countries, is reported in the *Guardian*, 'EU's secret ultimatum to Afghanistan: accept 80,000 deportees or lose aid', 28 September 2016: https://www.theguardian.com/global-development/2016/

sep/28/eu-secret-ultimatum-afghanistan-accept-
80000-deportees-lose-aid-brussels-summit-migration-
sensitive
— Italy's attempt to pay off a militia in Sabratha is
reported in the *Guardian*, 'Italy's deal to stem flow
of people from Libya in danger of collapse', 3 October
2017: https://www.theguardian.com/world/2017/oct/03/
italys-deal-to-stem-flow-of-people-from-libya-in-danger-
of-collapse; as is the suspension of NGO search-and-
rescue operations, 'Three NGOs halt Mediterranean
migrant rescues after Libyan hostility', 14 August 2017:
https://www.theguardian.com/world/2017/aug/14/
three-ngos-halt-mediterranean-migrant-rescues-after-
libyan-hostility
— A recent report on conditions in Libyan immigration
detention centres is in *The Times*, 'Food runs short amid
squalor of Libya's detention centres', 24 August 2017:
https://www.thetimes.co.uk/article/food-runs-short-
amid-squalor-of-libya-s-packed-detention-centres-
tpp98gkgl
— The Kenyan government official's statement on the
proposed closure of Dadaab was reported by the
Guardian, 'Fear forces refugees in world's largest camp
to return to conflict zones', 15 September 2016: https://
www.theguardian.com/global-development/2016/sep/15/
fear-forces-refugees-dadaab-kenya-worlds-largest-camp-
return-conflict-zones-human-rights-watch-warns
— An account of a Second World War British internment
camp, and how British citizens supported the inmates, is
in the BBC Liverpool story, 'Wartime camps in Huyton',
24 September 2014: http://www.bbc.co.uk/liverpool/
content/articles/2006/04/24/huyton_internment_camp_
feature.shtml

— An interview with François Crépeau, the UN special rapporteur on the human rights of migrants, is published by the *Guardian*, 'UN's François Crépeau on the refugee crisis: "Instead of resisting migration, let's organise it"', 22 April 2015: https://www.theguardian.com/world/2015/apr/22/uns-francois-crepeau-on-the-refugee-crisis-instead-of-resisting-migration-lets-organise-it

Acknowledgements

Jamal, Zainab, Ousmane, Caesar, Fatima, Hakima, Nisrin, Azad and Farhan: thank you for allowing me into your lives and for trusting me. Teresa: thank you for the stories. I hope this book tells the truth about what each of you experienced.

In the five years it has taken to research and write this, a huge number of people have offered me help, advice, places to stay – or a combination of all three. I'm extraordinarily grateful for this, and I will spend the next five years making sure you know it. In particular, this includes Yiannis Baboulias, Rasha Chatta, Mohammad Mirzay, Ioanna Panagiotopoulou, Rupinder Parhar, Taras Ratushnyy and Krassimir Yankov for their translation skills; Christopher Bertram, Joanna Biggs, Ismail Einashe, Owen Hatherley, Sarah Shin, Tom Southerden, Lyndsey Stonebridge and Helen Trilling for their perceptive, critical and improving comments on the manuscript; Ravi Mirchandani and Ansa Khan Khattak at Picador for their thoughtful editing and oversight; everyone at Verso for their enthusiasm and long-term commitment; and Karolina Sutton for taking an interest in the project at an early stage and pushing me to produce my best work.

The research for this book was funded through freelance reporting, and Paul Myerscough at the *London Review of Books*, Xan Rice at the *New Statesman* and Rachel Shabi, formerly at *Al Jazeera English*, are three editors who gave me encouragement and the space to try out my ideas. Small parts of the book appeared in different form in these publications. Freelancing can be an isolating experience, so I'm thankful for the journalists and photographers I've been able to work with while travelling – Jamie Mackay, Rebecca Omonira-Oyekanmi, Anna Psaroudakis, Rebecca Suner and Erini Vourloumis – for their companionship, good sense and the different perspectives they brought to situations we encountered. Samira Shackle and the rest of the *New Humanist* team have been supportive and forgiving colleagues, not least when I was away writing. And my family provided love and kindness, particularly in 2016.

Last of all, I'd like to thank Kathleen Commons for being both an inspiration in her work and an excellent person in general.